WALL STREET MONEY MACHINE

VOLUME 1

REVISED FOR THE NEW MILLENNIUM

The money is in the meter drop—you get in, you get out, you make money.

WADE B. COOK

WALL STREET MONEY MACHINE

VOLUME 1

REVISED FOR THE NEW MILLENNIUM

WADE B. COOK

Lighthouse Publishing Group, Inc.
Seattle, Washington

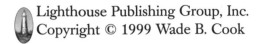
Lighthouse Publishing Group, Inc.
Copyright © 1999 Wade B. Cook

Library of Congress Cataloging-in-Publication Data

Cook, Wade.Wall street money machine, volume 1 :
revised for the new millennium / Wade B. Cook

   p. cm.
Includes bibliographical references and index.
ISBN 1-892008-60-2
   1. Speculation. 2. Stocks. 3. Futures. I. Title.
HG6041.C64 1999
332.63'228--dc21   99-17010
                                                CIP

"This publication is designed to provide general information in regard to the subject matter covered. It is sold with the understanding that the publisher is not engaged in rendering legal, accounting, or other professional services. If legal, accounting, or other professional services are required, the services of an independent professional should be sought."

"From a declaration of principles jointly adopted by a committee of the American Bar Association and the committee of the Publisher's Association."

Book Design by Judy Burkhalter
Dust Jacket Design by Angela Wilson
Cover Photograph by Zachary A. Cherry
Illustration by Jason Woodruff

Published by Lighthouse Publishing Group, Inc
14675 Interurban Avenue South
Seattle, Washington 98168-4664
1-800-706-8657
206-901-3100 (fax)

Source Code: WSMMRM99

Printed in United States of America
10 9 8 7 6 5

To Laura,

   my wife

         my love

                my friend

OTHER BOOKS BY LIGHTHOUSE PUBLISHING GROUP, INC.

101 Ways To Buy Real Estate Without Cash, WADE COOK
Cook's Book On Creative Real Estate, WADE COOK
How To Pick Up Foreclosures, WADE COOK
Owner Financing, WADE COOK
Real Estate For Real People, WADE COOK
Real Estate Money Machine, WADE COOK

Wall Street Money Machine, WADE B. COOK
Stock Market Miracles, WADE B. COOK
Safety 1st Investing, WADE B. COOK
Bear Market Baloney, WADE B. COOK
On Track Investing, DAVID R. HEBERT
Rolling Stocks, GREGORY WITT
Sleeping Like A Baby, JOHN C. HUDELSON
Making A Living In The Stock Market, BOB ELDRIDGE

Blueprints For Success, VARIOUS AUTHORS
Brilliant Deductions, WADE B. COOK
Million Heirs, JOHN V. CHILDERS, JR.
The Secret Millionaire Guide To Nevada Corporations
JOHN V. CHILDERS, JR.
Wealth 101, WADE B. COOK

A+, WADE B. COOK
Business Buy The Bible, WADE B. COOK
Don't Set Goals (The Old Way), WADE B. COOK
Wade Cook's Power Quotes, Volume 1, WADE COOK

Living In Color, RENAE KNAPP

OTHER BOOKS BY WADE COOK

Y2K Gold Rush
GOLD LEAF PRESS

CONTENTS

PREFACE

THIS BOOK is about getting cash flow rich, yet it is about safety and building steady income. I like many "how to get rich" books, and if I have a choice of reading a get-rich-quick book or a get-rich-slow book, I'll take "quick" every time, especially if it teaches a formula that consistently works.

The problem is to define what is meant by "quick." The answer is obviously found in seven basic questions:

1. How much do you have to start with?

2. Can you leave the original principal plus profits in your accounts to compound?

3. What vehicles (formulas) can you choose to use and to become expert in?

4. How aggressively can you apply the strategies and use the formulas for compounding your wealth?

5. How much risk you are willing to take? (Note: I'm not willing to take much risk at all and I hate losing money—you'll see my defensive maneuvers continually throughout this book.)

6. How much work are you willing to do? How much effort are you willing to expend?

7. How many weeks, months, and possibly years, will you spend trying and testing techniques and using all the guts, energy and wisdom you can muster so you can "get rich" overnight?

All wish to possess knowledge, but few comparatively speaking, are willing to pay the price.
                                                                —JUVENAL

And then the question comes up: "How much money is meant when someone says rich?" I'm going to give a hard answer to that soft question: "Two million dollars!"

If you want more, go for it; but think about two million dollars. At 10 percent a year, $2,000,000 will generate $200,000 per year. If you need more than $200,000 per year, then you have a problem. Even a five percent return generates $100,000 per year. Enough is enough. When I was worth only $2,000,000, I was very rich. I'm richer now, but only in degree. Rich is rich. True wealth, from a financial point of view, is simply having enough income to live the lifestyle you want.

Having assets that produce no income is technically one form of wealth, but not by my definition. We live in a monthly billing society. Having the cash flow, produced by a grouping of assets, while the assets are hopefully growing in value to produce more income, so that you can spend more constructive time with your family, go back to college, travel, give more to your church, and "be a better you," is being rich indeed.

It's not my intention to wax philosophical–there are enough philosophy books on motivation, overcoming fear, et cetera. This book is not one of those. It is a no-nonsense approach to income generation. You'll find here a few strategies that anyone with a modicum of sense would call "getting rich quick." For example: sometimes I double my money in four to five days–but only using $2,000 to $8,000–surely not with my whole portfolio. While doubling the $2,000 or $8,000, some money is sitting dormant in "bottom fishing" stocks that I hope will increase over the next few years. Other money is in some great blue chip companies, and still other money is making nice 20 to 40% monthly returns for me.

I'm into compounding. I'm into exponential growth. I'm into formulas which produce safe, sane, 20%+ monthly returns. It's this point that I want to dwell on. Every investment return mentioned in newspapers and magazines speak of annual returns. If I'm going to help you, the first thing I have to do is "un-brainwash" you concerning annual returns. Eliminate the word "annual" from your vocabulary. Annual is boring. Annual is lazy; annual doesn't get you thinking rich. "Annual" is worthy of elimination.

Start thinking about 10-day returns, or two to three week returns. At least think monthly. This forces you to start thinking like an income machine. Don't make investments unless they produce nice monthly returns, or shorter. You'll love the chapters on writing covered calls—a virtual cash flow, greased-and-ready-to-go, machine. You will learn a simple formula that can be repeated every two to four weeks. One month, you'll get a 28% return. Then on the same stock the next month, you get a 22% return. Then, if you sell that stock, the 22% goes to 38%.

Everyone is skeptical at first, but this is no joke. You're 14 to 30 days from making it possible. Now, if you want to slip back into your old "annual" habit, multiply 22% by 12 months for an annualized return of 264%. No kidding—my students and I have produced annual returns of 600 to 800%. You can too from time to time on part of your money.

The hard part will be to get your stockbrokers up to speed. These people are so wedded to old, stodgy, boring, risky methods, that it's no wonder they go in and out of business so fast. When I first decided to write this book, I was going to call it *A Cab Driver Takes on Wall Street*. Yes, I really was a cab driver, and yes, I learned a great wealth-building tool as a cab driver. That title has made it into a chapter heading. I'm bringing this point up because some of the methods these professionals employ need to be taken on and challenged.

This book, however, is not about pointing fingers and pointing out others' weak and boring strategies. Instead, I'll make a case for my cash flow strategies. They work. They generate income. But, in fact, you may need some of those boring strategies later on when you want to quit working a few hours a day and really retire. Then the 10% a year returns may be sufficient—once you're rich.

I make millions. I'll teach you how to do the same. I'm in the foxhole every day—doing what I teach. If all I do is teach seminars, then all I'll teach is "How to Teach Seminars." But I am an active investor. My recreation is making money day by day. I do it all the time. I will teach you how to do this, because I'm actively doing it.

If you want $200, $2,000, or $20,000 a day, read on. Direction is more important than speed. I've blazed the trail–come along for the trek of your life.

ACKNOWLEDGMENTS

ONE OF the points for successful investing that I stress in this book is the need for teamwork. Any work such as this, to come to fruition, requires a concerted effort by many, but the concentrated effort by a few. The Publications and Graphics Department at Lighthouse Publishing has gone the extra mile. My Research and Trading Department have provided timely information, insights, and more importantly, a high level of comradery for this process. This comes from their love of the machinations of the stock market and dedication to excellence.

Also my Team Wall Street instructors, who are in the trenches, doing the deals, and walking the walk. Their unique observations and willingness to share with our students is quite remarkable. Many of our students also deserve credit. They are wonderful. They love and support me, yet challenge me and cause me to refine, to improve, and to stay out in front of the pack.

And now to my love and companion, Laura. She is the better half, which has patience, concern, love, and support for the lesser half. Without these characteristics which she abundantly gives, my life would not be the same and many of these books and courses would be left unfinished.

But there is work to do to educate Americans on better ways to enhance wealth, to increase income, and to live more abundantly. So, to all who desire to do great things, I acknowledge your desire to improve and with God's help and strength, I stand by ready to serve.

MAKING GREAT INVESTMENTS

I AM about to stray from conventional investment wisdom and go off on my own path, but before I do, let me state the investment basics with which I agree. I firmly believe, and will stress repeatedly in this book, that the underlying premise in all stock market deals has to be that you like the company in which you are investing.

Do not buy stock, or options to buy the stock, or a convertible bond that may lead to buying stock, <u>unless you like the company</u>. My market research leads me to a lot of computer charts and other measures of a company's performance. However, even if all the numbers don't measure up, if I like what I see in the real world about a particular company, I usually buy stock in it. I am not oblivious to a company's financial status and projections—I enjoy reading quarterly statements and annual reports—but after all the numbers are crunched and all the words spoken, my investment decisions come down to a few basic points:

1. Can I explain what the company does in a sentence or two? Is the mission of the company so hard to explain that even a detailed analysis will not accurately reflect what it does to make money?

2. Does it have "jazz?" Is it exciting? Does the jazz create a desire to own the stock, and more importantly, will a lot of other people respond? Remember that supply and demand cause stock prices to rise and fall and are the outgrowth of market sentiment—created by news from or about the company.

3. What is the debt of the company? This is easy to find out from reports. I want to make sure no more than 45 to 50% of the assets are offset by debt, which can be the killer of most businesses. Lack of cash flow to cover excessive debt can drive a business into insolvency and, sometimes, into bankruptcy so fast it will make your head spin. I am very concerned about debt ratios.

4. What is the book value or the break-up value of the company? While you may have a hard time finding these numbers yourself, a good stockbroker or brokerage analyst can figure this out for you. There are also other value ratios to figure, such as price/earnings (see my remarks on price/earning ratios in "Common Mistakes To Avoid In The Stock Market" in the chapter 4), book value, and sales-to-book value. What I really want to know is this: Is the company valuable to other people? For example, is it a possible takeover candidate? Does it have assets (meaning companies, divisions, subsidiaries or products) which can be spun off into a new entity? In short, what is the break-up value of the company?

This leads to a system that has rarely failed me: Building wealth by buying assets at a discount. If you've seen my other books or seminars, you know that I cut my teeth in the real estate investment arena. My most lucrative angle to real estate was to make a profit going into the investment, not just coming out. This simply means the investment was undervalued. I picked up assets at a discount.

If you are going to buy stock and sell it for cash, remember, one of the fastest ways a company can improve is for the stock to come up to the price where it should have been trading—in other words, for the price to reflect the "actuality" of the company's status.

If you were to buy a company's stock close to its all-time trading high, as reflected not only in book value but also in its price/earnings ratio, then the chance for it going higher, obviously, is slim. A lot of factors would have to work together for an increase in its valuation. However, if you were to buy into a company at a substantial discount, you could either wait for news to get out on what a good company it is or wait for other institutional investors to start buying in. This way you could get out at a substantial profit a lot faster.

> 5. Where is the exit? This question has been my trademark. It is easy to buy stock but often hard to sell it at a profit. It is easy to get involved in real estate, hard to end the involvement. It is easy to get into personal relationships, and sometimes hard to get out. It is always harder to get out of something than it is to get in. So the emphasis should be on getting out. I always want to know where the exit is.

I'll explain this strategy more when I get to the rolling stock section. But it is important to bring it up here, even if you are holding stock for the long term. The simple point is this: is there enough interest in the company to trigger substantial buying and selling? When it is time for me to unload my holdings, are there going to be other people who will want to buy it? This does not come down to market timing, but to knowing my exit before I go in. When to get out of an investment, if you have not pre-set an exit point, might be when you would not get in.

CONTRASTING OPINIONS

Peter Drucker, in his famous book *The Effective Executive*, said it best: "Our decisions should be based on conflicting opinions." If everything is good, if everybody is bullish, if everybody is buying a certain stock, if the institutional investors are jumping in, I have a real problem, because the exit door can get very crowded when the opinions turn around.

Obviously, analysts working for several different firms are not going to come up with the same opinions about a particular company. It is effective, therefore, to have accounts at different places, to get their opinion reports, find out why certain analysts evaluate a stock good or bad, and why they have chosen to upgrade or downgrade it. I don't put complete faith in analysts' remarks since most of them are not making anywhere near the kind of money they need to be making in order for me to follow their advice. However, it is nice to surround myself with all of these different opinions.

My particular format is to learn as much as I can about a company and what other people are saying about it. Then I let it settle down for awhile and make the decision a few days or weeks later. The stock will always be around. Usually, two or three weeks after analysts upgrade a company and all the stockbrokers get really hot on it, the stock settles down to the original price anyway. You can then evaluate the company based on the fundamentals and the other things I have been writing about so far.

I want to make my decisions based on solid principles. I have found formulas that work very well for me. I also look at the different components of each particular investment and then make my own decisions. I have passed up opportunities on companies when I did not like some of the information I was receiving. A few times I have been burned by not investing in companies that other people invested in, but all-in-all I look back and say that trusting my own opinion (after surrounding myself with a lot of contrasting opinions) has worked best for me.

RISKS AND REWARDS

There always has to be a trade-off. The road to wealth is not a freeway. As a matter of fact, many times it is a very rocky road with many bumps, dips, and detours along the way. Not only are most people not willing to take the risk, but many are not even willing to get on the road. That is fine with me, but for those of you who have decided to play the stock market game, one of the greatest areas in which you can invest and receive the greatest rewards is your own brain power.

I know that sounds trite, but your success in the stock market will be directly connected with the efforts, knowledge, and energy you apply. The quality of your investment decisions is based on the quality of the information you feed into the thinking, meditation, and decision-making process. There is no substitute for good information, and there is also no substitute for timely action. Remember, even though the "how tos" are very important when it comes to determining how to make profits, the stock market is not so much a "how to," as a "when to."

If you want to invest in equities or debt and have no risk at all, the easiest place to put your money is in short-term government securities. With these investments, you can determine the rate of return or yield. Quite simply, there is virtually no risk. However, your profits will increase as you move on up the risk potential scale. I think that you would have to be completely naive not to realize that as you take more risks, the rewards become greater, as do the potential losses.

At some point along this risk versus reward line, you need to determine where you are happy and comfortable. This is usually determined by where you are in your life. Is there a need in your life right now for more income? Do you need more investments producing tax write-offs? Are you shopping around for investments you hope will grow and become worth a lot down the road? Very seldom have I met anybody who just needed more income without needing the tax write-offs and growth vehicle to accompany them—most of us need a blend of all three. However, increasing income or cash flow probably stands out as the most important.

Your need for tax write-offs will go up and down from year to year, depending on the income and losses you have. Your need for growth (you should be contemplating and investing for it at all times) will be heavier in your later years. However, your need for cash flow will always exist and will always be growing. This is evident not only from my years of looking at my own investment portfolio, but also from talking to thousands of people—those who have come through my seminars and relied on my company and me to help them learn the strategies for cash flow. Our goals have been to help people 1) maximize cash flow, 2) lower liability and risk exposure, 3) prepare for a great retirement, 4) make substantial amounts from either real estate, stock market, or business interests, and then 5) make sure that family members eventually get everything through what is called bequeathment.

I have come to realize that cash flow is king. Once again, this is a cliché, but one with so much meaning. The dynamic of cash flow reaches far into everything else we do. It controls our standard of living. It can control the simple "nitty-gritty" things, like which colleges our children will attend. It controls what car we drive, what house we live in, when we go out to dinner, and what types of restaurants we frequent. I have based the bulk of my seminars and books around income generation.

This income generation theme came into focus with one underlying concept: to create a grouping of assets that continually produce monthly income. You want the assets, not you, producing the income. Remember when you first started working? You were probably flipping hamburgers at McDonald's and making minimum wage. After you graduated from high school and went on to college, you probably started making $8 to $20 an hour. Later on, maybe you were put on salary, and made the equivalent of $40 to $50 thousand a year, and/or you started your own business.

All of these forms of making money are what we call earned income. From a tax point of view, earned income is taxed in a specific way and certain offsets can be applied. As you grow older and start accumulating wealth, you start generating what is called unearned income. Unearned income could be from royalties or rents, it could be dividends, capital gains, or any other way of making money whereby your money is making money, not you. Unearned income is probably the goal of most people reading this book. The theme of my seminars, my books, and indeed my whole life has been to teach people how to generate or acquire assets, usually on a leveraged basis, and to generate the kind of income they need to either grow into another lifestyle or sustain the lifestyle they have. This is not only for now, but also for their future—for a rich retirement.

Now back to risk and reward. I must emphatically say now, at the very beginning, I hate losing money! As you read on and get into my different strategies for making money, you will realize that a lot of what I do is designed to stop any cash flow drains or any reduction in asset value. A lot of what I do is defensive in nature.

Simply put, the first strategy in winning is to not lose. Yes, I have chosen some very unique ways of making money, and some of them will be new to you. I hope they are as exciting to you as they are to me. The strategies I am going to show you have been tried and proven effectively, but they fly in the face of conventional wisdom. I hope they'll make sense to you, even if they don't to institutional investors. Remember, we as individual investors can simply go for the income, while the people who are supposedly advising us want to make sure that we have a balanced portfolio, or that we buy their current investment "recommendation of the week."

You can create a balanced portfolio once you have excess income. So, the first job is to create the excess income, but we are always running into interference. It seems that every time we run down the field, a strategy sidesteps us or we get tackled by a particular stock. It is hard to make a living in the stock market because it seems that all the conventional forces are determined to keep us at the bottom of the pack, like a crab trying to crawl out of the pot with all the other crabs pulling it back down. I am reminded of a statement from Woody Hayes, the famous football coach. He had a good halfback on the field who kept getting tackled. Time after time, he tried to run down the field and was met with resistance. Woody finally pulled him over to the sideline and said, "Boy, run where they ain't!"

This is what I have done—sometimes inadvertently—I "run where they ain't." I set my own course, which is to continually develop more cash flow, allowing my family and myself to live off the income from these investments.

Now, if I can create excess income and also keep adding to my asset base (which will continue to produce more income), then, in fact, I'll get into a cycle of ever-increasing wealth and ever-increasing cash flow. Most people never get into this type of cycle (they go to work, pay the bills, go to work, pay the bills, and on and on) and it seems like there is never enough at the end of the month. I have tried to jump off that merry-go-round and get my money earning more money and keep that money compounding and earning yet more money. Once this is started it becomes a habit, and with ever-increasing cash flow I am also able to purchase the investments that will grow for the long term.

> *Knowledge always desires increase; it is like fire,*
> *which must be kindled by some external agent, but which*
> *will afterward propagate itself.*
> —SAMUEL JOHNSON

Today, I believe that the best way to make money is through an aggressive approach to real estate or an aggressive approach to the stock market. I have done the real estate deals and made my first fortune that way. When I started teaching seminars, I realized my true love in life was to share these strategies with other people. The benefits I receive from teaching are simply that I get to see people spending more time with their children, giving more to their churches, and spending those special moments with their spouses. The highest reward for me along this risk and reward spectrum, after working out some of the bugs and taking the risks myself, is to share some of these methods with other people.

Remember that you need to walk in the moccasin of the Indian if you want to really feel what the Indian feels. You need to have the experience yourself. If there is anything that I can do to help you learn a few short cuts, avoid some problems, and show you a better way of getting to your ultimate enhanced cash flow level, then my job as your educator, and this book, will be a success.

Look at your own life and try to determine what you should really be going for. I am going to make a case for building up your income and developing more cash flow, from a weird and contrary point of view. I use what I call "The Mack Truck" theory: you sign a deal, you make an arrangement, you go into business, you buy a property or make another investment, and then you walk out into the street and get flattened by a Mack truck. What do you leave behind for your family? What have you saddled them with? What responsibilities must they now take over? With your life, job, or business the way it is, if you were laid up for six months to a year in a hospital, what income would support you?

Some of the answers are obvious: you can get disability insurance, or for the ultimate bang in life, you can get life insurance. But, simply put, what would happen to you, your family, and your business? You may have a great business today, earning you a lot of money, but how fast could that change? Then what would your family do?

What I am driving at here is that you should build up income from a separate source. You can call this two-stepping your wealth if you want—people have called it that for many years. Two-stepping your wealth means that if you have a nice profit center now—a cash cow—and you are living comfortably, then take some of your profits and move them a step away from your business. I know from running my own business, it is easy to keep recycling all of the money into the business and get into a never-ending spiral of growth. While this may be good in the early years, at some point, you must take some of the money and put it into other types of investments.

A lot of businesses find excess funds going into 401(k), Keogh, or other types of corporate pension plans. Other businesses open up brokerage accounts or bank accounts in the name of the corporation or business and start investing money there. My point is to take some of the money and turn it into a business. Then, if there is a downturn in your business, you have income from another source that can support your lifestyle.

I know many couples who have worked this together, where the husband or the wife is intensely running the business while the other spouse handles the investments. You can share information and consult with each other, so it is almost like having two businesses going, with one being a money management business. However, if you are truly going to turn money management into a business in and of itself, then I think you will find the strategies here helpful. Most of them are designed to treat the stock market just like a business, which is to buy low and sell high, and put the emphasis on selling and creating income.

As A Business?

Those of you who have your own business know how hard it can be to start one and keep it profitable. I am amazed at how many people think they will have all the freedom they want when they own their own business. While it is, and should be, very rewarding, not only from a financial but an emotional point of view, running a business does require a lot of time and energy.

Remember the old nine-to-five days when you were working for someone else? Now, you own your business and all of a sudden you are working from six or seven in the morning until seven or eight at night, sometimes six days a week. You must think about your competition, what they are doing, where they are going, and what you can do to counteract their advances. You need to think about your own management, hiring and training people to handle different aspects of your business, and you need to worry about little nitty-gritty things, like time clocks and employee theft. You also need to worry about compensation plans and measures to protect your business, such as noncompetition and nondisclosure agreements with employees and management.

You have a whole host of things to worry about and now you want to enter the stock market? Guess what? Your best bet is to invest in a dozen or so companies all worrying about these same things. The reason is that you have leveraged knowledge that will help you succeed. In running your own business, you have learned many company strategies and you can look for good management in other businesses.

Remember, bet on the jockey, not on the horse. When we are investing in a company, the number one consideration should be its management. How good are the leaders, what are their experiences, and how will they handle adversity? If they have a great product, but a mediocre management team, the results will be only mediocre. On the other hand, if they have a mediocre product, a good management team will either enhance it, figure out a way to sell it, or create new products and services that will make the company successful.

SUMMARY

When I think of the many people I have been able to teach and consult with, I continually ask myself the question, "What is it that I need, and what is it that these people need to sustain ourselves as the kind of people we truly want to be?" It comes down to the simple economic fact of having income that will sustain us through our lives. You've heard of PMA: Positive Mental Attitude; well let's move on and go for PMI: Perpetual Monthly Income. This whole concept of developing assets that will produce income–even perpetual income–is my financial goal.

Outwardly, this has nothing to do with the spiritual or emotional areas of my life, yet I have learned by happy and sad experience that my financial status affects a lot of other things. I want to ask you a few questions, and I know that these are strange questions: Could you be a little bit better you if you had more money coming in? Could you give more to your church? Could you spend more time with your kids or grandkids? Could you give more to charities? Could you go back to college, take classes, and learn things that you haven't been able to learn?

My continual challenge in life is to balance these aspects. But now, in the financial arena, I want to share those things that will help you fundamentally alter your outlook on money. By the time you finish reading this book and applying these techniques, principles, and formulas, I want you to be successful and have more income, doing the things in life that you really want to do.

2

THE CAB DRIVER WHO TOOK ON WALL STREET

WHEN I was young, my goals were not lofty. I didn't want to be President or conquer the world. My dream was to become a college professor. To educate myself and reach my dream I needed income. I could not get any money from my parents, and because we were a middle class family, it was hard to get college grants and loans.

To generate income, I started up an insurance agency. I figured that if I wrote enough policies I could have continual income from premiums–at least enough to support me through college. But as hard as I worked to get policies on the books, it was still hard to get paid. I was successful, but it just wasn't enough.

So I made two moves that changed my life permanently. First, inspired by the book *How I Took a Thousand Dollars and Made Five Million Investing in Real Estate* by William Nickerson, I turned to real estate. I borrowed money to buy my first couple of properties.

Second, simply out of the need to buy groceries for my family, I latched onto a job driving a taxicab. Have you ever had one of those experiences that afterwards continue to change just about everything else you do? A simple idea exchange that becomes a turning point? Driving a taxi was just such an experience for me.

In order for you to understand what this is all about, you need to come back with me to my first day driving a cab. The company I started driving for, Yellow Cab Company in Tacoma, Washington, had a mandatory rule that entailed spending a day training with a cab driving trainer named Bill Marsh.

After being out with Bill for about 45 minutes–30 minutes at Denny's getting him a cup of coffee, 15 minutes actually on the road–I realized that I could handle this cab driving business on my own. As I watched what he did, it dawned on me that to be a successful cab driver you only had to do one thing.

I asked Bill if he would take me back to the lobby to get my own taxi. He said I had to spend the whole "mandatory" day with him. "Look," I said. "Could you please just take me back?"

Back at the cab company I talked to the owner/partner. "Mrs. Potter?" I said, "My name is Wade Cook. I'm a brand new cab driver. You don't know me, but is there any way I can just take a taxi out for the day?"

She replied, "Oh no, no. You have to spend the day with Bill Marsh."

I persisted. I explained to her that I knew Tacoma really well and told her that if she didn't like what I did by five or six o'clock that afternoon, she would never see me again. She listened and ended up giving me a little, beat-up, Dodge Dart for the day.

I took it out that first day and made $110–that was my net. The second day I came back with about $90 profits and the third day about $140. I was off and running. I began making between $3,200 and $3,800 a month. I needed about $1,200 a month to live on. I was able to take the rest, holding some out for taxes, and apply it to buying and fixing up houses. With this money, I purchased nine rental houses my first year. The rest of my real estate story is told in the books *Real Estate Money Machine, How to Pick Up Foreclosures,* and *Real Estate for Real People.*

My point here is the lesson I learned in driving a taxi–to me the most significant and powerful financial lesson I have ever learned in my life. In fact, since then I've hobnobbed with some of the greatest financial minds in the country (doing radio, TV talk shows and seminars in 43 different states), and nothing I've learned from any of those men and women is more powerful than what I learned my first day driving a cab. The lesson is simply this—*money is made in the meter drop.*

What does "the meter drop" mean? Every time you get into a taxi, the driver pushes the meter down (nowadays it's a computerized button), and it costs you $1.50 to $2. Whether it is a $5 run or a $50 run, you still pay $1.50 every time you get in the cab.

Many cab drivers only take big runs. In Tacoma they positioned themselves in town to get the run to Sea-Tac Airport, a $30 to $35 fare. At the same time, I was beating the cab to death by going for all the small runs. I would take the $3, $6 and $8 runs. At the end of some busy days I would have up to 40, 50, or 60 runs. Do you see the difference? I was killing them. Now, don't get me wrong, I've had my share of big runs too. Sometimes a little $6 run would turn into a $15 run because the person my passenger was going to visit wasn't home. However, it was those extra meter drops that really added up to a lot of cash.

REPETITIVE CASH FLOW

The meter drop made it clear to me that the bottom line to wealth is duplication and repetition. For example, a hamburger in Tampa Bay should taste just like a hamburger in San Francisco Bay, and McDonald's took advantage of this, not by selling one gigantic hamburger, but by selling billions of little ones—and french fries. Repetition made the McDonald's fortune.

About nine months after I started driving, Mrs. Potter called us all in for a meeting between shifts. While we were waiting for her to come in, all the cab drivers were bragging about how much money they were making. Bill Marsh sat there and said he had made more money in one month than anybody there. I casually asked him how much he made. With a note of triumph, he said, "One month I made $900." All the cab drivers started oohing over him, thinking that $900 was a lot of money.

Now remember, my lowest month was over $3,200. But I said with a smile, "Boy, that is a lot of money, Bill." No way was I going to mention to these guys how much I was making. They could see the rental properties I was buying and draw their own conclusions, but to this day, they still don't know, unless they've read my book.

On to real estate. At first, I did not follow the lesson I learned as a cabdriver. I went out and started the old buy-and-wait game. I waited for inflation, waited for Washington D.C. tax write-offs, and waited for other things I had no control over. After a year of playing the buy-and-wait game—the rental game—I had to sell one of my properties. I needed money. I sold the property, received some cash for the down payment and carried back a mortgage. The key, however, is that I didn't get all the cash up front. I sold the property under what you would call "owner financing."

I sat in my taxi, staring at the check I received from the down payment, and realized something: I had purchased this little property with $1,200 down; when I sold it, even after closing costs, I ended up with $2,200–$1,000 more than I put into this property in the beginning. And, I would receive net monthly payments of $160 for 28 years.

I just stared at the check. I had stumbled across a whole new way of investing. I thought, why am I playing this buy-and-wait game? Why am I turning my life over to renters? Why wait for tax write-offs out of Washington D.C., hoping some benevolent congressman gets a depreciation bill passed through Congress? Why am I doing things I have no control over? Why don't I just go out and buy properties to sell? Why not do the meter drop with my properties?

I figured that I could sell a couple more rentals right away and then target properties I could buy and fix up a little bit, then turn around and sell with this new "money machine."

Back then, I did not call it the "money machine." I called it "turning properties" or "flipping properties." Nevertheless, I thought to myself that I had to treat real estate like the "meter drop." Instead of getting in and waiting, why not just buy for the sole purpose of reselling? This way I could build up a huge base of deeds of trust and mortgages and have monthly checks coming in. In the end it was these monthly checks that allowed me, and can allow you, to live the way we want.

At that time I had a lot of rental properties, but they were only making a little bit of money. If one renter didn't pay one month, it ruined the profits for the whole year. I was constantly putting more money into taking care of these properties. Any of you who have had rental properties realize that no matter what kind of money you have lying around in the bank, any rental property will "eat it up" and take it away from you. That giant sucking sound is real.

The rental game is just not what it is cracked up to be. However, the Money Machine is a fabulous way to make money by literally forcing the issue–rapidly accumulating wealth. I did this over the next year. I went out specifically looking for properties I could buy and sell quickly. Again, it was the meter drop. Get the passenger in, get the passenger out, and get on to the next deal. After doing many of these properties, I was able to quit and retire at the age of 29.

On To The Stock Market

Faced with time and financial freedom, I ended up writing a book. I never did go back to college to get my teaching degree, but I did end up with a book in the bookstores. Since that time, I have written several more. I entered the lecture circuit and started traveling the country. My semi-retired state was really becoming a fun career. This also gave me the opportunity to make more money.

I knew I didn't want to put the excess money into savings accounts. I did buy a lot of second mortgages, which kept my cash flow ever increasing. In addition, $5,000 here and $10,000 there went into stock market investments.

I opened up a brokerage account and bought mutual funds, one of which had gone up in value 14% each of the previous three years. As soon as I bought it, it went down 2%. Quite a few stocks went up in value, but most of them floundered around and many went down. I figured the stock market was not for me because I was going to have to learn a whole new set of rules and vocabulary to be successful at it. Meanwhile, I was still involved with real estate and teaching seminars.

Then I got a call from a friend who at that time was a stock-broker. He wanted to take me to lunch and explain what he was doing with many of his clients.

At lunch that day, I listened to the most fascinating idea, which struck a chord with me telling me it was right and true, especially at that time. He wanted me to buy 100 shares of Motorola stock.

I bought 100 shares of this stock at $50 a share for $5,000 plus $40 in commissions. The stockbroker asked me to put the stock up for sale at $60. Those of you who are familiar with the stock market and have brokerage accounts realize that you can put an order in to sell the stock and take off for Hawaii. If, and when, the stock hits $60 a share, the sale will be triggered automatically by computer.

I put in the order to sell at $60 a share. About six weeks later, the stock hit $60 and the computer sold it. I had $6,000 in my account, minus about $90 in commissions. I made about $910 profit on this transaction. Then the stockbroker said to put in an order to buy the stock again at $50 a share. I put in an order for 108 shares at $50. About five weeks later the stock rolled backed down to $50 and the computer triggered a buy. Now I was the owner of 108 shares of Motorola at $50 a share.

At that time, the stock dropped down to around $48 or $49, and I was getting kind of worried. But it climbed right back up to $60 a share and the computer triggered a sale again. I had the excess profit in my account. The stock hit $60 a share several times and kept climbing up to $61 to $62, so I did miss out on some of the possible profits, but I made the consistent, reliable profits. I did this particular stock many times for several years.

This cab driver had found a way to do a meter drop on Wall Street.

3

MAKING YOUR
MONEY WORK HARD

I HAVE repeatedly espoused the working hard formula in my major course, the Wall Street Workshop™ and in my Zero to Zillions™ Home Study Course. I am convinced that many people do not know how to make a lot of money because they don't know how to measure the effectiveness of their money. I am talking about calculating a simple yield or a "rate of return."

It is really quite simple. To figure your rate of return, take the money you get back from a particular investment and divide it by the cash you have tied up in the investment. In real estate and other forms of tax shelter investments, you would calculate the cash you get back in the form of income, and you could also calculate the increase in the value of the property and tax savings you receive. You could spend a lot of time calculating specific rates of return based on different features of an investment.

When it comes to stock market investments, I am particularly interested in the cash-on-cash yield. I am not looking at a compounding yield, except as a fun figure to calculate from time to time. An actual cash-on-cash yield is measured by taking the cash I get back on an investment and dividing it by the money I had tied up.

The only concern I have is this: when most people calculate yields they have a tendency to calculate them on an annualized basis. For example, if you had $10,000 in a CD earning 5%, at the end of the year you would have $500 or possibly $540 in compounded interest. That would be a yield of 5% or 5.4%.

When it comes to stock market investments, use my formulas and you will notice that I do a lot of things in two-week to one-month periods. For example, I usually write covered calls for the next month out. I am generating one-month premiums or one- and two-week premiums. My rate of return then is a one-month rate of return, which is substantially different from an annual return.

If you wanted to calculate an annualized return, you could take a one-month return and multiply by 12, or take a two-week return and multiply by 26 (there are 26 two-week periods in a year). If you start thinking in terms of monthly returns and going after investments that produce large two- and four-week returns, then the whole nature and volume of your cash flow will substantially change. The point is to figure out how much you get back for every dollar you invest.

SPEND PROFITS, NOT PRINCIPAL
One of the earliest pieces of advice I learned when I started investing money was to spend my profits, not my principal. Let me relate that to using the money you are making in your brokerage account. Most of you, in setting up your brokerage accounts, will have all of the profits going back into different investments. At some point, though, the needs in your life will change. You will need to start living off the income from your investments. But until that point, let me share some ideas you can apply with the profits from dividends, capital gains, or option income.

You can immediately plow money back into stock. If you have a stock that has a "dividend reinvestment program," you definitely should take advantage of it. You will be able to buy additional shares of stock in the company with the dividends and without paying any commissions. Sometimes you can buy the stock at a 10% discount (so all of your money is going back into the stock at a discount).

One of the best newsletters in the country for learning more about this is called *The Money Paper.* Check the recommended reading section at the back of this book for more information on this paper. This newsletter will give you names of companies and even, for a small fee, sell you a single share from some of these companies so that, as a current stockholder, you can get in on its dividend reinvestment program.

When I buy a new stock for the first time, my brokers tell me if it has a dividend reinvestment program attached to it. If it does, the brokers set up the program so that each time a dividend is paid it goes to buy more stock in the company.

The dividend may be paid while the stock price is high. If you are doing the rolling stock strategy with this company, that could be a little uncomfortable, but not too bad. In lieu of doing it that way, you could just have the dividends paid directly to your account or even have a check sent to your home.

Let me say it one more time: spend your profits, not your principal. Another way of saying this is to spend your interest, not your capital. Leave your capital base intact. Use it to spin off income to live on.

BET ON THE JOCKEY

One concept that will always prove successful in investing is simply this: Bet on the jockey, not on the horse.

TEAM	PRODUCT	=	RESULTS
C +	A	=	C+
A +	C	=	A
A +	A	=	A+

You see, if a company has a really good product (let's say an "A" product), but you have a "C" team of mediocre people handling the product, then you are going to have mediocre results. Conversely, if you have an "A" team, a really great group of people running the company or investment idea, even though the product or project may be a "C," the team will be successful, either bringing the "C" product to its potential or dumping it and finding other products. They will win.

When looking at investing in an apartment complex or other project through a limited partnership, look at the people handling it. What is their experience? How long have they been in the business? What other success stories have they had? What have their failures been? It is the quality of people that will determine the outcome of the company. Another way of looking at this is to learn from an old statement that my father made to me. He said, "Wade, if you are not going to be a star yourself, latch onto a star."

WHAT DRIVES A STOCK UP?

I like to find stocks that are going to have a lot of upward pressure. I remember when I was driving a taxi; from time to time I would see a Plymouth Fury in the garage. We had a few small cars, like Dodge Darts, but most of our cabs were Plymouth Furies. I knew the engines in these Chrysler products would last forever, if the right cars were purchased and taken care of.

The mechanics knew this too. Sometimes the Furies would have bald tires or the interiors would be torn up. Sometimes the paint job would look shabby, but rather than doing the little patch–up work on the exterior, the mechanics brought the cars in to check out the engine pressure.

That seemed to be all they were concerned with: the pressure of the engine. Individual car owners would be concerned about the look of the car, but not them. Engine pressure determined how long the cars would last and how much power that they would have.

How do we apply this to the stock market? I like to buy stock in companies that have a good chance of going up. Call this the "pressure"–a lot of upside potential. It could be in either a sector or an industry group, or it could be a stock coming out of bankruptcy. New ideas, technology, new applications, mergers and acquisitions, stock splits, and new management all can provide pressure to drive the price up.

This pressure applies particularly well to turnaround candidates, stocks that have been in decline but show signs of charging forward again. Let me show you how to find them and gauge their potential.

Look in the newspaper, going down the left column of the stock page, and look at the highs and lows for the year. If you see a company's high for the year at $15 and a low at $13, and the stock is currently trading at $13.50, this is not a turnaround candidate. Don't get me wrong–this stock could go from $13 up to $30 or $50 a share, but move on down the page and find this: a stock with a high of $13.00 but a low of $1 and currently trading at $1.50.

Now this company could be heading for bankruptcy and the stock could stop trading in a very short time, but at least you know there is turnaround potential. Don't think that just because you bought it at $1.50, it is going to go up. All you really know is that there has been something wrong with this company and it's a good time to do your homework.

QUICK NOTE: In the stock market pages, a small "vj" in front of the company name signifies that the company is in bankruptcy. (Please read in chapter 5 about bankrupt companies.) Again, all that you learn here is that it is a turnaround candidate. Now it's time for you and your stockbroker to do your homework and find out if this company can come back out of the doldrums.

What can cause it to rise? There are a few things: 1) a change of management; 2) new licenses or applications of existing products; and 3) mergers with other companies. I like these kinds of companies because a lot of people have given up on them.

Remember the old stockholders who bought the stock at $12 or $13 a share and then watched it plummet. Some of these previous stockholders sold out at $8, some at $6, some at $4 and now the stock is clear down to $1 a share. Ask yourself, do these people want to get involved again? The answer is usually no. But those of us coming in new see the company and its turnaround potential. This presents a great way to find stocks through a procedure I call "bottom fishing."

BOTTOM FISHING

Last fall my children and I stopped by a nursery and purchased some daffodil bulbs. Daffodils are one of my favorite flowers. Since I come from the Northwest, you can see why. We are famous for our daffodils up here. In Southern California they have the Rose Parade, we have the Daffodil Parade.

We took some time, dug our holes, and planted the bulbs in the ground. Once we filled in the holes with dirt, my children stood back and immediately wanted to see the flowers. I had to explain to them that the flowers would not come out until after the winter. In the spring they would start to grow. I am confident that when spring comes and they see the results of their work and realize how beautiful the daffodils are, they will be as excited as can be.

Bottom fishing is buying low-priced stocks with the hope that the company will either turn around or grow in value–this is what we are hoping will happen. Plant the bulbs. If you have good fertilizer, good soil, the right amount of water, the right kind of bulb, and a little luck, you will get the results you wished for. Not all the bulbs will grow, but I am confident that the few that grow and bloom will make a big difference in my stock portfolio

TYPES OF BROKERAGE ACCOUNTS

When you go to open your brokerage account you must realize that there are three different types of firms. The information here will help you make a decision on which type of account or accounts to have.

The first type of account is at a "full-service broker," including some of the largest and oldest brokerage houses: Merrill Lynch, Smith Barney, Piper Jaffray, et cetera. These brokerage houses will charge larger commissions, but they will also give you research data, reports, and make a lot of information available to you. They will call you when they have a good deal.

The second type of brokerage account is with what is called a "discount broker." In this category, I would place Charles Schwab, Fidelity Investments, et cetera. They are about mid-range on the commission scale. I particularly like Charles Schwab, and I have many accounts there. Very user friendly, Charles Schwab has a computer tie-in service called "Street Smart" and "ESchwab" that lets me become a stockbroker at home.

The third type of broker is called a "deep-discount broker." You cannot open up a financial magazine or any other financial paper without seeing several of these firms advertised. Falling into this category would be Accutrade, National Discount Brokers, Jack Smith & Co., Kennedy Cabot and a host of others. Their commissions are very low, say $25 per trade, and sometimes it doesn't matter how much stock you trade.

One strategy I have a hard time agreeing with is to use all the information you get from a full-service broker and handle all your trades with a deep-discount broker. I don't like ripping off ideas like that.

Let me tell you what I did. I hired a full-service broker because I like doing business with them, and their services are quite extensive and rewarding. The extra commissions I pay have more than been returned to me in terms of information I have learned about companies and investment strategies. A good stockbroker makes you money, they don't cost. One broker made me $63,000 on one trade. This amount can pay for a lot of commissions on other deals. No Internet account has brought me this kind of deal.

I have even moved some of my accounts to the full-service broker from the other types of brokers. First, I negotiated for the lowest possible commissions I could get. Don't think you need to have a lot of money to do this. I only put in around $5,000 to open the account. Obviously, the broker was hoping I'd recommend him to others. He gave me a discount rate of 40% off the standard rate after further negotiation. Request the "investment club" discount from your broker. (Note: I am not a broker and do not ever make recommendations, nor do I ever get anything when my students make trades through their brokers.)

You can have accounts at all three types of brokerage houses or just choose one that you like. It depends on your level of expertise and how much research you want to do. Remember, the deep-discount brokers and many discount brokers will not give you any advice at all. When I mention something to Charles Schwab brokers on the phone, there is complete silence, even if it's something simple like, "Well, I bought this stock at $3.50 and I am going to sell it again at $8.50. That's a $5 profit." They do not respond at all.

So, if you need to have a response, if you need ideas, if you need a sounding board, then you may want to consider a full-service broker. While I may not agree with that advice at all times, at least my full-service broker is there and I can use him as a sounding board for what I want to do.

MARGIN ACCOUNTS

When you open up your brokerage account, it is my highest recommendation that you open up a margin account. Many of the stocks we are rolling are "designated stocks," the stocks trading under $5, which do not have margin capabilities. But working with higher-priced stocks will give you margin-trading capabilities. Let me explain what this means. I'm not saying that you should use the margin. Margin is a form of debt. Be very careful with debt.

The brokerage firm will be willing to lend you money based on the security of the current assets you hold in your account. This means that if you put in $10,000 cash or securities you will be able to buy $20,000 worth of marginable securities. This lets you double your investment base.

To explain the way this works: If you purchase securities with $10,000 cash, the brokerage will allow you to purchase $20,000 worth, in essence loaning you the other $10,000. There will be a small interest charge on this loan. Recently, the interest rate has been 7.5%. This charge is deducted from your account each month. Remember only use margin occasionally.

Let me move on with this and explain to you some of the other "shop talk" that can be used with your investments to help you get maximum benefits. If you have $20,000 in stock in the account, you obviously get the growth and dividends on that stock. If the stock goes down in value, your broker may ask you to bring in more money, which is called a "margin call." However, if the stock goes up in value, you may be able to buy more stock with your increased leverage.

When you call your broker, ask, "What is my buying power?" That is exactly the term you should use. You've spent the entire $20,000, but a few days later you may have a buying power of $800. This means your stocks have gone up in value and you can buy $800 more stock. You could call up two weeks later and have another $600 in buying power. This means your stocks have gone up in value again. You can leverage your money in quite an effective manner.

Then again, you may call a week later and not have any buying power. In fact, you may have a margin call, and need to bring in $400. Obviously, you should not spend all of your money, but keep some cash available in the account. There is a difference between your cash available and buying power. Any good brokerage house can scan its computer to tell you what these amounts are in a matter of seconds.

Can you get into trouble with the margin account? The answer is yes, when you have a margin call and no money. A full-service brokerage firm will do everything it can to stop you from getting into trouble. If your stocks drop in value, the firm will sell off those excess securities over your margin amounts if you don't bring in cash. The only uneasiness would arise when you have a margin call from time to time. To solve this, simply keep some cash available to cover it. I really like margin accounts because they let you enhance your asset base so rapidly. In writing calls against our stock we double the rate of monthly returns as we only put up half the money. However, as great as these returns get, all debt should be approached very cautiously.

In regard to your pension plans, if you set up a pension plan with any brokerage house or insurance company, it is almost guaranteed you won't be permitted to trade stock on margin. Lately some firms with certain pension trust documents may allow for margin trades on some of your money.

This lets you rapidly accumulate wealth in a pension plan. However, you already have the capability to do rolling stock, or writing covered calls within your pension plan or IRA. If you are going to set up a Keogh plan, corporate pension plan, or a 401(k), please give a call to Anderson Law Group, PLLC (1-800-706-

4741) or contact them at www.alglaw.com first, because we are the best in the country at doing this. Not only will we set up your pension plan, but we will be the "behind the scenes" administrator. You will be the trustee and only you control the money. Also, we do not charge an annual "asset maintenance fee" of 1.5 to 2.5% like the other firms do.

Having a margin account means most stockbrokers will allow you to double your purchasing power with the cash in your account. For example, if you put in $5,000, most stockbrokers will allow you to buy $10,000 worth of stock. What do they get out of this? Number one, they earn interest on this money, which will be debited from your account every month. Number two, they are able to sell more stock, thus earning higher commissions.

The stockbroker will require collateral on this type of account, choosing only marginable securities that he or she likes and is willing to use as collateral. Going back to our example, if you have $5,000 in an account, and you are able to buy $10,000 worth of stock—you are in fact borrowing $5,000 from the stockbroker. The benefits are great in that you now own twice as much stock. If you are applying some of the principles I present, like rolling stock or writing options, you will be able to buy more stock and diversify your stock holdings. You can make extra money go a long way. If your brokerage doesn't like the stock they will not allow you to purchase it on margin.

ONE QUICK POINT: When you have more money in your account or when you have more experience, your stockbroker may allow the margin account to go down to anywhere from 40 to 32%. To buy $10,000 worth of stock, you may get to the point where you would only have to bring in $3,400. This is a higher degree of leverage. Once again, your stockbroker has to feel comfortable with this. At the very beginning with new accounts, stockbrokers are going to be very cautious of the types of stocks they allow you to have. After many years of keeping my accounts in one place, I have earned some leniency with my stockbrokers. At the beginning they would not allow me to margin stocks under $5, especially penny stocks or low-cost stocks listed on the computer bulletin board. After awhile, some of them allowed these types of stocks to be used as collateral. Lately Internet stocks have taken off, but most are very volatile. It's not uncommon for a brokerage firm to require 70% margin or so on these stocks.

Be warned that if any of the stocks in your margin account go down, there could be a margin call. You would have to bring in more cash or other securities to act as collateral. Likewise, if the stocks in your margin account go up, it could increase your "buying power." I have tried to figure out some relationship between cash available and margin buying power, but there seems to be no way of calculating it. Each stockbroker has his or her own way to calculate your buying power. Basically, as the stocks go up you have more buying power, and as the stocks go down you have less.

My last point on margin accounts is to be very cautious with this debt unless you have extra cash available. You may not want to use up all of your buying power. For example, if you put in $10,000 and you have a buying power of $20,000, you may want to spend only $14,000 of the buying power so you do not get caught behind the eight ball.

ABOUT MARKET MAKERS

When the stock is trading, there is a lot of movement during the day with buys and sells going on between them. Many times you will call up for information on a stock and hear that it is $3\frac{1}{8}$ bid, $3\frac{1}{2}$ ask, or that it's $3\frac{1}{8}$ bid, but $3\frac{1}{4}$ last trade.

What is this? When someone buys a stock, he usually pays the ask. He sells the stock at the bid price. How did a trade get in at $3\frac{1}{4}$? Market makers purchasing the stock at $3\frac{1}{8}$ are really trying to sell the stock at $3\frac{1}{2}$, but they may sell it for some price in between the bid and ask. Many times when I called up my broker I am told they make a market in a particular stock, which makes me feel more confident. I can get the stock at a somewhat lower price than I would normally have to pay if I were just buying at the ask. I would venture to say that, most of the time, the savings make up for the commissions I pay. It would be hard to deny that the assistance of a full-service broker, who is acting in your best interest, can sometimes make up in savings the amount or even more than what you are paying in commissions.

CHOOSING AND USING A GOOD STOCKBROKER

I have thought a lot about this section. This is covered extensively in the Wall Street Workshop™, as well as in the Zero to Zillions™ Home Study Course on audio and videocassettes. We're going to do a paradigm shift. I am going to teach you how to look at choosing and using a stockbroker from a whole different perspective by employing a method that I hope will be functional and get you up to speed very quickly.

I learned in my real estate days that a good real estate agent could make a person very wealthy. I am convinced a stockbroker can do the same thing. Unfortunately, most areas in which you invest limit your ability to get to know your stockbroker. This is especially true if you use a deep-discount stockbroker. How can you get to be friends with your stockbroker? How can you learn your stockbroker's strengths and weaknesses? How can your stockbroker learn your strengths and weaknesses? How can you ensure that your stockbroker knows what you can and cannot do? How can you be sure of what your stockbroker can and cannot do? How can you develop a working relationship with someone who is constantly changing and who you do not work with on a personal basis?

First, determine what type of brokerage firm will best serve your needs. I want to know that a stockbroker enjoys his business and is willing to get up early to be at the office when the market opens. Does he enjoy it enough to study and research the market? Does he truly enjoy learning? Does he read *The Wall Street Journal* or other papers? Does he make it a policy to be up-to-date on all the latest information? Does he engage in his own personal transactions? Would he get involved in the same transactions he advises you to undertake? These are all very important questions.

Next, choose a brokerage firm that will allow you to build a good long relationship. In the beginning, the relationship may not appear to be valuable, but it is crucial if this relationship is to become profitable to you in the long term.

Another area of concern in dealing with a stockbroker regards having fun with your investments. Are you laughing and joking and having a good time? I know this sounds strange, but if you are not having a good time, you are not likely to be very successful at trading. The stock market is not only about numbers, it's about feelings and emotions. It's about timing. It's about learning when to get involved in an investment and knowing when to get out of an investment.

The key here is whether or not your stockbroker enjoys the business and is having fun. If he does, it can become contagious, not only to you, but also to his other clients. This can start a chain reaction of valuable information. Other clients you don't even know will bring your stockbroker other deals and tell him about other companies that he may not be aware of. Your stockbroker will determine if any of this information is valuable, and he will share the information with you. A good stockbroker will become a clearinghouse, producing a lot of good information through his access to a wealth of sources and an extensive computer network.

A PERSONAL NOTE: One main reason I chose my current stock brokerage was that I was attracted by its financial consultant, or stockbroker, who is very knowledgeable and aggressive. My definition of that is street savvy. Even though he is young, he seems to grasp not only the macro but the micro process of stock and option maneuvering.

I thrive on information. I want to know everything I can about a company before I invest in its stock or purchase options on its stock. Every stockbroker has access to Standard and Poor's, Bloomberg's, and several other information services, many of which are very costly. A stockbroker can spend thousands of dollars a year just to have access to the maximum amount of information available. If he does, then I can be assured of receiving reliable, updated information from a variety of sources. I can base my decisions on several contrasting opinions. That's why I really like the bigger brokerage houses. They generally have more of the "little" services that at first don't seem to be of much significance, but in fact can be very helpful.

One of the things I like to know is the cost basis I have in the stock. If I am trying to decide whether to purchase several more shares of a stock I previously bought, I want to know what I paid for it. If I am trying to sell it, I definitely want to know how much I paid. Since I keep several brokerage accounts in different pension plans and corporations, the cost basis can be different for each stock in each account. My accounts require an abundance of inquiries, and I need stockbrokers who are ready to assist me with this.

My stockbroker can tell me within a matter of seconds what my cost basis is, through the computerized services he pays to have in his office. The number he brings up on his computer tells me this information plus what commissions have already been paid. I get exactly "to the penny" how much money I have invested in a particular stock. These services help me make important decisions, and he pays the fees. In the long run, these services also help my stockbroker, since I am buying and selling more stocks than normal, enabling him to pick up extra commissions.

Remember when I mentioned the word "fun?" Let me carry it to another level. I don't know about you, but I like to do business with friends. For instance, if I have a friend at church that is a good car mechanic, I have a tendency to ask for his services. If I have a friend who owns a grocery store, I want to shop at his store. If I don't have friends in a particular profession, such as dry cleaning or shoe sales, I will search out and make friends in that profession.

Why not carry this through to the stock market? Are you friends with your stockbroker? Can you become friends with your stockbroker? Usually, friendships are developed, or at least fortified, outside of a business setting. Sometimes you can't do this with a stockbroker because his life is so busy during the time the stock market is open that there is really no time to develop a personal relationship. Fortunately, however, even in a business setting, you can build a good friendship. What this means to me is that the stockbroker actually knows me. He knows what I am after. He knows what gets me going and knows the kind of money I like to make. He realizes that I am looking for investments that will continually support my family and me if everything else in my life fails. Also, he is a friend who will call when good deals come around.

When was the last time your stockbroker called you? I am not talking about the stockbroker who calls you about the latest, hot deal—a stockbroker you have never heard of before. Those calls are just a waste of time to me. I'm talking about somebody who really understands the quality of the companies I am looking for. I need a stockbroker who understands the different formulas I am using to determine which stocks and options I need to buy and sell, and who can help me when I want to get out of these different types of investments.

Another point about friends is that you get to know their good points as well as their bad points, their strengths and their weaknesses. If you have a stockbroker who is primarily into options, then why not capitalize on his field of expertise? If you have a stockbroker who really understands covered calls and the formulas that go behind them, then why not make good use of this knowledge? If you are looking for "start-up" companies and IPOs (Initial Public Offerings), then find a broker who specializes in that particular area. You could have a variety of stockbrokers helping you with a range of investment ideas.

Most stockbrokers, however, are "general practitioners." They offer many types of services. Although they may have a certain area of expertise, they are at least conversant and proficient enough in other areas to help you earn money in a variety of ways.

As I mentioned earlier, are your stockbrokers doing the deals themselves? If they are not doing the deals, they are probably not following the stocks very closely. When a stockbroker is actually doing the deals there is a real tendency to keep up with those particular stocks in which he or she is investing. I learned this concept years ago in the real estate field. I could hardly ask a property tax question of a CPA (Certified Public Accountant) and get an answer, unless he himself was investing in real estate. If he was into real estate and keeping up with investments, he usually kept up-to-date with all the tax law changes that affected real estate.

The same is true in the stock market arena. An old axiom in the life insurance industry stated that you would probably never sell a policy bigger than the one you own on your own life. So the question to ask your stockbroker is, do you believe in this same policy, which would imply, do you believe in the company you are buying stock in? If you do, are you willing to share that information with your friends, your clients?

I want my investment experiences, and yours, to be pleasant ones. Even if I lose money on a particular investment on a given day, I want someone who can sympathize with me. When I am making money, I want someone who will pat me on the back and congratulate me. Likewise, I want to be able to do the same thing. I know my stockbrokers, from time to time, have received awards. They have received recognition in the industry and I want to be there as one of their biggest supporters.

You would be amazed at how a "built-in" friendship can bring out the best in everybody. This is especially true when brokers know exactly what you are looking for. This is also true if you know your stockbroker's experiences and limitations. Once you have learned this, you can work together, like a well-oiled machine.

4

MAKING YOUR MONEY WORK HARDER

As I travel the country doing radio and television talk shows, I emphasize that I treat the stock market like a business. I am constantly asked what that means, as if the interviewer does not understand the parallels between investments in the stock market and a business. People start businesses for many reasons, the foremost being to make a lot of money. Even if they start up a business for freedom or to create tax write-offs, the point is that a business is operated to make a profit. If it is run wisely, the business owner can and will get rich.

Stock market investments require the same discipline. The following points will show how to treat the stock market like a business:

1. The term "buy low and sell high" is so common that people ignore it, especially those who do not know what it means. Let me express it another way: buy wholesale and sell retail. It is easy to say, so you are probably asking, "Okay, how do you buy stocks at wholesale and then sell at retail?" Here's how:

a.   Buying stocks wholesale means buying stocks that are on dips, bottom fishing stocks, or investing in severely low-priced stocks that have a chance of turning around. In order to be profitable in any business it is essential to buy wholesale and sell retail. Doing this with the stock market means taking advantage of the volatility of certain stocks, buying when they dip down to a good bottom resistance level. Wholesale buying can be accomplished by selling calls or puts– generating income, which adjust your cost basis downward. See *Stock Market Miracles* and *Safety 1st Investing* for more information on selling puts.

b.   Find stocks that have gone down due to mismanagement, losses, or some other catastrophe and are ready to bounce back. I call these "turnarounds." Wait for the stock to bottom out. Purchase it when it starts to come back up.

c.   Another angle to this would be to buy stocks or options for the sole purpose of reselling them at a small profit: not trying to make a huge profit. You should already know the price movement of the stock by looking at the charts on TC2000 (Telechart 2000®).

2.   A business for most people has to be fun and exciting. If it is not, they will quit or not be very good at it. Another point, most business owners get to be experts in their fields, often starting out by breaking off from a bigger company to specialize in their area of expertise. If one can get good at stock market strategies, to him it becomes a business, i.e., rapid turnover, super discount buying, et cetera.

The same holds true for the stock market. While there are many strategies that can make you rich, certain strategies may fit your investor profile better. The ones I like the best are the ones that generate cash flow, with monthly profits that are deposited into my account or mailed to my home. Why not specialize in those types of investments? Another way of saying this is that I am not into investments for the long term; I am into seeing how much cash can be generated from them in the short term. This can best be done with covered call writing, and can also be done with rolling stocks or options, especially options on stock split companies.

ONE POINT: Know when to get out of the investment. You also need to know this when you are running a business. At what point on a particular product or service (that is not selling) should you lower the price or stop selling it? In the stock market, you also need to know when to get out. I have covered knowing when to get out of options in other chapters.

Excitement is generated when you make money. It is easier to get out of bed in the morning if you know you are going to make a few thousand dollars by the end of the day. Create a business that generates excitement for you, and if excitement for you is a nice balanced portfolio, great, go for that. If excitement for you is monthly cash flow, then go for that. If excitement is fluctuating bond prices and rolling bonds, then go for that. Whatever gets you excited, then specialize in that area and you will have a higher propensity for being successful.

3. Consider what is the highest and best use of a particular stock. For example: some stocks generate nice options premiums when sold. Some stocks do not have call premiums available. Other stocks are good for rolling. You need to research each stock and ask what is its highest and best use.

Likewise, you need to look at yourself and ask what your highest and best use is. Should you be leveraging your time by teaching the stockbroker what you are looking for and having him use his time to find and bring you good deals? If you really like working with numbers and working the formulas, then your highest and best use could be to get good at the numbers and formulas, and then work them by putting the emphasis on closing positions. You buy so that you have something to sell.

4. The last point on running your own investments like a business is this: If you have operated your own business, then you know what it takes. Not many people in this country know how to start up a business and successfully run it to the point where they get rich. There are many businesses operating that just get by and, as a lot of you know, most businesses in this country fail. It is not that the owners fail, just that the business does. The owners usually pick themselves up and start other businesses. Eventually, if they are persistent, they succeed.

The point is that when you run your own business, you understand pricing, buying wholesale and selling retail, employee relations, and taxes (in all of its different forms, local, state and federal). You learn about competition, market share, and what it takes to be successful. You do this because you are intensely involved with your own business.

Now you can convert all that information over to your stock market investments. For example, use your own business experience and measure that against what other companies do. You can choose companies by knowing what the management is up to–this is the key. If you have operated your own business, you understand the key is personnel. It is nice to have a good product and service, but if you have a mediocre team running your product and service you will get mediocre results. Conversely, if you have a mediocre product and service but a great management and marketing team, you will have superior results. As mentioned before, this is "betting on the jockey, not on the horse." You need to apply the same knowledge you have about running a business to stock market investments and use that knowledge as a magnifying glass to look closely at other companies.

You can tell if a company is going to make money by the value of its product or service, or just by doing your homework on the company, or sometimes even from its annual reports.

Here are some examples:

1. Has it created a market niche?
2. Does it have safeguards against competition?
3. Can it do well in downturns, or is it cyclical?
4. Does it have proper tax structuring in place?
5. What is the quality of the management staff, all the way from marketing to accounting to leadership, and how do they measure up?

In summary, we need to get from our stock market investments exactly what we personally need at any point in time. We need to use the market at hand, whether it is an up market or down market, and find plays in that marketplace that will generate the cash flow, tax write-off, or growth we need. It is nice to get a blend of all these things. One last point: you cannot go broke making a profit. First and foremost there should be a dedication to generating excess profits, so that you can stay in business despite setbacks.

COMMON MISTAKES TO AVOID IN THE STOCK MARKET

The following ten items are given here in an effort to help you "leapfrog" your way to wealth. There is no reason for you to make all the mistakes I have made in my years of stock market investing. A wise person will either follow in the footsteps of a guide or see through the eyes of someone who has been there before. Yes, experience is the best teacher; however, it is too expensive. If you can learn anything from this book to help you make and keep more of your money, then my time as an educator will have been well spent.

> *There are three classes of people in the world. The first learn from their own experience–these are wise; the second learn from the experience of others–these are the happy; the third neither learn from their own experience nor the experience of others–these are fools.*
>
> –PHILIP DORMER STANHOPE

1. Investors do not "gear up" and "get fit" for their opportunities. They start out thinking small. I am reminded of an old Japanese proverb that says, "The frog in the well knows nothing of the ocean." While we cannot invest billions of dollars like money managers with large funds, we can at least get our accounts ready to use some of the same investment principles they use.

For example: We can do a simple thing like setting up a margin account. This will allow us to trade on margin–to trade by using borrowed money. In most instances, you will be able to borrow at least double the money you put in. Once you have put more money into your accounts, you will be able to put up less money and purchase stocks on margin. This may be better than 50%. It's almost as if you need a specific target to help pull yourself up and realize there is a bigger world out there.

Other strategies: 1) Blending cash flow, tax write-offs and growth, 2) realizing monthly returns are obtainable, not just annualized returns, 3) learning how to think creatively–how to solve problems and how to second-guess companies. For example, learn when a company may be considering a stock split. This would occur around the time the board of directors meets, or when there is a large stock price increase or great earnings.

Sometimes it becomes a case of not seeing the forest for the trees. You need to gear up, get above the fray, and look at your portfolio in particular and the stock market in general from a lofty perch, just to be able to see the direction you want to go, as well as which way the trends are moving.

2. Another common mistake occurs when investors, such as yourself, do not choose a good stockbroker. Investors should only choose stockbrokers who like their business or who are very good at what they do. They need to choose those who have specialized in the field they themselves might want to invest in, such as options and/or spreads, or any debt–oriented investments, like bonds and convertible bonds.

The right stockbroker can become your best asset and investment partner. I am also going to extend this one step further and say that most investors do not surround themselves with a good support team. Investors should get unbiased feedback from CPAs, attorneys, stockbrokers, and real estate agents on a continuous basis, thus helping them "home in" on their target and learn to make wise decisions.

3. Most investors do not treat the stock market like a business. When I speak on radio and TV, I am often asked, "What do you mean, treat the stock market like a business?" To me, treating your stock market investments like a business means you are putting the emphasis on selling, not on buying. Anybody can invest in housing or stocks. The real problem is in knowing when it is time to get out of the investments. When is the best time to capitalize on and maximize the profits?

Another aspect of being in business is that you are producing something that was not there before. A different way to treat the stock market like a business is to "buy wholesale" and "sell retail." You will probably relate to this better if you have been in business for yourself. You will begin to analyze and look at companies from a businessperson's perspective, looking at the profits, debt, employees, and market shares, which are all-important factors.

Along with investing in the stock market, I have also read every business book that I can get my hands on to make sure I am keeping up with the latest trends. From time to time, I ask myself, "If I did not have my existing company, what business would I get involved with?" Usually, it would be the same business I am already working in, because I enjoy the educational field and helping people make money and protect their assets. This is exactly what I want to be doing at this time in my life.

But, if I were to go into another business, for example computer software or communications, what would I need to do to start such a business? How would I be able to expand globally? What would I need to do? I would have to map out a strategy of what I needed to do and begin by looking for companies doing the same thing. I got started looking at companies like At Home, Broadcom and others. Consequently, this allowed me to make large investments in Intel, Microsoft, IBM, DELL, and others that are involved in this type of technology. Many of these companies are experiencing worldwide expansion.

So treating it like a business means acting like a businessperson, establishing my stock market accounts in business entities that allow me to pay fewer taxes, grow in value, and produce cash flow to live on.

4. Another common mistake investors make is they do not learn and work the formulas. There are several mathematical formulas that can help you make more money and continue making money through repetition. There are formulas for writing covered calls and selling options. Other formulas will determine rates of return and yields. And there are still more formulas for learning when to buy and sell an option on the stocks you have purchased. One of

the major keys to wealth building is getting a formula that works for you. Even though you may want to keep tinkering with it to make it better, work the formula. Make it into a formula for success, then you will be successful.

5.   Another problem to avoid is having an unbalanced portfolio. For example, some people will invest only in options, which can be highly risky. They should have stocks and do option plays, as in writing covered calls. They should limit the portion of their portfolio invested in options. At the beginning, they should keep the percentage very low, since options are risky. They should learn where they are on their own personal time line, whether they are in the accumulation phase of their life, the maintenance phase, which would be the "just trying to keep it" phase, or the spending and retirement phase. According to their criteria at this time, they need to balance different types of investments and balance out, by using different formulas (for a more complete understanding of balancing formulas see *Safety 1st Investing*).

Other decisions are determined by whether a person is after 1) cash flow, 2) tax write-offs, or 3) growth from their investments. Most stock market investments, except Section 29 Energy Tax Credits, along with a few other limited partnership investments, or REITs, do not produce tax write-offs. If the investments are growing and producing cash flow at the same time, that can be a bonus in itself. However, in the stock market you usually get one without the other.

For example, say you want to invest in a company where the stock is growing but operations are also producing big earnings. Producing earnings tends to "pull up" the growth of the stock price of the company. However, the emphasis can be placed wherever you want it placed. I personally put the emphasis on cash flow. I believe your need for tax write-offs will change from year to year. Your need for cash flow will always be there in an ever-increasing amount. Your need for growth will increase in later years. Therefore, you should concentrate on cash flow, not only to support yourself for the present but also to make more investments that can produce tax shelters down the road. This strategy will produce more cash flow and perpetual monthly income in the future.

6. The key to making money is to know when to get out of an investment. This decision is really quite simple. If I already own an investment, I will continually ask myself, "If I did not own this investment, would I buy it now?" For example, if there has been a lot of buying on a particular stock causing it to rise in value, it will probably not go up much more. I will ask myself, "Would I buy the stock again, right now at this price?" If the answer is no, then I usually sell the investment.

If I know something about the company; for example, if it looks like it is going to do a stock split or has great earnings coming up, I may ask, "Would I buy this stock, knowing this information?" If the answer is yes, I'll go ahead and hang onto the investment. When getting out of options, I use my take small profits rule. That is, if it is going to take a huge move in the stock for me to double my money in the option, I will get out. Again, there may be other extenuating factors. You can see how my formula works by reading the section on formulas.

7. We as investors do not take enough time to study, research, and ponder the different investments we are contemplating. One of the things I am convinced of is that we need better and more timely information.

For example, I like companies that have more than one analyst doing the research, and because I have brokerage accounts in several different firms, I am able to get analysts' reports from all over. I like this because a lot of times there are varied opinions, all with value. Once again, when I study these companies I am able to base my decisions on these analysts' contrasting opinions. My only problem with using published research is that it is often written by advertising companies associated with the particular company. It is almost like reading a major public relations piece. Even when you see articles in magazines, there always seems to be a slant to them, either positive or negative. Therefore, I like third party opinions, total news analyses without any editorial comment.

I rely on *Investor's Business Daily*, *The Wall Street Journal*, certain magazines such as *Individual Investor*, *Worth*, *Financial World* and the *Dick Davis Digest*, along with several others. You can find the list of magazines I subscribe to along with newsletters I read in appendix 4.

8. The biggest single outlay for many small investors, especially small business owners, is in the taxes they must pay. If this is the single biggest payout and concern, then why is saving money on taxes not the single biggest area of study? Virtually every time you go into a bookstore, you should buy every book you can on tax strategies. You should learn about tax credits, like Section 42, Section 29, and NOLs (Net Operating Losses). Do you realize that one year's worth of energy and effort may affect 19 different tax years? You can go back three years and get all the money you have paid in taxes, wipe out the taxes for the latest year and create losses for the next 15 years. Tax credits can apply to all these different years.

One simple thing you can do is to consider when to sell your investments, based on how long you've held them. Do you realize that long–term capital gains are still in effect, even though they have been minimized compared to before? You could sell an investment in January of one year rather than selling in the previous December. You could put this taxable income off into the next year and sell off a losing investment in December to cover other gains right now. You can also set up different entities, especially a Nevada corporation and pension plan, to allow you to have different tax year ends, or use money made in different state tax jurisdictions to lower your state tax bracket. These all enable you to put increased amounts of money into a pension plan. Once the money is in the pension plan, you now have your money growing tax free.

You see, a corporate pension plan or a Keogh plan takes all of your investments and turns them into tax free investments. You have all heard about tax-free investments, like municipal bonds. Now, all of your investments can be treated the same way when you set up a tax-free entity. The long and short of it is simply this: most investors do not realize they can save a lot of money on taxes; therefore, they do not invest in tax-saving investments.

9. Most investors do not prepare for change and are caught short when it comes. Remember, you should take advantage of the current market. At the time this chapter was written, there was a steady bull market. There are three bull markets for every bear market, and bull markets last an average of about three to five years, whereas bear markets last only about nine to eleven months. So I really gear up to invest in bull markets. I don't think you can get rich just by waiting to invest in bear markets. Take advantage of the market that exists at the time. Meanwhile, realize that every time there is a big run up in the stock market, there will be a lot of profit taking. A lot of the major funds will start dumping stocks to capitalize on these profits. Even in bull markets there are dips and many pullbacks–these create buying opportunities. For more information on bull and bear markets, pick up a copy of my newly revised book *Bulls & Bears* (formerly entitled *Bear Market Baloney*).

One of the key elements of successful investing is this formula: "You should always know the exit before you go in the entrance." Look for this same philosophy in the rolling stock section and several other places throughout this book. Do not become involved if you do not know what results you want. Be sure you are going to make money now. This involves buying some stocks that are sub-wholesale or stocks with a high probability of growing back quickly. You can look at buying stocks specifically to write covered calls where you can possibly pick up option premiums right away.

If you invest in companies that are very popular and seem to have news or reports out often, and if the news is usually good, then the stock may go up. However, if there is a market turnaround or if that particular sector of the investment arena dies, that particular company's stock may fall out of favor, especially if all the fund managers are investing in it. Many fund managers invest in the same stocks. You could see a stampede for the exit. It may get very crowded as the stock drops quickly.

Be careful and do your own research. Maybe you will find the little–known companies that have a high rate of return along with a high potential for increase. As long as they are not tied up with where the herd is going, you can reap good returns.

The final comment I'll make on preparing yourself for change is that you need to balance the risk. There is always going to be a trade-off between risk and reward. For example, when you are investing in bonds, you can get a substantially higher rate of return by investing in a slightly lower grade bond. While the risk is minimal compared to that of a higher bond, the rate of return is substantial.

Everything in life is a trade-off. You need to find out what your tolerance for risk is, and then you can go for the gusto. I, for one, hate losing money and I will do anything I can to not lose money. This is why I have come up with all these strategies to help me decide when to buy and when to get out of a particular stock. I will do almost anything I can to make sure I do not lose money in stocks and/or options, even though I may miss out on some tremendous plays because I simply am not willing to take such big risks.

10. Last but not least, we as investors too often do not structure our legal affairs, using an array of legal structures such as Nevada Corporations, Living Trusts, Pension Plans, Family Limited Partnerships, and Charitable Remainder Trusts. We should learn everything we can about how to properly structure ourselves in each state and learn which state laws affect us. We should learn about different entities and their functions.

The five areas we are most concerned with are:

1. Helping people make money, through teaching seminars and writing books, along with offering home study courses. These educational tools deal with stock market, real estate, and business strategies.

2. Helping people minimize their exposure to risk and liability.

3. Helping people reduce, sometimes even eliminate, income taxes and other forms of taxes.

4. Helping people prepare for a great retirement by setting up tax-free entities.

5. Helping people prepare for bequeathment. We want to make sure your family gets everything you have worked so hard to build up, in a tender, loving, caring way.

Proper structuring will help you save money on income taxes now, get ready for a great retirement, and reduce your estate taxes. You will love this information because you can sleep better at night. Your family will love it because they will be able to get everything you have worked so hard to build up with as few hassles as possible.

Simply put, most people do not make vast amounts of money in the stock market because they are not ready for it. They don't work at it by studying and doing the things necessary to guarantee their success, or at least to minimize the risk of failure. I am dedicated, as an educator, to help you prosper more and build up your monthly income so you can spend more time with your family, give more to your church, and really do what you want to do with your life. I hope this information will help to get you on track, keep you on track, and boost you to reach your financial dreams.

STOP THE PRESSES!

I've always wanted to say that. I got my chance just minutes before this book was off to the presses. I just couldn't let this book out without results of several of our latest option plays on stock split companies. To say they are phenomenal would be a giant understatement. They're outrageous.

The book was ready to go, but I had typesetting put this in here. You can go to the fourth appendix for the balance of this hot information. To get your attention, I'll list one annualized return and I'll do it big.

$$3,469\%$$
$$(12\ Days\ 114\%)$$

Okay. That was exciting. "Sure," you say, "you can do it, but what about me?" So, I put here several testimonials from my students. There are more in the back of this book.

"Our investment accounts are very small, limiting us to smaller plays. We find our favorite strategies involve buying and selling low-cost rolling stocks or options. The best return on investments we have had have been in Boston Chicken (27%, 53%, and 53%), Danka Business Systems (6 and 50%), and Eli Lily (51%). These were all one-month returns"

—KATHY BARKER

"Wal-Mart was trading at $92. I purchased 200 of the May 90 calls at $7.75 each. The market was closed the next day on Friday. By the following Thursday I sold 100 of the options, or one contract at $12.50 and I put this money in my account. With commissions I had $1,615.91 in that trade. I took out $41,250 in cash and still have one contract of options. That would have given me an additional $592.05 capital gains if I had cashed out on Friday. There is no way that I can lose now. That was a 93% return in four days."

—HOWARD SPIVA

"I found that Unilever (UN) dropped three or four points one afternoon for no particular reason. I picked up some December calls at $2⅝ right before the close of the market. The next day the stock opened $3 higher and continued to climb for the first part of the morning. I sold them at $6, for a $3⅜ gain. This was a 77% return in one day!"

—WES JARVIS

"A recent trade involved Dell Computer. We brought three contracts of the May $90 calls on 1/27/99 for $13¾. Cash out was $4,125. We sold the same calls on 2/2/99 for $26¾ for a net gain of $3,900 (less commissions). That comes out to about 94% return in seven days."

—VERNON REDD

"Thanks to Wade Cook Seminars for teaching me the things that my broker never got around to sharing with me. As a graduate of your Wall Street Workshop™ seminar, I would like to share a trade I made using the knowledge you folks taught me. On November 16th I bought one contract of Onsale, Inc. (ONSL) March $20 in-the-money calls for $6⅝ in my margin account. The investment for one contract was

($6.625 x 100) divided by two equaled $331.25. The contract sold two weeks later at $42.125 times 100 = $4,212.50. The gain was 1,171.66% in 14 calendar days."

—DON SKINNER

"I'm just endorsing Wade Cook Seminars because every time I go to one, my income goes up. If my income is going up why shouldn't I be excited? I'm writing covered calls, buying a few options, and doing rolling stocks—just the basics. I am finding a 20 to 35% per month income. I am simply implementing the tools provided and the teachings by the staff."

—DAVID EWER

5

ROLLING
STOCK

THIS CHAPTER is about repetitive cash flow. No one I know has come up with a name for the type of investing I call "Rolling Stock." A few brokers call it "channeling," if they know about it at all. It works on stocks that roll up and down in repeated waves. As you get familiar with a particular company, you can run a chart on it as far back as five years or more to find out how it has performed. There are 25,000+ publicly traded companies in America. I am confident there are literally hundreds of these companies rolling between certain price points at any given time.

I have found hundreds of them. Some roll fast and some slow, but for many months or years they have rolled between certain price points. I like to find the ones that are rolling very quickly, like every five to seven weeks, and use the peaks and falls to my advantage.

I have had several that rolled quickly and then slowed down. I have had others that took off and started rolling quite a bit. I will explain the reason for that later, but first let me give you two rules to follow.

1. You have to know your exit before ever going in.

I learned this from an attorney. When I walk into a movie house, I'm always looking for an exit. If something goes wrong, I want to know where the exits are and how I can get out.

When I was buying real estate I always kept in mind what I was going to sell it for. I had a game back then called "Friday." It has only one rule. I bet you can guess what it is. Don't buy anything unless you can sell it by Friday.

From time to time, real estate agents came to me and said, "Wade, we have this hot house for you to buy."

I would reply, "How much can I make by Friday?"

They would say, "No, no, no. This is a house you will love for your retirement."

My reply: "No. How much can I make by Friday?"

You see, in those days I did not need tax write-offs and growth for the future. What I needed was cash flow. And to generate cash flow, I needed an early exit.

Your need for tax write-offs will go up and down from year to year. Your need for growth, especially for your retirement years, is really strong at certain times in your life. *But* your need for cash flow will only increase. Because of this (as well as for other reasons), never go into a deal without determining how you can get back out again.

2. Don't get greedy!

Let me tell you a quick story to illustrate.

Soon after I started teaching rolling stocks in early 1994, a gentleman named Kurt attended one of my seminars. He heard the following examples of my own rolling stock investments.

My wife really likes frozen yogurt cones so we invested in a company called The Country's Best Yogurt (TCBY)–it was her favorite store. I would buy stock in TCBY (TBY) for my wife for Mother's Day or birthdays. I know some people buy flowers and candy, but I was trying to build up our asset base. I used that as an excuse to continue buying assorted securities. With the revised

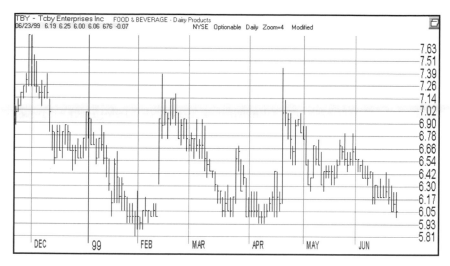

TBY - Tcby Enterprises Inc   FOOD & BEVERAGE · Dairy Products
06/23/99 6.19 6.25 6.00 6.06 676 -0.07   NYSE Optionable Daily Zoom=4   Modified

addition I thought I'd put a chart of TBY right here. It's rolling again.

I purchased the stock at $6 a share and noticed the price went down to $5.50. I started following it in the newspapers. It went up to $6.50 and then to $5.50 and then back up to $6.50. The next time this stock hit $5.50 (after watching it for about six months), I bought a bunch of it. I left my wife's shares alone, and I purchased the stock through my other account. At $5.50, 1,000 shares was $5,500, plus commissions. Then I put in an order to sell the stock at $6.50. It took four to five weeks for it to hit $6.50. After selling at $6.50 and computing the profits, I had $6,500–a $1,000 profit (minus about $100 in commissions) which I had made in about a month. I continued with TCBY for about five years.

My favorite rolling stock is a Canadian company trading in the United States called Cineplex Odeon. I discovered it because I really like going to the movies. When I visited the first Cineplex Odeon theater, I realized what a nice theater chain it was. I bought some of the stock at $3 a share. At that time I was buying other stocks for holding purposes, like Disney, Nordstrom, CBS, and some other big company stocks. I started buying Cineplex Odeon for the same purpose and noticed that my $3 stock went down to $2.50. I continued to watch it go from $2.50 to $3.50. I decided to purchase more. Every time it went down to the $2.50 range, I'd buy. I would sell it at the $3.50 range, sometimes at $3.25. Once in awhile the stock went up to $4, but remember, don't get greedy. (Note: Cineplex Odeon has been purchased by Loews Cineplex.)

I am not a stock analyst. My sophisticated analysis is that my wife and children like yogurt, and I particularly like to watch movies. If you are looking for me to do all kinds of research on these types companies, I'm just not your man. Sometimes I hear about companies and mention them on our Wealth Information Network™ (W.I.N.™), but I'm not going to do a detailed analysis on the stocks, checking out why the highs are high and the lows are low. I won't analyze the volumes at different points in time. I'm just too busy making money to get involved in that. I rely on other professionals (stockbrokers, et cetera) to do this work.

After hearing my stories in the seminar, Kurt ran an analysis on the stocks I mentioned and set up charts to see the highs, the lows, and the volumes.

He came back the day after I spoke about Cineplex Odeon. I had mentioned that, in the last four to five years, I had rolled in the $2.50 to $3.50 range about 15 times, sometimes making 75¢ per roll and sometimes making $1. He told me there was no way I could have worked it 15 times, as I had claimed. It had only hit its $4 peak six times over the last four-and-a-half years. He brought in his charts to prove it.

I currently subscribe to TeleChart 2000®, which I really like. It may have been TeleChart 2000® or another charting company he was using. He had taken another color of ink and had drawn lines from one high to another, which was about $4, six times. Sure enough, every six or seven months it would reach its peak at $4.

I looked at him and said, "But Kurt, you have missed the whole point. When did I tell you that I sold the stock at $4?"

I looked at the rest of the class and said, "When did I sell this stock?"

They all shouted back, "At $3.50!"

I asked him if he would go home and find out how many times the stock went down to $2.25 and back up to $3.25, or down to $2.75 and up to $3.50. In short, how many times could he have made 75¢ to $1 in those ranges by buying and selling? His findings: thirty-five times in the last four-and-a-half years. It was about five years since I'd started buying this stock. I hope you catch what could have happened.

Let's get more specific. You have only a small amount of money to start investing—let's say $2,500. Each time Cineplex Odeon gets down to $2.50, you buy 1,000 shares or $2,500 worth. You put in your order to sell the stock at $3.50, or maybe even 500 shares at $3.50 and 500 shares at $3.25 or some other scenario you feel comfortable with. When the stock hits $3.50 (again you can be in Hawaii on vacation), the computer will trigger a sale and you will have $3,500 in your account three days later. (Remember that these are merely examples. As of this printing, Cineplex Odeon is no longer rolling and has been bought by Loews Cineplex. The stock no longer trades as before.)

Now you put in your order to buy the stock once again at $2.50 and the computer will trigger a buy when it hits that price point. Once again, you will have 1,000 shares in your account. This time, though, if you wanted to, you could take that extra $1,000 in profits and purchase another 400 shares. This time you could have 1,400 shares rolling instead of just 1,000 shares.

To summarize, don't get greedy and don't always sell at the high. Sometimes you will miss out on some of the profits you could have made, but if you get greedy you will miss out on all the little $1 rolls. Think about this: if you could roll $2,500 and make 75¢ to $1 a share, you could make over $30,000 over a five year span with the same $2,500. Isn't this leverage at its best?

One of the questions people ask when they see this rapid turnover of stock is, "Well, what about the commissions?" I'm incredulous when someone asks me that. What I see all the time is people tripping over pennies on their way to dollars, worrying about things they shouldn't be worrying about.

If you spend $2,500 and buy 1,000 shares of stock through a deep-discounted broker (see the sections on types of brokerage accounts you can set up) and each trade is $25 to $45 in commissions, you realize how foolish that question is. You buy $2,500 worth of stock, the commissions are $50, and you sell that same stock for $3,500 and your selling commissions are $60, or even more. This still leaves you with $890 in profit.

Another one I made a mini-fortune on was America West Airlines. When I started doing this I was living in Phoenix and flying a lot on America West. I started buying the stock at $12 to $14 a share, and then the company went into bankruptcy. The stock went down to about $6 a share, then $1 to $2, and for a while in that bankruptcy process, it even fell below $1. I started buying it. I'd buy it at 75¢ and sell it at $1.50. I'd buy some more at $1 and sell it at $2. This stock was rolling every week or two. It would roll at about $1 per share.

The next question I get is, "How do I find these companies?" My answer to that is really quite simple. I find them by looking for them in the real world. I look at hundreds of charts to see these roll patterns. When I first started doing this, I actually thought Motorola was the only company that rolled in a certain range. I thought I had hit the mother lode. Then I noticed that as well as the yogurt company and the theater chain company, there were other companies doing this.

I have a new way of finding these companies, and it will take a roundabout explanation to get you to an understanding of this concept. All through the spring of 1994, people urged me to get my own computer Bulletin Board System (BBS). I must admit to you I didn't even know what a BBS was–I thought it was some British thing–but the idea intrigued me, especially when I learned it was possible to have our own internal computerized BBS. We set out to do this in May and June of that year. The BBS has been replaced by an Internet site at www.wadecook.com.

We wanted to provide timely information, which is so hard to get. For me to write a newsletter and have it proofread, printed, and sent out to you would take two to four weeks. The information would be old and stale by then. In fact, the rolling stock could have rolled from $2.50 to $3.50 and back down again by the time you revised the newsletter. But now, with the Internet site, people are able to subscribe to the service and log on twenty-four hours a day, seven days a week, and find out what Team Wall Street and I are doing every day.

QUICK NOTE: I am a cab driver, not a stockbroker. I do not have any investments for sale. I will not get anything out of the profits or losses you make. You will invest in these stocks at your own risk; therefore, you need to do your own research and use your own professionals to make decisions. I do have the right to give out educational information about what I am doing. Our Wealth Information Network™ (W.I.N.™) is simply an information-based Internet web site service and you can get information on subscribing by calling 1-800-872-7411. It is also important to know that W.I.N.™ is more than just a "stock" Internet service. There are all kinds of tax updates, asset protection strategies, corporate strategies, real estate strategies, sayings, quotes, and news you can use that will make your financial life more enjoyable. Now it is on the Web at www.wadecook.com, and has our trades listed in a tutorial way.

Back to how I find the stocks. Now that I have e-mail, people send me information about companies they think may be rolling, companies that look like good turnaround candidates or bottom fishing candidates. Every day or two I get faxed information or charts of companies. I have found many better rolling companies than Cineplex Odeon and TCBY. We are rolling 10 to 20 companies at any given time, and we are constantly looking for more.

Using my own brain, I can handle the numbers and keep track of only three or four companies at one time. By having a good notebook and computer system, I can keep track of 20 companies at a time. We constantly have to be on top of the 20 companies we're rolling. This means that if a company doesn't roll very fast and there is another one rolling a lot faster, we will replace the slow company with the quick company. I like them to roll every five to seven weeks.

We're constantly adding to and taking from this list. Even within the list, sometimes the range changes. For example, a few summers ago Cineplex Odeon was over $3 for so long that I thought it would never come back down under $3. I thought the new roll would be starting at $3 and roll up to $4, or $4¼, because the stock did get over $4 for a while. I started buying it at around $3 and selling at $4. Then for the past few years before it was sold to Loews, it got down to \$1½ and \$1⅝ and would roll up to \$2⅜ and \$2³⁄₁₆. The point: the roll ranges change.

The long and the short of this is that Wade Cook and W.I.N.™ have become a clearinghouse for investment ideas. I get information on about a dozen companies for every one that I talk about or mention on W.I.N.™

The next question that comes up is, "What if the stock goes down to zero?" Well, that has never happened to me in six years. I don't have a very good answer for that. You shouldn't be investing in companies when their stock might go down to zero. Talk to your broker about "stop loss" orders.

I know that sounds facetious, but we (my Trading Department and brokers) do a lot of homework on these and watch them for a long time. These are not cheap little low-volume stocks. Many are on the New York Stock Exchange, including both examples I used–TCBY and Cineplex Odeon. Many of the other companies are on NASDAQ, but they are usually \$15 million-plus companies. I usually like companies that are \$100 million-plus, which are considered small caps and mid caps. Even though the stock sometimes goes lower than what I purchased it for, I have to be patient and wait for the stock to go back up to its sell point, or sell at a loss and redeploy my money elsewhere.

The final question is, "Why do you buy cheaper stocks?" The answer to this is simply volume. If you buy Motorola at \$50 and it goes to \$51, you have made a profit of \$1 per share. If you buy a stock at \$5 and it goes to \$6, yes, you have still made \$1, but with a substantial percentage increase on your money. If you could buy a stock at \$1 and have it go to \$2 you would double your money. I had one stock that rolled from 25¢ up to 50¢. I bought America West Airlines at \$1 and sold at \$2 and sometimes bought at 75¢ and sold at \$1.50 This was literally doubling my money. So it is not just a matter of being able to buy more shares, but the right to use some of the profits to pay the bills.

The problem with these inexpensive stocks is that you cannot purchase them on margin. Most brokerage houses will only allow you to use margin on stocks that are trading over \$5 and have a level of trading volume and/or corporate earnings to justify the price. They, the brokerage houses, don't want loan collateral to fall in value. For example, I can buy twice as many stocks that roll between $6 and $8 through a margin account. This really enhances my full potential. However, the smaller stocks ($1 to $2) are not tradable on margin; therefore, you have to have cash in your account to equal the price of each stock you buy. The results are still rapid, but you lose some of your borrowing-margin capabilities.

Sometimes I do this type of formula on bankrupt companies. Why? I do not like bankrupt companies in general. Even though they may have entered Chapter 11, they may still go completely out of business. But, by rolling large companies, this could be a chance for a great opportunity if there is a comeback.

How does all this relate to rolling stock? I don't really like companies when they are going into bankruptcy and I'm not really fond of them if they have a hard time coming out of bankruptcy. However, that one- or two-year period of time between the filing of the bankruptcy and its discharge can be very volatile–with a lot of rolls. The company could have some serious problems, but the price of the stock and the roll pattern has nothing to do with the value of the company. The value of the stock is determined by "news." These stocks become news driven. The roll movement up and down is a function of news–good and bad. Call it OMF (Other Motivating Factors) or the technicals–volume moves, support and resistance levels, or whatever–the stock does not move up or down based on earnings or other fundamental improvements or declines in the company. In short, rolling stocks are a function of the "technicals" not the "fundamentals." (Note: See *Stock Market Miracles* or *Safety 1st Investing* for a comparison of fundamentals, technicals, and OMFs.)

How does this help increase our trading profits? Simply that looking at charts like the following is the best way to find and time our buy and sell points.

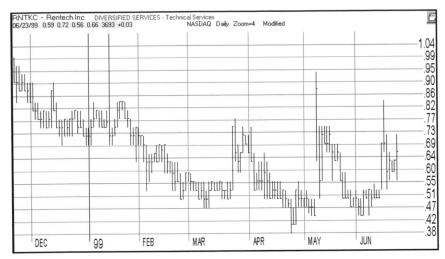

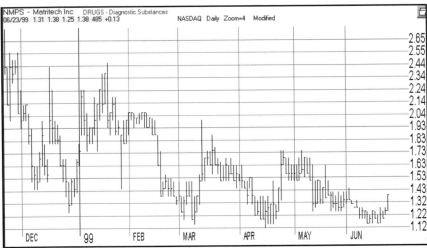

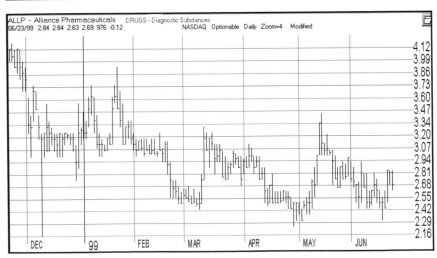

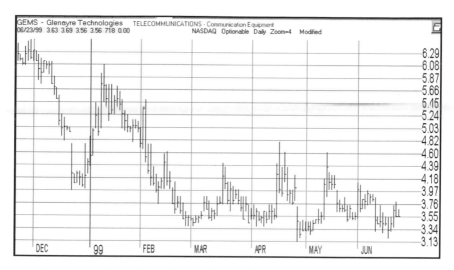

GEMS - Glenayre Technologies   TELECOMMUNICATIONS - Communication Equipment
06/23/99 3.63 3.69 3.56 3.56 718 0.00   NASDAQ Optionable Daily Zoom=4   Modified

For example, when I was investing in America West Airlines (AWA), a company previously in bankruptcy, the newspaper reported on the company every day. If the news was favorable, the stock would jump up; if the news was negative, down the stock went. For example, if AWA was going to get new planes from a leasing company in England, even though it was in bankruptcy, the stock would jump up. A couple of days later the bankruptcy judge would not allow an influx of borrowed money, and the stock quickly went down. A week later, AWA would get an extension on its bankruptcy filing, learning that Anset Airlines in Australia was putting in more money. The stock would jump back up. Then a week later more bad news and down it went. In these situations good news and bad news play out quickly.

Many stocks are driven by news. If you are playing the rolling stock game this can be a good way to make money. For example, other people may want to buy this stock at $1 and hope that it goes from $1 to $10. This may happen in a one-, two-, or ten-year period, but meanwhile the stock goes up based on good news and then just trickles back down because of no news or bad news. As a result, we can roll it several times. The volatility or movement of the stock is determined by news and not by any intrinsic value of the company. Hence, a lot of money can be made.

Look now at five charts of more expensive stocks. We can play these as a plain stock play, but the stocks are high priced.

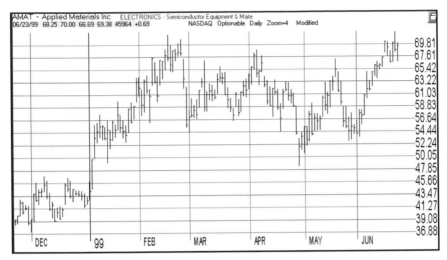

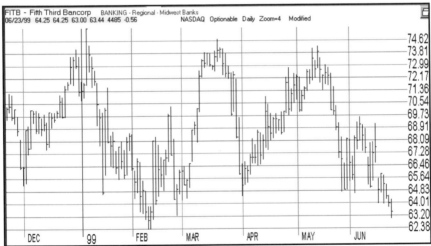

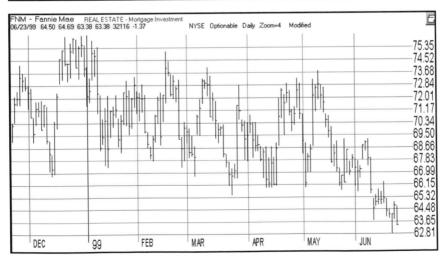

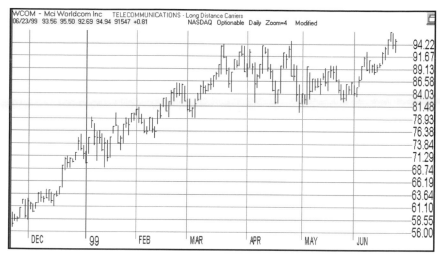

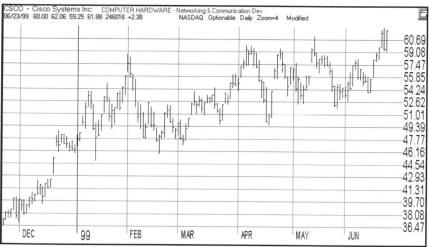

We may have to buy call options when the stocks are low and sell these calls then the stock rises. We could also buy puts when the stock price is high and sell these same puts as they increase in value as the stock price falls. More is written on rolling options elsewhere. Options let us use a form of leverage to play the up and down movement of the stock.

6

ROLLING STOCKS HERE AND NOW

IT WAS my first love. It was my only love. There was a time when I needed cash. My business life was falling apart. A stockbroker showed me a stock that traded between certain price points. This stock moved up to its resistance point and then down to its support level. It did this repeatedly, up and down. It moved sideways in repeated waves. When it hit the top of its curve, the resistance level, the stock price began to fall. Support at the bottom, resistance at the top. I watched and learned and observed these patterns.

You see, I didn't have any money to lose, and the profits had to be cash profits–spendable, real profits. In short, I needed a sure thing. Now, while every stock that has fit this pattern has not performed exactly like I wanted it to, many have.

Taking into account the patterns, the repeated waves, I was ready to act. I was ready to roll with the stock and generate steady cash profits. Many months I had to take out the profits to pay the bills.

I called this "rolling stocks." The stock rolls up and down in repeated waves. It's a real moneymaker. It's not very exciting, but who says steady income should be that exciting?

It has been years now since I coined the phrase "rolling stocks." This strategy has helped thousands cash flow the stock market. This concept and the coined phrase have been defended successfully in a Federal Copyright Infringement lawsuit. When I first came out with it, brokers and financial pundits who had never tried it, or had never really studied it, made fun of it. Now, they embrace it.

It's not an earth shattering idea. It is just a workhorse. Some people start with very little and build up enough income to better their lives. Now that these many years have passed, and so many more trades are under my belt, let me give you some added insight.

UP, DOWN OR SIDEWAYS

I think the fact that many people have also come to realize is that the market, and every stock in the marketplace, is either going up, or it is going down, or it is going sideways.

Doing rolling stocks is a system of taking advantage of a sideways movement in a stock price. We look at charts or watch stock prices. We notice support levels and resistance levels. We look for repeating patterns. We look for a channel. We observe and plan beforehand our entrance and exit points.

Look at the five charts of rolling stocks on the next pages. Obviously these were rolling at the time of this writing. They may not be rolling, or the prices (roll range) may have changed before you read this. Please check current prices and roll ranges and then practice trade 15 to 20 times on various stocks before you use real money. Let your broker see these so he can get used to this strategy.

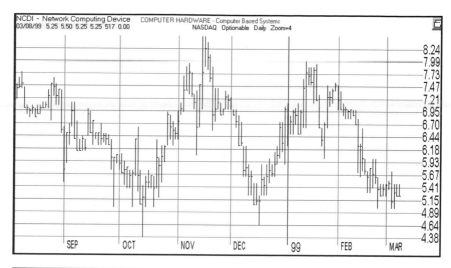

NCDI - Network Computing Device   COMPUTER HARDWARE - Computer Based Systems
03/08/99 5.25 5.50 5.25 5.25 517 0.00   NASDAQ Optionable Daily Zoom=4

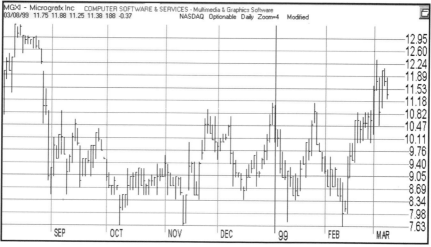

MGXI - Micrografx Inc   COMPUTER SOFTWARE & SERVICES - Multimedia & Graphics Software
03/08/99 11.75 11.88 11.25 11.38 188 -0.37   NASDAQ Optionable Daily Zoom=4   Modified

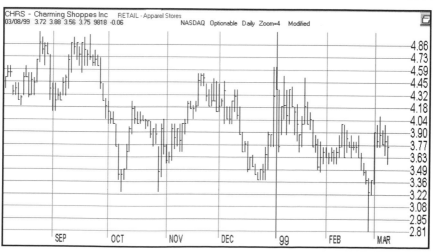

CHRS - Charming Shoppes Inc   RETAIL - Apparel Stores
03/08/99 3.72 3.88 3.56 3.75 9818 -0.06   NASDAQ Optionable Daily Zoom=4   Modified

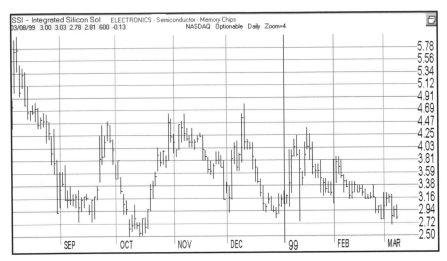

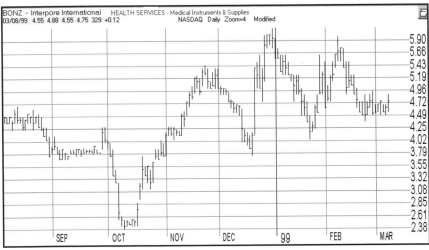

TECHNICAL OR FUNDAMENTAL?

I've written extensively on these two aspects of measuring companies and stock and option price. Remember that the fundamentals tell you what to buy or sell, and the technicals tell you when to buy or sell.

We do rolling stocks as a pure rolling stock play on less expensive stocks. Usually our rolling stocks are in the 50¢ to $8 range. We like stock that rolls from $1½ to $2¼ in repeated waves. Many of the companies with 75¢ stocks, or even $7½ stocks do not look that good from a fundamental perspective. However, rolling stocks, or at least the low price points and high price points, are a function of the technical viewpoint.

Many of these stocks have no earnings. Sometimes they have entered bankruptcy or have just come out of bankruptcy. Whatever the case, the roll pattern comes from the news. Some price changes are 100% news driven.

Remember that technical methods show us the entrance and exit points. Think about this: A stock has good news, it goes up from $2 to $3, but then a huge block of stock goes up for sale, driving the price down to $2 again. At $2, and one month later, the company signs a new agreement to sell more products and the buying starts all over again. At $3, it starts back down.

To repeat, rolling stocks is a function of the "technicals."

UPWARD, DOWNWARD BIAS

We like predictability and in a perfect world we would like to see a stock roll between $2 and $3 forever. However, roll patterns usually have a bias. It rolls in this $2 to $3 range, but soon the bottom or support level price is $2¼ and the next few months it moves up to $2½. The top price also moves up to $3⅛ and then $3¾. There is still 75¢ to $1 in the roll, but it is moving up.

The opposite could also be true. It is rolling but with a downward bias. Watch out for these. Monitor the downward bias stocks more closely.

A DIFFERENT VIEWPOINT

Another way to look at rolling stocks is to only buy (or own) them on their way up, and then sell (do not own) them on their way down.

Sometimes we do not buy the stock at the very bottom of its roll range. We also don't always sell at the very top or most opportune sell point. Remember to not get greedy. Don't glean the vineyard. You don't need to make every penny on every roll. In fact if you try to make $1⅛ on a 75¢ to $1 more predictable roll range, you'll lose out on many rolls. Your profits will increase as you take the shorter and quicker rolls.

PATTERNS

My years of investing have taught me many things. One is to

get better at the power of observation. I watch these roll patterns carefully. I've seen three distinct patterns. They look like this:

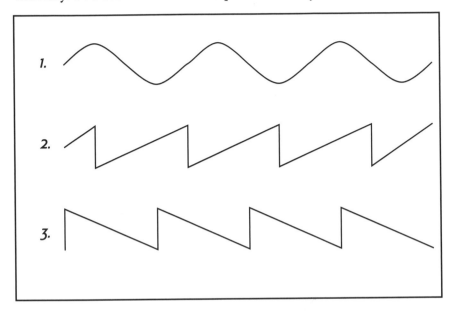

1. The roll is smooth. The pattern fairly consistent
2. The stock price takes weeks or months to climb up to a certain point, then, wham, it comes down overnight.
3. The stock price spikes up then trickles down. Then it spikes up again.

COMMENTS

With patterns 2 and 3, sometimes we can explain and even predict the quick up or down, but usually it happens unexpectedly and for no visual reason.

With pattern 2, I would think that 2 would be the most common, but in real life the pattern in 3 is very common. The stocks spike up, usually on some sort of news, and as the news plays out, or gets stale, the stock dribbles down.

And pattterns 1, 2, and 3 each could have an upward or downward bias, as mentioned before.

MORE EXPENSIVE STOCKS

All we've looked at here so far has been cheaper stocks. I think anyone who has been in the market at least six months has noticed roll ranges on more expensive stocks. These rolling stocks get noticed but may have a hard time playing, as they are so expensive. Look at these charts.

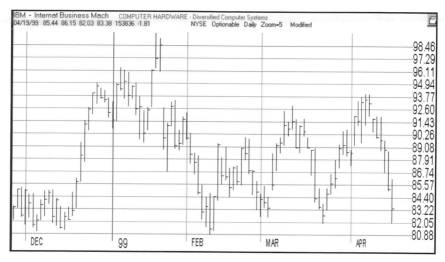

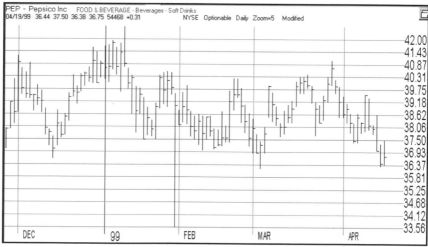

You always have the opportunity to buy and sell these stocks. Another way, a way that will tie up less money, is to do rolling options.

If the stock is rolling between $115 and $130, we can buy call options on the stock when the price is low and expected to go back up. Remember we want to catch it on its way back up. Say it bounces off of $115 and is at $116, even after hitting $117 earlier in the morning. It starts up again. We could buy the $115 or $120 call out one to two months.

As the stock gets to $126, we could sell those calls for a nice profit, and then buy the $130 or $125 puts as it falls.

These better known stocks are easy to practice trade. Get good at this on paper before using real money. Also, watch for good and bad news.

These quick movements are based on the "technicals." Here are a few things that you can monitor.

1. Volume movements (money flows).

2. Earnings reports and other financial news.

3. The quarterly news releases by the company and outside sources.

4. Analysts reports (upgrades and downgrades).

5. Other stock news in the same industry.

6. Check the market in general. Yes your targeted stock is down, and you think it is ready to go back up, but the whole market is down. Don't try to buck the trend. Make the trend your friend as Steve Wirrick, one of our instructors, says.

7. Don't be afraid to take a quick profit. Some of these stocks and options can be caught and captured on quick bounces. Example: Your targeted stock hits $115. You buy the $115 for $4, the stock jumps to $119, and your $4 (or $4,000) becomes $7 in two hours. Take the $3,000 profit and go to the movies. Lather, rinse, repeat.

These options give us a chance to play the better stocks with less money at risk. Don't ignore all the other rules of option investing (including controlling the risk) just because these roll patterns look so good. Be careful to choose the right strike prices and select the appropriate month for maximum protection even if you have to sacrifice some of your profits for safety's sake.

ROLL THE MARKET

Now on to a macro view. Up, down, or sideways. What about the market as a whole? This chart looks like a rolling stock with an upward bias. Look at the peaks and valleys. Look at all the opportunities.

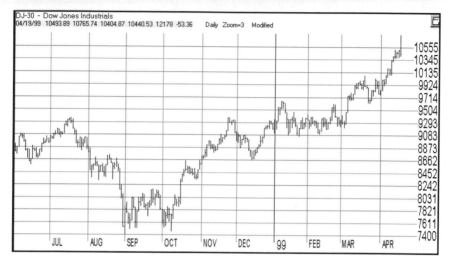

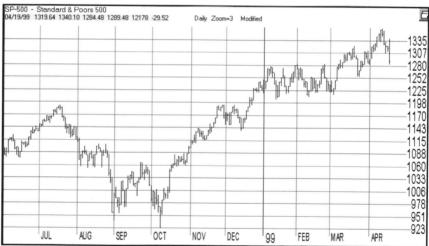

The DJX represents the 30 stocks of the Dow, or DJIA. The SPX is the Standard & Poor's 500. That's the 500 largest companies in America.

Could we play the market like a rolling stock? The answer is "yes." We do it with buying call or put options on the particular index we like. We buy calls on dips, and sell those same calls on peaks, or on a nice increase. We can also buy puts on peaks and sell on dips.

To a certain extent playing the whole market is easier and safer than one particular stock. You know the market will be there and you know it moves up and down almost daily. We're after safe, predictable cash flow and once we've practice traded the market and only put up a small amount of money at risk, we could see nice steady cash flow.

SUMMARY

Rolling stock is still my first stock market love, but it's not my only love. For many beginners it is a great way to start. It's amazing the things people learn about the market, the companies, and about themselves as they employ their strategies.

Couple rolling stocks with other strategies like options and the chances of winning increases. Also you can do option spreads on rolling stocks and you can write covered calls on the stocks over $5 (if they have options).

Rolling stocks is the best bread and butter cash flow strategy in an otherwise crazy market.

7

MY TAKE ON DAY TRADING

DEFINITIONS OF words change. Changes occur by usage, or more specifically usage in a different way. The word, "trader," or "day trader," or "day trading" has undergone just such a change.

Let's look at the way it used to be. The word "trade" is a general term and would incorporate all activities of commerce. In the stock market, a trade is simply buying or selling of a security. You would and still do hear, "nice trade," "800,000,000 shares traded today," et cetera.

The Internal Revenue Service, in its quest to pigeonhole activities and thereby define what can be deducted and expensed, laid hold of the word "trade," as in trader. A trader in securities is a person who makes a living at trading stocks. To be a trader, a significant portion of that person's income would need to come from trading activities. If so, then the activities associated with trading–commissions, research, and miscellaneous expenses–would be deductible against profits made.

If an investor is not considered a trader then many of these expenses are not considered expenses and therefore not deductible. I think even a novice would see the advantage of this "trader" designation. In a general sense the word trader is still widely used. The specific IRS definition is also used.

There is, however, a new definition and this new usage is associated with day and intraday trading. We used this word throughout 1996, 1997 and 1998. To use the word "day trades" meant one or two day trades. Sometimes one to three week trades. It meant "days" to us. We would buy an option on Coca-Cola on Monday and sell it on Thursday. We would sell a Ford put on Wednesday and buy it back on Friday. These quick turn trades, and to be sure, much more aggressive plays than the typical buy and hold type plays, made us a lot of money and generated a fair amount of criticism.

It's still amazing to me that well meaning stock market gurus and journalists don't see the wisdom of using options to limit risk, capture profits on stock (puts), and generate income. Options allow inordinate profits on small (reduced risk) investments.

Bringing up these criticisms is important and you will see how these comments affected my seminars and me as the last few years evolved. The last few years have seen the development of a new type of trading. This new format has changed the meaning of the word "day trader." To a certain extent I think the changed meaning has added a bit of danger to the stock market arena.

Many times as definitions change, people who know or use the old definition do not make the transition and the line between the two meanings get blurred. First let's look at the change, then we'll look at the blurred lines and the danger associated therewith.

DAY TRADING – A NEW DEFINITION

A new type of trading has emerged. It is called day trading, or more specifically, SOES trading. SOES stands for Small Order Execution System. Here's how it works. A brokerage firm, licensed and on-line–either directly or on the Internet–sets up a room or office next to their main brokerage office. They allow people to sit in this outer office and do trades. The broker picks up a few cents per share per trade. They can make hundreds of thousands of dollars on these small per transaction amounts. Now, if they also charge a set-up fee, a daily computer usage fee, and a $5,000 training seminar to get you up and running, then this type of business should be profitable to them. But what about to the customer?

Another aspect to SOES trading is an underlying philosophy of "cash is king." You see, from the offices I've seen, they do trades intraday. By the market close, all trades are back to cash. Also, all trades are stock purchases and not options. This type of system ignores the great and exponential profits of options investing. They encourage people to only buy stocks with so much extra risk that would be abrogated with options.

It's ironic that Wade Cook, our educational and resource centers, and my students are getting lumped into this new definition of day trading, yet SOES trading is so distinctly opposite of what we teach and do.

I'm grateful for an opportunity to explain our methods, to make clear what we teach and do. This is important to me now to make this comparison. Why? Awhile back ABC's *Good Morning America* TV crew showed up at our Wade Cook Financial Education Center, in Santa Ana, and filmed our center—our computers, TeleChart 2000® system, et cetera.

This film crew and news reporter lumped us with other day trading brokerage centers. They knew nothing of what we really teach or do. They did not explain that most of the SOES concept is not what we teach at all. If they wanted to record that we're into education and empowering people to make correct and better decisions then I probably wouldn't be writing this. They missed an opportunity to see a wonderful new approach to investing in the stock market. They missed out big time.

> *Practice yourself...in the little things; and thence proceed to greater.*
>
> —EPICTETUS

Another point before I get into a comparison or actually a differentiation between Wade Cook and SOES. For years I've said that we're the best stock market seminar in the country. "We're number one, Ichiban, Numero Uno, but when I look around there's no one in second place." When it comes to experiential learning, when it comes to helping our students get results, we are the best. We stand alone.

I've also stated that it is difficult to explain how good our Wall Street Workshop™ is because a good way to explain something is to compare it to something else–something the listeners can relate to. Kind of a "it tastes like chicken" scenario. Well, up until now there has been nothing to compare our methods to, but now there exists this new SOES method which is seemingly sweeping the nation. I'll show you later how it's not sweeping the nation.

Here are my thoughts on an important comparison between two different concepts for investing in the stock market.

NUMBER ONE - THERE IS A DIFFERENCE BETWEEN INVESTING AND TRADING

Investing involves equity ownership. As in real estate or investing in your own business, investing means to trade cash, or some other valuable medium of exchange, for an ownership position. You vest in that ownership position immediately. I contend that ownership for the long-term is a key to wealth.

Study ancient wisdom in the Bible. Land and flocks were so very important. Indeed, is not the conflict still raging in the Middle East about land ownership and "birthrights?" I agree home ownership for many is important. Acquiring assets that provide for a great future and retirement is essential. Simply put, we need assets that produce the ownership benefit of income. Knowledge of how things work is also important.

So what does this mean? Fundamentally I teach, "Treat the stock market like a business." This means that with part of your money you buy wholesale and sell retail. You take a small amount of cash, get in, get out, make a profit, and then use this profit to pay the bills or to invest in great companies for the long-term. Underlying everything I teach is how to employ your assets and knowledge in ways which will help you accumulate a huge asset base, which will stand the test of time.

Getting back to cash by 4:00 P.M. Eastern Time is against everything I teach. Cash is not king; cash is a servant to work for us wisely. The stock you bought at 3:00 P.M., hoping for a $2 jump up, may need overnight or a few weeks to make its move. A $4 option may produce far more profits with far less risk for a quick profit. An investment of $80,000 (1,000 shares of stock) that goes up to $82,000 is a nice $2,000 profit. But what if the $4 option on 10 contracts, or $4,000, rose to $5,000 on the same stock movement. $1,000 profit on $4,000 is much better than $2,000 or $80,000 or even $40,000 on margin.

What if the stock tanks to $72,000 during the short period of ownership? That's an $8,000 loss compared to a $4,000 loss in the option. I'm not through. If the SOES method is to get back to cash by the market close and they're losing money on the trade by selling too soon, they're guaranteed the loss and the investor gives up the opportunity for the deal to turn around and become profitable. You can lose just as much by selling too soon as hanging on too long.

> *Make up your mind to act decidedly and take the consequences. No good is ever done in this world by hesitation.*
> —THOMAS HENRY HUXLEY

Anyone who has been in the market even a short period of time has seen overnight or short one-week profits made. I've talked to around 11 people involved in SOES trading and all except one said they were either at break even or at a loss. Most were at a loss, though their brokers were getting paid nicely. Win, lose, or draw the brokers make money.

This brings up my next point.

NUMBER TWO - WE ARE PURE EDUCATORS

Tell me and I'll never forget; show me and I may remember; involve me and I'll understand.

We sell books and seminars. Period. We are not brokers. We have no investments for sale. More importantly, we get nothing out of what our students do.

Our style is to think and invest smart. The method of "getting back to cash by market close" can, over the long-term, only benefit the broker. I'm always asking the question, "What does everyone get out of the deal?" Follow the money.

Another part of our style is to tutor people by walking the walk. We put all of our trades on an Internet site. The whole world can see what we do. I don't want to hear criticisms from these ne'er-do-well journalists until they put all their trades up for every one to see. I'll even host a site for them.

An interesting sidelight, then I'll get back to the SOES comparison. I challenged one of my harshest critics to put all his trades up for me or anyone else to see and after a long time of challenging him he finally admitted he had never made the trades I teach, like rolling stock, writing covered calls, stock splits options (five methods), and numerous spreads. "You've never done a deal, or walked the walk, and you criticize me?" Silence.

Another aside: that last sentence has more truth than you'll realize at first. You have to be there in their office. That will be point number three. But before that, wouldn't it be interesting to have the broker, or educator, put up all their trades for everyone in the outer office to see. The SOES stockbrokers are on the other side of the wall raking in commissions and taking in-the-spread fees ($\frac{1}{8}$ or $\frac{1}{16}$ per share). They also charge commissions plus this small in-the-spread amount. Let's see if they are walking the walk by putting their trades up for all to see. Let's continue by getting back to the SOES office.

NUMBER THREE - WHERE?

Most of my students are busy. They have jobs, businesses, and families to attend to. Some do their investing at home. Some trade on the Internet electronically. We even have a "day trading" seminar taught as part of our Support seminars. I'm into anything that makes people more proficient and more efficient, but all this is done at *where they are.*

Most of my students do their investing on the phone–cellular or stationary. They do their trades wherever they are. Most are on the run. I've seen SOES offices. These offices resemble a room full of slot machines to me. Seriously, people sit at computer screens all day hoping for a hit. Once in awhile one yells out–just like when the bells go off in Las Vegas. Because of this time and place commitment, I do not see this style of trading sweeping the country. It's not natural.

I know this sounds really critical, but I just can't see me, or most of my students, sitting at a computer pulling the lever all day long. It's not natural.

> *A man can succeed at almost anything for which he has unlimited enthusiasm.*
>
> —CHARLES M. SCHWAB

NUMBER FOUR - NO RECOMMENDATIONS

Like a typical SOES office, we make no recommendations on stock. We don't care about a particular stock anyway. We care about formulas for cash flow. We show people how to find, analyze, and determine which formula will work for maximum cash flow for their individual needs.

People are always asking for a hot stock tip. I don't give these. I give hot formula tips. Tips on how to learn and work a system. Now let me add here that the SOES method is a system. As with any system, you can learn it, make it yours, fine-tune it, and be successful. If you want to pay the fees and sit at a screen all day long, then I wish you well.

Before I go on, I want to make another quick side point. A few state government agencies have looked at our company. They've made all kinds of accusations but when they truly look at us they find that we're purely an educational company. For years some of them have tried to link us with brokerage firms or mutual funds that raise money. They wanted us to meet their investment advertising criterion. We are not able to be pigeonholed like this because we don't take and invest other's money. SOES trading brokers do manage money to a certain extent. For all intents and purposes you have a broker client relationship. We don't.

Also, I think many brokers have badmouthed us because they may have thought we were like SOES traders or like other brokerage firms who put on seminars. They wrongly thought that we would steal their clients, when the opposite is true. Even to this day we're trying to build the relationships between clients and brokers. We'll educate both on how to work better together. Look at these quotes from actual stockbrokers:

"I am a stockbroker and a financial advisor and have been in this business for 10 years. I attended the Wall Street Workshop™ in June of 1997 and was profoundly changed in the way that I view option trading. Not just option trading, but all of the strategies that Wade Cook presents. I have used these strategies many times over and have placed over 201 trades using these formulas and have made some serious money for my own account. I have also shared these with some clients, who have asked, and they have had tremendous success also. You take the volatility we have seen in the markets over the past year, and you cannot help but see how Wade's formulas work. Even though I attended the workshop in 1997, these formulas are timeless and are more prevalent today. There is a lot of talk about option strategies and day trading strategies going on out there, but Wade's concepts have been tested and proven to be a leader in the industry. I would recommend Wade Cook to anyone who wishes to enhance their knowledge of investing. I would *radically* encourage other brokers and financial advisors to step up to the plate, to put aside their own opinions, and go to a Wall Street Workshop™. After all, it's going to make such a difference in their financial life. What have they got to lose? When I was at the workshop, I was the only broker in the audience. I wish all Wall Street Workshop™ graduates continued success!"

—KEVIN R. SULLIVAN

Trust only movement. Life happens at the level of events not of words. Trust movement.
—ALFRED ADLER

NUMBER FIVE – LEVERAGE

Stocks are even more risky than options when traded quickly, the SOES way. One simple reason for this is that stocks cost so much more than options. Options allow for less cash therefore less risk. The high cost of a stock could be spread out among several option plays and thereby limit risk from a diversification viewpoint.

Trading is about getting a bigger bang for the buck. Proxy, or option investing, allows for this. You can also play index options on the DJX, the S&P 500 (SPX), or the S&P 100 (OEX) (my favorite).

Options allow for spreads, straddles, and a host of other well founded and time honored systems. Options allow for magnified profits.

"I will retire from my current position on March 15th (my birthday) and only trade. Thanks to you and other master instructors, I have taken $30,000 in November to $200,000 by the end of January. I am assisting elderly parents, and two neighbors that are in ill health as well."

—Craig Hancock

"During the workshop I made two trades which netted $2,125 profit on a $4,825 investment or 45% gain in one day. On the following Monday, I tried one trade on my own using your techniques and in two days made $1,500. Wow! My wife and I sure are excited. We know we have more to learn so we signed up for Cook University. We have become very dedicated and enthusiastic about your cash flow strategies. Just very simply thank you very much for opening this new realm of investing."

—Jim Grasso

"A recent trade involved Dell Computer. We bought three contracts of the May 90 calls on 1-27-99 for $13³/₄. Cash out was $4,125. We sold the same calls on 2-2-99 for $26³/₄ for a net gain of $3,900 (less commissions). That comes out to about a 94% return in seven days. How do you like that Jane Bryant Quinn?"

—Vernon S. Redd

I have never met anyone trading stocks that has made this much money in such a short period of time with such a small amount of money.

IN SUMMARY

Let's return to the definition of "day trading." I hope that this new SOES type of trading definition does not become the new definition for day trading. But alas, it seems to have done so. Once again the TV and news journalists who want a quick story, and who don't want to explore what is actually going on, will lump all of these perceived trading styles as one.

Back to the *Good Morning America* piece. They interviewed two of our students who told great stories. In the background were computers. From a quick view our center looked like any other broker's office, but at our center the students will do the research, check charts, and get on W.I.N.™, our Internet site, but when it comes to placing orders they would have to get on the phone and call their brokers. Then, their trade may be a two-hour or two-week trade. More than likely it would be a one-month trade as would be required in a typical writing covered call, sell put, bull put spread, or bear call spread situation. These news reporters take a quick glance and write their misinformed or under-informed stories.

However, I'm writing partially this to define who we are. I don't want any misunderstandings. If you're thinking of tying into the Wade Cook system I want you to be well informed and know exactly what we do and don't do.

I've written elsewhere, "get yourself in the way of progress." Load up your brain with cash flow formulas, which can be learned, practiced, and fine-tuned. Use small amounts of "at risk" money to generate big returns. Then keep learning and get to be an expert. SOES trading allows for some of this. I don't have anything negative to say about SOES trading–I just think there's a better way.

8

STOCK OPTIONS

ONE WAY to quicken your rate of return is to use a small amount of money to control a large block of stock. The following information is given with this goal in mind. An option to purchase stock is the right (not the obligation) to buy or sell a particular stock on or before a certain date, called the expiration date. The whole idea of being able to leverage money is not only exciting, but one of the cornerstones of true wealth accumulation. Very seldom will you find any estate that grew to be the size it is without using some type of leverage, particularly in real estate investing, wherein a buyer puts down a small down payment, say 10 or 15%, and purchases a large block of property. The other side of leverage in real estate is debt. So, comparing option investing in the stock market with real estate investing can be done only to a limited extent. An option to purchase stock is not a down payment, as it does not go against the purchase price. It does allow the purchaser of an option to control a block of stock and to profit if the stock goes up or down.

To get heavily into the different strategies that will help you make money in the options market, we need to define certain terms. There are four different types of options. The only one we are going to discuss here is the option to purchase or sell stock. We will ignore index options, foreign currency options, and interest rate options.

When investing in options, you must first understand that these are derivatives. A derivative is an investment made on an underlying investment. Shortly before the writing of this book there was a lot of bad talk about derivatives. However, derivatives are an important part of our economy, especially on a worldwide basis. Companies protect their sales profits to foreign countries by buying calls and puts on a foreign currency. If the currency exchange rate fluctuates and possibly wipes out their profits on a particular transaction, they can protect their profits by buying options. These are derivatives.

Options on stock are also derivatives. If you don't like the idea of buying derivatives, then you should go to the chapter on writing covered calls (or selling puts in *Stock Market Miracles* or *Safety 1st Investing*) which explains selling derivatives, not purchasing them.

There are two types of stock options. One is called a "call" which gives the investor the right to buy a particular stock and the other is a "put" which gives the investor the right to sell a stock. Sometimes I will refer to these as "calls" and "puts" or sometimes I will call them a "call option" or a "put option." Without trying to confuse the matter, the investor needs to know that he/she can buy a call or sell a call and he/she can buy a put or sell a put.

Let us discuss the call option first. When an investor purchases a call, he/she is controlling a block of stock with a small amount of money. Options are always written in 100 share contracts. If a call option on a particular stock, at a particular time, is $1.25, that would immediately calculate to $125 as "one contract." One option at $1.25 x 100 shares = $125. Obviously, there would be commissions on top of this.

QUICK NOTE: Relatively speaking, commissions on options are usually smaller than they are on stocks.

When one is buying a call, one is hoping the underlying security goes up. There is not an exact relationship between the stock price and the option price, but a relationship does exist. This relationship is spoken of in terms of a "delta" which we will cover later. There are really two different marketplaces. There is the stock market and there is the options market. Just as the stock market has several different exchanges, the options market also has several different exchanges. These markets act independent of one another, but usually there is a pretty close relationship between the prices at these different exchanges. The movement between the stock and option prices is a continuous course of study. The option price usually lags behind the stock price, sometimes by hours, but often by only minutes.

Quite often, options are poised to move, and do so quickly, in anticipation of stock moves. Because small fortunes can be made or lost so quickly, the option market (meaning the market makers) is much more intense, more careful, quicker to act and react than the stock market. I've often said the options market is smarter than the stock market, and now after more than a decade of such investing, this statement has borne out to be repeatedly true. I've written of this unique relationship elsewhere. But I want to make one point and issue a challenge to you at this time. I think we can learn a lot about stock movement by studying option prices, option movement, and the reaction of the option market to news about companies. More on that later.

The main reason for investing in options is embodied in this next sentence: When there is a small movement in the stock, there is a magnified movement in the option. Let me say that again in terms of real life experiences. When there is a small movement in the stock, either up or down, there is a magnified movement in the option. Look at the following table and you will see what I mean:

FORD (F)		STRIKE PRICE: $65.00
Ford is currently (May) $62, the July option for a $65 strike price was $1.75 when purchased.	STOCK $62.00 $63.00 $64.00 $66.00 $68.00 $70.00	OPTION $1.75 $2.25 $3.00 $4.00 $5.00 $6.50

I did an upward movement on this stock for this diagram so you can see what happens to the price of the option in relationship to the price of the stock. I could have done a similar diagram with the stock going down in value and the $1.50 option would drop to $1.00 or 50¢ and possibly down to no value whatsoever. So, with this in mind and before we get onto the comparisons of the movements, let's talk about how risky options can be.

Options expire at 11:59 A.M., Eastern Time (ET) on the Saturday after the third Friday of the month. Effectively for all of us, that really means 4:00 P.M. ET on the third Friday since the stock market closes at 4:00 P.M. and the options market close a few minutes later. I live in the Pacific Time zone (PT) so it closes at 1:04 P.M. to 1:06 P.M. Friday. There may be computer match ups of trades (actual exercising of the options) after that point in time but when we call our stockbroker at 1:04 P.M. in Seattle or at 4:04 P.M. in New York, the market is closed and option purchasing is closed. The buying and selling of stock is halted an hour or so later. (Note: in the next year—sometime in 2000—most stock exchanges will be extending their trading hours.) The expiration month could be any month you choose in which options are written. Options usually exist six and seven months beyond the current month, longer in the case of LEAPS®. (LEAPS® stands for Long Term Equity Anticipation Securities.)

Because options expire, they are risky. They are called "fixed time investments." This is one reason you definitely should read the booklet put out by the Chicago Board Options Exchange (CBOE) entitled *Characteristics and Risks of Standardized Options*. You can get this booklet for free from your stockbroker. As a matter of fact, when you open your account to trade in options your stockbroker will definitely give you this booklet. If you have attended one of my seminars, I hand out this booklet. While some of this material is very technical, it contains a lot of really good information. It not only explains the different option plays, but also the risk of these different plays. We will talk about some of these risks and how to mitigate them later. Let's get back to the point at hand.

As I stated previously, when there is a small movement in the stock there is a magnified movement in the option. If you look at the diagram, you will see Ford at $62 with a $65 strike price call option of $1.75. Again, for this diagram, I am just using the "last trade" price. In the options market, as in the stock market, there is a bid and an ask. For example, it may be $1.50 bid by $1.75 ask, which would be $1.50 by $1.75. The option price, when the stock reaches $64, could be a $2⅞ by $3. I listed the price that I think you would pay. I am making up these numbers right now but they are reflective of what goes on in real life.

You can see when the stock grows from $62 to $64 the option has gone from $1.75 to $3. Think about this: the stock has gone up about 3% but the option has nearly doubled in price. Additionally, when the stock goes from $64 to $68 it goes up about another 5.8%, the option goes up another $2 to $5. This $2 move reflects almost a tripling of the money from the $1.75 price to the $5 price. If you had purchased 1,000 shares of Ford stock, you would have paid $62,000. If you had a margin account, you could get the same 1,000 shares by only putting up one half the cash or $31,000. However, if you purchase 10 contracts (remember, each contract constitutes 100 shares) at our original price of $1.75 you could purchase 10 contracts at $175 each, making the total cost $1,750. You would still control the same amount of stock, or 1,000 shares for $1,750. When buying options you do not receive any dividends on the stock. However, you still control a large amount of stock with a small amount of money.

The $1,750 is now worth $5,000. We call our stockbroker and sell all or part of our position. We do not have to wait until the third Friday, or expiration date, to sell these options. We also do not have to buy the stock. In fact, we can purchase these calls for the sole purpose of selling them once there is an increase in value. We could have sold them before for $2.25 or $3.50 or $4.50. We could wait and if the stock continues to rise the option will do likewise–so long as there is time left before expiration.

We could sell five of our call options contracts for $5, or $2,500, and hold on to the other five contracts hoping for a further increase. However, if, while waiting, that stock takes a dramatic surge forward, within hours the option could be worth $9. Five contracts would be $4,500, but before we call our broker the stock falls back and the options by midafternoon are only worth $3. I used this example to show how fast these options can move.

There are two major plays when investing in call options on stock.

1. Buy a call option and hope the stock goes up, then buy the stock at the agreed upon price (called the strike price).

That however, is not the reason I purchase options. If you want to do so, you are on your own. What I do is the second play.

2. Wait for a buildup of value in the option itself and then sell the option.

For example, when the stock moves from $62 to $64, our $1.75 option, or $1,750, becomes worth $3,000. This small $1.25 move to $3 allows us to nearly double our money and get out. This 2% movement in the stock represents nearly 100% movement in the option. Again, another small movement of $1 and we could get out at $4. If we were to do so, that would be $2,250 on our $1,750 investment. We would have a $2,250 profit ($4,000 minus $1,750 purchase price = $2,250) minus commissions. Now, to see how good this form of leverage is, let's compare it to buying and selling the stock. You'll realize quickly that had you bought and sold the stock you would have made more money. Let's take a look. To buy 1,000 shares of Ford at $62 would cost $62,000. Sell it at $66,000 and we would reap a $4,000 profit. Nice move. Nice profit. More profit than buying the $65 call option for $1.75, or $1,750 and selling this option position when the stock hits $66 for $4, or $4,000. That's only $2,250 net profit, not $4,000–$4,000 net profit doing stock, $2,250 net profit doing options.

Which one looks better to you? Some who are reading this will still go with the stock, because up or down, you still own the stock and the stock doesn't expire. However, most of you will look at the amount of cash involved in each side of the comparison and realize that options let you profit substantially more with so much less cash tied up. Sixty-two thousand dollars to make $4,000 or $1,750 to make $2,250. One is a 6.4% return ($4,000 ÷ $62,000 = 6.4%). The other a 77.8% return ($2,250 ÷ $1,750 = 128.57%).

One last point about risk: If Ford goes down to $56, or $56,000, you've lost $6,000 (if you sell). The option may be worthless, but you would only lose $1,750. Yes the stock and the option may come back up, but in a way you have more risk with the stock.

> **TO REITERATE:** A small movement in the stock could and usually does mean a magnified movement in the option. I don't want to beat a dead horse here, but again, if the stock goes down to $25 to $26 on or before the expiration date, and doesn't even come close to the $30, our $1.75 option could be worthless.

I read recently that only 15 to 20% of all options ever get exercised–which means there are a lot of gamblers out there betting a stock is going to go either up or down–gamblers who are losing their bets. I don't know where these numbers originate, but I don't think it is too far from the truth. I've read other articles and reports where 80% of all options expire worthless or are never even acted upon. The options market is riskier than the stock market because the options expire.

Think about this, if you purchase Ford stock at $62, whether the stock goes up to $64 or down to $56, you still own the stock. If you purchase the $65 call option at $1.75 and the stock goes down to $56 then your option becomes worthless, you lose your $1,750.

I dislike losing money so much that I have come up with several defensive strategies. As a matter of fact, most of the strategies I use in my option plays are defensive in nature. Again, the first rule of winning is to not lose, and I will employ that here to the "-nth" degree.

Options offer an ability to capture large profits. I have repeatedly stated the risks. Okay, okay–they are risky. Now let's see how to lower and if possible, nearly eliminate losses from options. To do so we need to educate ourselves. We need to understand the language or jargon.

We need to learn options inside out. Here's an interesting comparison. You are learning how to play baseball and there is a man on first with one out. Your coach yells, "Okay double play depth," and you don't know how to do it. You don't know about forced outs–getting the ball to second base on a hit grounder before the runner from first gets there. If you don't know about this part of baseball you won't know how to make a double play. To play baseball you need to know "what plays are available."

It is the same with stocks and options: what plays are available? This chapter will help you see the words and plays. Actually, these brief explanations of option plays need to be brought out and discussed before you can see how to us them with any cash flow formulas. How can you know what writing a call or selling a put means if you don't know what a call and put are?

IN THE MONEY
In regard to call options, when the stock price is above the strike price, the stock is said to be "in the money." For example, if you go back to our Ford diagram (page 88), you can see that when the stock is at $66 on a strike price of $65, a $66 stock is "in the money" by $1. You can also see, by paying $4 for this option, part of the $4 (the premium we are paying for the option), is actually buying that portion of the stock that is "in the money." We have purchased the right to buy the stock at $66 and it is already at $66. This $1 is what is called intrinsic value of the option. The balance of the $4 or the extra premium we are paying is what is called the time value. Another way of putting this would be that the remaining $3 is extrinsic value to the option. The term extrinsic value is very seldom used, time value and intrinsic value are used morte frequently.

AT THE MONEY
When the price of the stock is exactly the same as the strike

price, for which you are agreeing to buy or sell the stock, this play is said to be "at the money." In our example, the $1.75 option, $60 strike price is "at the money" meaning, the stock price is the same as the strike price.

OUT OF THE MONEY

In a call option, when the stock price is below the strike price, the stock is said to be "out of the money." In our example, the $62 stock is "out of the money" by $3 and the $63 stock price is "out of the money" by $2. Once again the strike price is $65. The option premium is the price you pay or receive for buying or selling an option.

Options start at $5 and then increase in $2.50 increments. So the strike prices are $5, $7.50, $10, $12.50, $15, $17.50, $20, $22.50, and then $25. Once they hit $25 dollars they go in $5 dollar increments, $25, $30, $35, $40, $45, $50 and on up to $200. At $200 they are in $10 increments.

At the $65 call strike price, the $62 stock is $3 out of the money. At the $60 strike price the $62 stock is $2 in the money.

In the money and out of the money put options are just the opposite. If the stock is at $62 and the strike price is $60 for the put, the stock is $2 out of the money.

If the stock price is below the strike price the stock is in the money; say, $3 in the money on the $65 put.

BID AND ASK

In the stock market there is bid and ask on a stock; there are different market makers or specialists controlling the bid and the ask, based on supply and demand. The same is true in the options market. Behind the scenes exist the OCC (Options Clearing Corporation). This corporation, throughout the day and night, matches up all the buy and sell orders. It makes sure if you do have options to sell and you are willing to sell at the bid or if you want to purchase options at the ask, all your orders are taken care of. Just like in stocks there also can be a large discrepancy between the bid and the ask and there can also be a tight spread between the bid and the ask. Again, this is reflective of the supply and demand for that particular option. One of the things you can do to make sure there will be plenty of buyers when it is time to sell, is to check the OI (Open Interest) on the options. Typically speaking, you would want to make sure you are only investing in options where there are at least 100 contracts.

For example, if you buy five contracts on a large option at $80 on a particular stock, it would be nice to know there are a lot of other people interested in that particular option, either buying or selling it. If you buy 10 contracts on an option and are the only one purchasing it, say on a thinly traded stock, you may get hurt when it is time to sell because there are not a lot of other buyers for that particular option. So ask your stockbroker to check the OI. (Side point: Stick with large, widely traded stocks.)

> ***ANOTHER POINT:*** There are two option styles or formats: American Style Options and European Style Options. An American Style Option is an option that can be exercised on or before the expiration date. European Style Options can only be exercised on the expiration date. In the United States we only trade American Style Options on stocks. The purpose for bringing it up here is to stress, if you are buying an option on a stock, you can exercise the buy and/or sell of the option or the stock anytime before the expiration date.

In the United States we do use European style trades on most of our index options. See *Safety 1st Investing* chapter 13 on index plays and options.

OPENING YOUR ACCOUNT

When you open your brokerage account, you need to tell your stockbroker you want to trade in options. He may be reluctant to do this at first and want you to put in a certain amount of money to cover yourself. A lot of this is just internal brokerage controls. Don't let him tell you there are all kinds of rules and regulations about having to have $50,000 or $100,000 in your account. Lots of people open up accounts with as little as $2,000 and have been able to trade options. He will make you sign a release or waiver, basically stating that you understand the risks of options. Even if you're never going to trade an option, this is one thing you should do when you open your account, so "if and when" you are ready to trade in options you will have the account cleared for this type of trading.

Most brokers will also not let you trade in certain options at first such as naked puts or other advanced and highly profitable, but much riskier plays, until you have more money in your account and more experience. Again, each brokerage firm differs in the experience level they require and the hoops they will make you jump through to trade in options. However, do your best to trade in all kinds of options. One thing you can definitely do is make sure you can write covered calls, even in your IRA.

WAYS TO AVOID LOSS

There are five things I do to avoid losing money in option plays. Obviously, if I avoid losing money then I should be making a lot of money. I have learned to make a lot of money in options but I avoid several plays where others often get involved. I continue to be very profitable in most of my plays. Again, one of the secrets to winning at the stock market is to be able to act quickly, and to win more times than you lose. Here are the five hints that will help you mitigate any losses and make a lot of money:

1. NEWS. I act on good news. Sometimes I act on rumors if I think they are well founded. Even when the rumors don't pan out, I have sometimes made money on those plays. When I hear about a company taking over another company, mergers and acquisitions going on, a company selling off a division, or a company doing a stock split (which I will mention in chapter13) that is the time to act on the news. I usually act close to the strike price. For example, if the stock is currently $80 and I think there is a lot of really good news, I usually buy the $75 or $80 option. If the stock has already moved up to $83 on the news, I may still go ahead and buy the $80 option, which is slightly "in the money" rather than playing "out of the money" options. If it is really exceptional news and I can buy an option a little bit further out, I may go ahead and buy an $85 or $90 option (if I think the stock is going to get that high). Remember, I am not gambling on the stock and the stock

does not have to get up to $90 to make money on a $90 call. If the stock is currently $82 and I buy a $90 call for $1 and the stock goes to $84 to $85, the option may go from $1 to $2 or $3. I can triple my money and get out long before the stock gets to the strike price I have chosen. Remember we do not have to wait for the expiration date. This trade could have been two hours, two days, or two weeks.

2. THE PERCENT-TO-DOUBLE RULE. Some of your stockbrokers will have a computer program available that has a "percent-to-double" column. When you call him up and are exploring several possibilities on buying options on a particular stock, you can ask him what the percent-to-double is. What this means is, what dollar movement in the stock is necessary for you to double your money on your option. Again, you don't have to double your money on your option to be profitable. You can buy an option at $1 and sell it for $1.37 and still make money. But, it is nice to know, if you want to double your money in your options, what kind of movement you need in the stock.

Many brokers do not have the percent-to-double (%dbl) formula available on their computers, but some can derive it in other ways. Remember, this formula is a computer model that crunches numbers to predict a scenario. Historically, this model has been very accurate. What you want to know from it is how much the stock will have to move in order to double your money in the option price.

When stockbrokers look at an option price, some computer programs will also display a percentage-to-double column. For example, if the stock is at $26 and you think it may go up to $34 or $35, you might buy the $30 call option for $1.25. When you buy a call option, you hope the price of the stock goes up, so that if you exercise or sell the option, you will make money.

Ask your stockbroker for the percentage-to-double. You never know what it will be–10, 17, or 23%. What this means is that the stock will have to go up that percentage (say 17%) in order for you to double your money in your option. I think that in most instances 17% is too much; I like to see about 6 to 10% to double options. Granted, you may know something about the company (for example, a stock split) that is likely to drive up the price of the stock, and you may want to ignore the 6% to-double formula. I like the formula, because, basically, the stock only has to go up 6% for me to double my money in the option. Time has a lot to do with this.

In my example, if you bought an option on a $26 stock at $1.25 and the stock went up 6%, to $27.56, you would double your money in the option. In other words, your option would go from $1.25 in value, up to $2.50. If there is still plenty of time left, you may want to reconsider whether you should sell the option or not. But, if you decide to sell at this time, you could double your money. Many times I have tripled my money on options because the stock has gone up so fast that the percentage to double was actually too low. Usually I will put an order in to sell the option at a certain price when I buy it, but that is not always the case. Because I like to do these on a little longer-term basis, I have plenty of time to monitor them and see what happens.

The percent-to-double formula is given here as a monitor to protect yourself against becoming involved in options on stocks which require too much movement for you to make any kind of money.

3. FIFTY PERCENT RULE. When buying "in the money" options we employ this rule. This rule helps us not to pay too much for the time value (extrinsic value) of the option. I don't think any of us mind paying intrinsic value as we are actually buying the portion that is actually above the strike price or "in the money." For example, say the stock is currently at $27 and you purchase the $25 call option out several months. The price you pay is $3 for this option at a $25 strike price. You can see that of the $3 you are spending, $2 is already "in the money" and $1 is "time value." To calculate this rate, you simply take the amount of the option that is time value, and divide by the price of the option. So, in this case, you would take $1, the extrinsic value, divide it by $3, total cost, and you get 33%. My strat-

egy is to make sure the time value is not more than 50% of the option value. Don't get me wrong, from time to time I have purchased options with a higher percentage ratio, but usually only on stocks I know are exceptional, like in a stock split or the fact that I know something else about the company. However, as a general rule, you will avoid getting into trouble if you're not paying too much for the time value of the premium.

4. DELTA FORMULA. One way to stay out of trouble with options is to make sure there will be a good relationship between the movement of the option and the movement of the stock. This relationship is expressed with the Delta Formula. I've seen the actual formula, and it's too tedious to print here. However, using the formula is definitely worth exploring. Let's use an example:

A stock is currently at $82. You're hoping to see it go up, so you buy a call two months out at the $85 strike price for $3.

STOCK	OPTION
$82.00	$3.00
84.00	4.00
85.00	4.75
86.00	6.75
87.00	7.75
88.00	9.75

As the stock moves up, the call option moves up. When there is a $1 increase in the stock, and it reflects a $1 increase in the call option, it is called a Delta of 100 (or 100%) Do you see the relationship? Likewise, if the stock goes up $1, and the option goes up 50¢, the Delta is 50, or 50%. Deltas are between 0 and 100. To avoid problems, buy options with a Delta above 60 to 70; eighty is preferable. Remember, the closer to 100, the better.

Put options are the opposite. As the stock goes down, the value of the put option goes up. If a $1 drop in the stock means a $1 rise in the option, the Delta would be 0. With puts, you want a Delta closer to 0. Some brokers' computers may show this as a (-) negative 100. For example, a call Delta of 80 would be a put Delta of 20, or a negative (-) 80. Your stockbroker will have the number available. To avoid problems with put options, look for Deltas under 20 (or below -80.)

5. STOCK SPLITS. This is not only one of my favorite ways to make money, it is also one of the main ways I avoid losing money. There are two kinds of plays: a short-term play and a long-term play. When a company announces a stock split, it is a prime candidate for option purchasing on dips, because there is a tendency for the stock to go back up to the original price. I have written extensively on this in other chapters so you can read about it there. I also think, once a company has done a stock split (if the company was in the $40 to $50 range and splits down to the $15 to $25 range), that it becomes a perfect candidate for writing covered calls. As a $60 stock splits 3:1 and goes down to $20, then starts to climb back up, there is great potential for writing $20, $22.50 and $25 calls on it. Again, you can read about this in the covered call section.

PUTS

The put is the right, not the obligation, to sell a stock at a particular price. When you buy a call option, you are hoping the stock will go up in value; when you buy a put option, you are hoping the stock goes down. If you were looking at a chart on a company and see that the stock was trading between $18 and $22, and the stock gets up to $22 and you think it will go back down to the $18 range, you can buy a put on the stock at either $22.50 or $20. As the stock moves down, the value of the option moves up. What you are doing is purchasing the right to put the stock to someone at a particular price, in this example $22.50. So, if the stock gets up to $22 and you buy a $22.50 put option for say, $1 and the stock goes down to $20 and then $19, you have purchased the right to put the stock to someone at $22.50. If the stock is currently at $19, you see there is a $3.50 difference. You can make money again by buying the stock at $19 and selling it to someone at $22.50. However, just like in the call option, the play is not only on the stock but also on the option itself. The value of your put option goes up in value as the stock goes down. So the stock goes down to $20, your $1 option could become worth $2. If it goes to $19 your option could be $3. You could sell your put at this time for $3 and make a nice profit of $2. If you had purchased 10 contracts that would be a $2,000 profit.

I want the you to know that I am not really big on doing puts. I am big on calls and planning on the company's stock going up. I take advantage of dips in the stock to buy call options. Mentally, I want to always be thinking about things going up. I know I miss out on some plays, but this is just my personality and it has served me well. So, I will continue to invest in stocks going up and not get involved in the negative side of the market, always hoping and thinking that things are going to go down. You see, if you're always hoping for a jet to crash so a company's stock is affected, or medicines to hurt someone, it changes your outlook on life. I bet on optimism. This is my personal bias and you can take it for what it is worth.

> *Optimism is a [medicine.] Pessimism is a poison. Admittedly, every businessman must be realistic. He must gather facts, analyze them candidly and strive to draw logical conclusions, whether favorable or unfavorable. He must not engage in self-delusion. He must not view everything through rose-colored glasses. Granting this, the incontestable truth is that America has been built up by optimists. Not by pessimists, but by men possessing courage, confidence in the nation's destiny, by men willing to adventure, to shoulder risks terrifying to the timid.*
>
> —B. C. FORBES

I do want to mention another aspect of puts. There is one other play that is really quite phenomenal. As a matter of fact, of all the things I talk about in my seminars, it is one of the most exciting. It is probably one of the highest yielding and one of the best ways for making money. The reason I am going to mention it here is because it is so important. I am not going to give it that much space, simply because there is a small downside to it and part of that downside is the fact that most of you reading this book will not be able to do it. Why? Because you do not have enough money in your account or enough experience to do so. I've covered this strategy extensively in *Safety 1st Investing*.

The strategy is selling puts. Remember, when you buy a put, you hope the stock goes down. Now, I'm not buying, but selling a put. Remember that when you sell something, you take in money; when you buy something, you spend money. So, when you sell a put, you will actually take in cash.

When do you do this? You sell a put when you think the stock is going to go up. So you are saying, "I thought we were talking about buying the call when we think the stock is going to go up?" Yes. You could buy a call or you could sell a put.

Let me give you an example. Let's say a stock is around $14 a share. It has been up to the $18 or $19 range and gets some temporary bad news. You feel this stock is going to go right back up to that $18, $19, and $20 price. You could sell a put on this stock at a $15 strike price. Let's say you receive a $1.50 for doing so. If you are doing 10 contracts that would be $1,500 into your account. Now, by selling a put you have sold to someone the right to put that stock to you at $15. Now remember, you think this is an $18 to $20 stock, so you don't mind owning this stock and purchasing it at $15 a share. Another way of saying this is that you have agreed to buy the stock at $15. You have been paid $1,500 for this obligation.

Let me say that once again to make the point a little stronger. You should never sell puts unless you like owning the stock of the company and particularly like owning it at that strike price. You need to be willing to buy the stock at that price and also have the money to do so. Remember, when you buy something, you are buying the right, not the obligation. Now, by selling, you have the obligation to perform. So, when you sell someone the right to put a stock to you, you have to perform, if it is put into effect. So, you need to be willing to come up with $15,000 in this example to purchase 1,000 shares of this stock at $15, or $7,500 on margin.

Remember, you sold the put for $1,500 and if you have to buy the stock at $15,000 your cost basis is down to $13,500 because you have already received $1.50 per option. If this stock goes up to

$18 or $19 and you had it "put" to you at $15, it is just that much more profitable. If you sell the put at $19 you would make $5,500 ($19,000 minus your cost basis of $13,500 = $5,500, minus commissions).

Once again, buying a call on a stock you think is going to go up and selling a put is not the same play, even though it is on the same stock. When you buy a call, you are spending money to do so. When you sell a put, you are receiving money to do so. However, once again, both of these plays are on the same stock that you think is going to increase in value.

> *CAUTION:* There is one minor problem that could turn into a major problem if you are not prepared for it. Your stockbroker is going to make you have enough cash in your account to cover your obligation if and when you do have to purchase the stock. You would have to hold about 20 to 30% of the stock price, or about $3,000 to $5,000 in your account. Your broker will allow you to sell naked puts but not without the backup cash to cover yourself. So, if you sell several of these, it could tie up a large amount of cash until the expiration date.

As I mentioned earlier, your broker will only allow you to sell puts once you have more experience. This method is a phenomenal play and a great way to generate extra cash in your account. All of these strategies share the same theme: building up your cash flow. While I personally like selling puts and it is one of my favorite strategies, I only do it from time to time, and then only when I have extra cash in my account. Usually my cash is tied up in covered calls and options. It takes a fair amount of cash just sitting there to be placed on hold when selling puts.

SUMMARY

If you are extremely careful in buying and selling calls and puts, and employ the methods I use for avoiding losses, the whole nature of option plays can be quite profitable and can be put to use to generate a lot of cash flow. These option plays, in conjunction with other plays mentioned in this book, can really enhance the asset accumulation strategies you need to develop in order to produce that extra cash flow.

However, I would not use a substantial portion of your investment portfolio for doing options. In a typical month I use a relatively small amount of money in these different options. Remember, they are very risky, and you need to start slow and get good at them. Practicing on small deals forces you to understand how these strategies play out. Again, a small portion of your money into options can produce phenomenal results. I have had many months where 15% of my money in options has made more than all of the other plays together. Sometimes I wonder why I am not applying 50 and 75% of my money to options, but I would rather have my money in more safe, sane investments, like covered call investing, even though I could make more money by employing more of it in pure options.

I am into safety, not only by having a diversified portfolio but also by having only a small portion of my money invested in that portion of the stock market which has extra inherent risk.

9

WRITING
COVERED CALLS

IF YOU want a wild way to double your money every few months, this chapter is not for you. However, if learning how to get consistently solid monthly returns of 14 to 34% is attractive to you, then read on.

I had my first exposure to writing covered calls with Novell, Inc. (NOVL) shortly after a stock split. I liked this company and had high hopes it would climb back to $60 or so, which it had done several times previously after stock splits. I started buying a little at around $20 to $22 and bought a lot of stock every time it dipped to $16 to $19 a share.

I accumulated 3,800 shares. After the stock failed several times to pop back up, I decided to sell. I told my stockbroker to sell all my shares at $20 per share. He said, "If you are going to do that, why don't you write a covered call on them?" I said, that was the second time I'd heard about "writing a covered call" and asked him to explain. I spent several hours that first day and have since spent many years, studying this remarkable process. In that time, I've turned it into a highly profitable, repeatable formula. The sophistication we have now developed has made this a real winner. After years of teaching this at our Wall Street Workshops™ it literally has become a powerful money machine for countless thousands.

"I purchased two stocks when I thought they were poised to take off. They did and when they started to downturn, I wrote covered calls on both stocks. About a week and a half later, the third Friday came and went and I regained control of my stock. To my good fortune the stocks began to rise again I wrote a covered call on one and the other one spiked up so fast that when it started to downturn I sold the stock. In just under 30 days my brokerage account had gone from $5,000 to a whopping $11,600! Now I realize that this kind of return is somewhat of an anomaly, but the gains have not stopped. As of writing this it has been two and a half months since I bought my first stock and my brokerage account is at $15,000. I have tripled my money!"

—Robert Harris

"Starting in December 1998 and doing just six covered calls each month our base portfolio has increased 20% in value and our call premiums have been $4,500, $6,500 and $7,700 for rates of return 15, 22 and 26%. At this time, we are able to help our youngest daughter and son-in-law on the down payment on their first home."

—Donald and Joan Holicky

"I am making approximately $7,000 a month just with your covered call strategy."

—Richard Losco

"I made $20,000 writing covered calls during the three weeks prior to the workshop using Wade's formula from the *Wall Street Money Machine*."

—Gregory Martin

But I'm getting ahead of myself. Let's go back to that first play.

My broker explained that writing a call is simply selling a call option. If you actually own the stock (long) and sell an option to someone to buy your stock, you are in a "covered" position. I will explain more of the details and implementation strategies as we go along, and I'll give several functional, advanced strategies in the following chapters.

Let's get back to Novell. I asked my stockbroker how much I would receive for selling these call options. He checked his computer for options and told me the next month call options, with a strike price of $20 (the price I was agreeing to sell at) had a bid and ask of $1 x $1.25. Now I could place an order to sell at $1.50 or $2, or whatever, and maybe I'd get hit, but maybe not. In this case I sold the options for $1. Since I had 3,800 shares, that generated $3,800. Options are in 100-share contracts, so technically I sold 38 contracts at $100 each. Either way, it was $3,800 minus the commissions.

Options clear in one day. Stocks clear T + 3 (trading day plus three). Stocks you buy are actually recorded in your account three days after you buy. You also have three days to get the money into your account. The same goes for stocks you sell–they move out three days before the money comes in. However, with options, it is one day (T + 1) for the cash to clear into your account.

Back to the story. I asked, "You mean I can get $3,800 cash in my account tomorrow for selling the right to someone to buy my Novell shares within the next month (actually on or before the expiration date–the third Friday of the next month) at $20?"

"That's right."

"This is a no-brainer, do it!"

The stock continued fluctuating between $18 and $21. That first month it was around $20.50 on the expiration date, and I got called out of 1,100 shares. I know this sounds odd. If the stock is over $20, why didn't I get called out of all of them? All I can say is, when the stock price is close to the strike price, sometimes you get called out, sometimes you don't. We need to explore several things to make this understandable.

A FEW IMPORTANT POINTS

1. American Style Options–the only type of stock options that we use in this country–can be exercised any time on or before the expiration date.

2. Only about 15 to 20% of all options get exercised. There are lots of people gambling that a stock will go up (buying

calls, selling puts) or down (selling calls, buying puts). When their bets don't pay off, they lose. You'll notice my aversion to losing money rippling throughout this book, and you'll see my defensive maneuvers to eliminate losses. If options were too risky, I wouldn't tangle with them. Just remember, most options do not get exercised by the people who own them.

3. If the stock is way "in the money," meaning, the stock is substantially above the strike price, you will get called out. For example, in our story, if the stock is above $21, you will have it purchased from you at $20 (called out).

4. You don't have to do anything to sell your stock. You will find out the Monday following the third Friday if your stock got called out. It's all computerized.

5. "Called out" means you sold the stock. Your confirmation slip will say something like "account assigned."

6. Do you have to sell? Yes, and you don't have a choice. Remember, this all happens electronically. There's a lot of computer activity going on Friday night and Saturday morning to match up buyers and sellers. Technically, options expire at 11:59 A.M. on the Saturday after the third Friday of the expiration month.

7. Is there any particular order to who sells what? No. Sales are by a random computer lottery. You might only sell a portion of the shares you own. You might sell all, or none.

Many times my stocks have been close to the strike price and I have been called out. I heard one of my students had been called out on 1,000 shares of stock at $10 when the stock was at $9.75. I have had this type of trade reconfirmed by several brokers. It doesn't make sense, does it? Why would anyone buy the stock for $10 when they could have purchased it on the open market for $9.75? It just shows you how crazy the stock market is.

WHO BUYS THE CALLS?

Now, let's explore this transaction from the other side and delve into the risks associated with writing covered calls.

Say someone walks into his broker's office or calls on the phone. He really likes Novell and thinks it is going up to $21 to $25 a share. He checks on the option price for the next month and is told the same bid and ask I was: $1 x $1.25. He buys 38 contracts for $1.25 plus commissions. Option market makers make a profit by selling at the ask and buying at the bid. Again, it's all done on computers. You don't know who this person is. He doesn't know who you are and he definitely doesn't know you are selling these options as covered calls. To him it's just a call option. Actually, a perfect 38 contract purchase probably does not exist. Joe in Boston bought 10 contracts, Harry in Atlanta owns 10 more, and Sally in Chicago owns 18.

They are gambling the stock will go up. Their risk is a loss if the stock goes down or if it just flounders around $20. If the stock goes down to a $17 price range, they would be fools to buy it at $20 (exercise their options), since they could buy it for $17 on the open market. If the stock goes to $22 to $25, they have made a nice profit.

Joe, Harry, and Sally could buy the stock at $20 and hold or resell, or they could sell their call option for $2 to $4 before the expiration date. Either way, it is profitable to them if the stock goes up. Remember, an option is a fixed time investment. They have to do something or the option will just expire.

ALSO NOTE: An option is the right (not the obligation) to buy or sell. However, when you sell an option, the person buying it has the right to exercise it or not, while you have the obligation to perform. Hence, your stock, if you are called out, electronically comes out of your account.

Let's go back to Novell. After 1,100 of my shares were sold, I still had 2,700 left. So, I called again and the options for the next month were at $1.25 x $1.50. I sold and took in another $3,375 (2,700 x $1.25). That month the stock did its "volatility thing" and I got called out of 1,000 more shares. Then it ran way up before I sold the next batch. It was around $22. By this time I was writing covered calls on a variety of stocks and getting quite good at it. Actually, I was starting to work formulas and turning the process into a business, but once again, I am ahead of myself. We will get to all of these ideas later.

I asked about the $20 strike price, and the calls were about $2.25. You see, the stock was now "in the money." It was above the strike price. While on the phone, I also checked the $22.50 strike price, and it was $1. I sold 700 shares (seven contracts) at the $22.50 strike price, generating another $700 cash and I sold the other 1,000 (ten contracts) at the $20 strike price for $2.25, generating $2,250.

I started getting a glimpse of a whole new cash flow machine. It was like my real estate days. Here were assets that would produce income of 20%, sometimes 30%, in monthly cash flow. My mind was calculating a business plan.

In order for you to understand how powerful this strategy is, I need to cover a few more points. Think of this:

1. You can buy stock that goes up so you have a capital gain (I will deal with the negatives later).
2. You get a premium for selling a call option.
3. You get any/all dividends paid on the stock while you hold it.

Also keep these two points in mind:

1. MARGIN ACCOUNTS. I have covered this in other sections, but to really excel at my covered call formula, you might want to employ margin trading. Simply put, you only have to put up half the money to buy the stock (some of you will put up even less, since you have more money in your accounts and more trading experience). By putting up half the money, you double your return, which leads to the next point.
2. COMMISSIONS AND MARGIN INTEREST. I have continually told people to "quit tripping over pennies on their way to dollars." If you use this strategy effectively, commissions and margin interest will be peanuts compared to the profits.
    a. Commissions on options are proportionally cheaper than those on stocks.

b. If you do only 100 to 200 shares, the commissions could eat up a substantial portion of your profits. You have to do transactions in chunks of 400 to 500 shares minimum. All of my examples in this book will be transactions of 1,000 shares. You can do 100 shares of more expensive stocks (especially volatile stocks) and sell premiums for a nice percentage return.

FIGURING A RATE OF RETURN

Now we need to take time out and deal with the calculations on our rate of return. You calculate a rate of return (yield) by dividing the cash in (profits) by the cash out (investment).

Go figure!   cash in   = _____% yield
                    cash out

Lets say we spend $3,500 to buy 1,000 shares of a $7 stock. (1,000 x $7 = $7,000 divided by two for margin = $3,500) and we take in 50¢, or $500 for selling the $7.50 calls. The expiration date is two weeks away.

$$\frac{\$500}{\$3,500} = 14\% \text{ yield}$$

This is a two-week return! If you take 26 two week periods x 14%, you get an annualized return of 364%. (Nobody ever gets this 14% every two weeks for 26 weeks. We put in the annualized return just for fun.)

While we are talking about yields, I would like to bring up another point. Everything we do, every yield we read about, mentions annual returns. We go into a bank and see a poster with a CD yield of 5.65% with an effective yield of 6.02%. What is this? Obviously the interest rate is 5.65%, but because of daily, weekly or monthly compounding, we earn more–actually earning interest on interest, so our $10,000 will actually earn $602 for the year.

Permit me to beat up on our assumptions, our mores, and our customs and get you thinking like a cash flow millionaire. The first

thing I have to do is "un-brainwash" you and get you to quit thinking in terms of annual anything. We need to think in terms of
weekly or monthly cash flow. This will change your whole financial paradigm, and hopefully your life will never be the same.

Again, I learned this in my real estate days when I played a
game called "Friday." It only had one rule: Don't ever buy a house
unless you can sell it by Friday (see *Real Estate Money Machine* for
details). Also, I've recorded a real estate cash flow seminar called
"Income Streams" on cassette. Call for your free copy at 1-800-872-
7411.

We live in a monthly billing society. Everything I do is for
income. Everything I teach is to get more monthly checks coming
in for my students.

Back To The Formula

We'll go to other deals, but I want to mention the three main
ingredients (rules) to this recipe. I'll explain these in more detail in
the next chapter, but you need to start getting a handle on the
mechanics of what makes the "Wade Cook Covered Call Formula"
work so well!

1. Use margin—you'll see it work on all these examples.

   NOTE: You can't do margin (See page 140 for more information on this) in an IRA.

2. Use stock in the $5 to $25 range for your best returns.
   There is a reason for this. You see, if you buy a stock for
   $6.50 and write a $7.50 call, you'll receive 75¢ to $1.25 for
   the premium. If you buy a stock for $48 and write a $50
   call, you'll receive 75¢ to $1.25. If you buy a stock for $98
   and write a $100 call, you'll receive 75¢ to $1.25. You see
   the call premiums are about the same if you're selling close
   to the next strike price. You can buy a lot more stock at $9
   than at $99 per share. This is true of normal stocks. Highly
   volatile stocks might have higher premiums, but be careful:
   the stocks can also take dramatic dips in price. Basically we
   write covered calls to get called out. We buy on dips and
   sell the call on strength—all the time hoping that the stock

will run up above the strike price so we get it taken away from us

Other considerations:

   a. The assumptions above (75¢ to $1.25) could have been
       50¢ to $2, but they are generally the same all the way
       up to the higher-priced stocks.
   b. I'm using a one-month-out expiration date for these
       assumptions. If you go out two to three months, the
       premiums are larger, but you have to leave your money
       tied up for that period of time. Most stocks we use are
       in the $15 to $25 range. Why? There just aren't that
       many good stocks in the $5 to $15 range.
3. You need a certain volatility to make this work really well.
   You see, a key to this process is to buy low and sell high.
   Let me put that in business terms: Buy wholesale, sell retail.
   Now let me put it into covered call terms: Buy the stock on
   dips, wait, and sell the call on strength.

To really understand this point, we need to explore another strategy. It's important for you to understand this and equally important to understand your limitations with this strategy. It's called writing uncovered calls, or, to use a more street-smart term, going naked.

It is not that hard to explain, but it is difficult for many to grasp because many have such a hard time realizing they can sell something they don't own. If writing a covered call means selling (for cash flow purposes) a call option on stock we actually own, then writing an uncovered call is selling a call option on stock we don't own. How can you do this? You just do it. You are giving someone the right to buy stock from you at a set price. Your risk is in the stock going up.

Let's say the stock is floating between $8 and $12 a share. When it goes up to $12, you sell the $10 call for $2. Again, we will use 1,000 shares or 10 contracts. You pocket $2,000 cash and you have no outlay of money. You're naked in the stock. If the stock floats down to $10 or below and you don't get called out, you're clear. You keep the $2,000. Actually you keep the $2,000 no matter what. If the stock stays at $12 or goes higher, you'll have to buy it at whatever price it goes to. If it goes to $14, you will have a $4,000 capital loss. Yes, this loss is mitigated by the $2,000 option premium income, which presents an interesting point: The stock would have to go up substantially for you to lose. This particular stock would have to act totally out of the ordinary to have this happen.

Now to a minor problem. I write naked calls a lot. I make "big bucks" doing so, but most of you will not be able to do this type of play—not until you have more experience and more cash in your account. It is not that there is anything wrong, except your stockbroker will prohibit you from this type of trading until you have satisfied his criteria for naked call writing.

One more point. If you do this type of trading, your stockbroker will require you to have enough cash in the account to cover the potential purchase. In our example, that would be $10,000 ($10 strike price x 1,000 shares) or $5,000 if you have a margin account. You will have to keep it on hold until the expiration date. Remember, you've sold a call, so you have the obligation to fill the order if you are exercised on. Also, if the stock goes up substantially before the expiration date, your broker may require additional deposits.

We write calls in a naked position when we think a stock will go down. In the last example the stock would have to go down under $10 for us to not get called out. What if we want the $12.50 call instead, we push up $1, or $1,000. Our risk is substantially less in that the stock just needs to stay below $12.50 through the expiration date.

Before we go on, this last discussion makes a nice segue into another point about writing covered calls—our risk.

Do we have a risk in writing a call on stock that we already own? Yes, and it needs some consideration. By writing a call, we have agreed to sell the stock at a specific price. We have limited our upside potential. As option writers, we have an "opportunity lost" risk. If you think you have a winner (i.e., a stock you bought at $10 and think may go to $30) you shouldn't sell the $10 or the $12.50 call. You might make more by waiting it out.

You may also calculate that buying and selling the stock several times and collecting premiums at each rising strike price every month is the way to go. There are certain stocks that we use over and over again. Others are temporary one-month deals. I purchased several around $9 to $10 and sold calls at $10 and $12.50, reaping nice premiums. Later, I jumped back in at the $18 to $20 range. I hope by now you've subscribed to my Internet web service called W.I.N.™ Through it, you can find out what I'm doing–the stocks, the premiums, and the strategies I employ on a daily basis. See this Internet site at www.wadecook.com.

I've hinted at this, but I want to make sure it is perfectly clear. When we sell an option, we get to keep the premium no matter what. It is not like a down payment wherein it applies to the stock price. We don't have to apply it or give it back. It's ours if the stock goes up and we get called out, and it's ours if the stock is below the strike price and we don't get called out. These premiums are a money machine. Later you'll see how compounding these 14% to 24% monthly returns can really enhance our wealth potential.

Back to our $7 stock. The stock went up to $8 and we were called out. Again, this simply means we sold the stock at $7.50. We bought this stock at $7 so we have a 50¢ per share capital gain or $500. Now we have a total of $1,000 in cash profits–$500 from the call premium and $500 from the capital gain. Our rate of return is now 28.57%. Just for fun, the annualized return is 743%. We have our $3,500 cash back in the account, plus the thousand dollars.

Let's look at another one. Recently, IDT Corporation (IDTC) was at $22⅞. Let's work the formula. One thousand shares times $22.875 = $22,875. Divide by two for margin and we have $11,437.50 invested. We sold the $22.50 strike price for $3⅝ ($3.625) since there was plenty of time before the expiration date. The stock dropped to $18 before going to $23.50, and we were called out. Let's calculate our profit. $3.625 x 1,000 = $3,625. That is a 31.69% return for a few weeks ($3,625 divided by $11,437.50 = 31.69%). But we were called out at $22.50. We have a loss of $.375 per share ($375), so we have a return of 28.41% ($3,625 - $375 = $3,250; $3,250 divided by $11,437.50 = .2841; or 28.41%).

In my seminars, I use the phrase "give back," meaning we have to give back part of our $3,625 profit. We net $3,250. This was an "in the money" call. It was only "in the money" by 37.5¢. Now, if the stock goes down a little, as IDT Corporation did at first, and we don't get called out, we get to keep the whole $3,625. Only by being called out do we have to give back the $375.

Let's look at another scenario. The stock goes down to $18. The next month's premium is only $1.62 for $22.50 call. We are not willing to sell for that. We place an order to sell the call at 2\frac{1}{8}$. This will be $212.50 if the order gets filled. We place the order, GTC (Good Till Canceled). It may take one to three weeks to get up to 2\frac{1}{8}$. Remember, a small movement in the stock could mean a magnified movement in the option. Also, it may not go up and we may not get filled. As a matter of fact, the stock might take another dip and all we can get is 25¢ or $250. Please note we're discussing a second premium written on the same stock the next month.

Our next example is a wild one. It will show several strategies and will also let you see our risk come home to roost. In early May, I heard about a pharmaceutical company in phase three testing of a new product. I had just lost a little on another such company and was leery. The stock was around $9. One thousand shares would be $9,000, or $4,500 on margin. I sold the May $10 calls for $1. This generated $1,000 in cash, a 22% two-week return. The stock wandered from $8.75 to $10.50. On the expiration date it was $9.75, and I didn't get called out. I kept the $1,000.

I then checked on the June $10 call options. At that time it was 75¢. I felt the stock was volatile enough and had enough news coming out to wait. I put an order to sell the June $10 calls for $1.25. About a week later, the stock was over $11 and my order was filled. I sold my calls for $1.25, and another $1,250 hit my account the next day. The stock floated back down to the $9 to $10 range and I didn't get called out. Then, within a few days, the stock shot up to near $12. I probably should have just waited it out, but I asked about the $10 July calls, and while at it, I checked on the July $12.50. The $10 strike price options were going for $2.25 and the $12.50 options were going for 75¢.

I had a hard time making up my mind so I split them up—sort of divide and conquer. I sold the first five contracts at $2.25, generating $1,125 (500 shares x $2.25) and another five contracts at the $12.50 strike price for 75¢ or $375.

The rationale behind this split strategy may be apparent to some, but not to others. Also, I use this approach quite often, so let me explain this in the next chapter.

Now, let me tell you what happened. The news was good and the stock ran up to $17. I was called out of the $10 strike price (500 shares). This generated capital gains of $500 ($10 – $9 = $1 x 500 = $500) and $1,750 ($12.50 – $9 = $3.50 x 500 = $1,750). Add this to the $1,000 first premium, and the $1,250 second premium, then the third and fourth premiums of $1,125 and $375. You can see my $4,500 produced a nice $6,000 income in just 10 weeks.

This is exciting, and while not all of the stocks and premiums are this good, many come close. They, at least, make up for the ones that we don't make very much profit on.

How Do You Find These Stocks?

I find companies for good covered call writing everywhere. You learn more about my criteria—stocks between $5 and $25, some volatility, and marginability—in a following chapter. Here is how I find them:

1. I read a lot. I keep a pad and make a list of every stock (in this range) I read about. If it's in the news, it helps with the volatility. When I get to a phone, I call my broker or fax him a list. He faxes or calls the current prices back to me—both stocks and calls. He knows what I'm looking for. Read on and I'll explain this.

2. I teach seminars and have W.I.N.™ Students and clients are constantly giving me information on different stocks. I turn around and share them with the other attendees or people on W.I.N.™

3. My stockbroker tells me about covered call possibilities all the time. Many stockbrokers barely know about writing covered calls, while others are very knowledgeable.

I want to show you a typical list of stocks and options I get back from my brokers. Remember, this is at current prices. You would have to see a chart to check on the swings of the stock.

You'll observe several numbers down the right side of the example. I want to explain certain aspects of this. I'll also show you how to look at this type of chart and cut to the chase on the ones that look good.

Our assumption is these trades are happening this and next month. Eight trading days remain in June and 28 trading days remain in July. In real life, the purchase of the stock and the sale of the option on the stock may be spread out over several weeks.

STOCK	SYMBOL	PRICE	MO	STRIKE	OPTION BID	ASK	NOTES
Able Telecom	ABTE	$6¹⁵/₁₆	June	$5	$1¹⁵/₁₆	$2¹/₁₆	
Holding			June	7.50	¹/₄	⁵/₁₆	
			July	5	2¹/₁₆	2¹/₄	
			July	7.50	⁵/₈	³/₄	#1
Avid Technology	AVID	16¹³/₁₆	June	15	1¹³/₁₆	2¹/₁₆	
			June	17.50	⁷/₁₆	⁹/₁₆	
			July	15	2⁹/₁₆	2¹³/₁₆	
			July	17.50	1¹/₄	1⁷/₁₆	#2
E.Spire	ESPI	10¹⁵/₁₆	June	10	1¹/₄	1¹/₂	
Communications			June	12.50	³/₈	¹/₂	
			July	10	1¹⁵/₁₆	2³/₁₆	
			July	12.50	¹⁵/₁₆	1³/₁₆	#3
IDT Corporation	IDTC	20¹⁵/₁₆	June	20	1¹¹/₁₆	1¹⁵/₁₆	
			June	22.50	¹¹/₁₆	¹⁵/₁₆	
			July	20	3¹/₈	3¹/₂	
			July	22.50	2	2¹/₄	#4
Premiere	PTEK	14¹⁵/₁₆	June	12.50	2⁷/₁₆	2³/₄	
Technologies Inc.			June	15	⁷/₈	1¹/₈	
			July	12.50	3¹/₈	3³/₈	
			July	15	1⁷/₈	2	#5
Humana Inc.	HUM	14⁹/₁₆	June	12.50	2¹/₈	2¹/₂	
			June	15	¹/₂	³/₄	
			July	12.50	2¹/₂	2⁷/₈	
			July	15	1¹/₄	1¹/₂	#6

NOTES:

1. You can get a larger premium by waiting. However, you have to leave your cash tied up another month. If I can get a larger premium on the next strike price up, I may go ahead and do it.
2. The July $17.50 call produces a smaller option premium than the July $15, but makes an additional profit (capital gain) if I get called out.
3. This is a difficult stock price, but if you own the stock and it is trading at the top of its range, you would do well to sell the call on strength, buy it back on weakness, and perhaps sell it again.
4. This is another difficult stock price. But you own it and have already taken in two months of premiums. The stock has recently reversed a downtrend and is moving up. Sell calls out of the money. You will have a good chance of getting called out.
5. This stock is at a great price and the options have nice premium.
6. This stock has a great looking chart and is trending up. You could write the calls now and expect to be called out, or you could wait to sell the calls and probably take in a larger capital gain.

Remember, a small movement in the stock (either up or down) means a magnified movement in the option (either up or down). Wait for an uptick before you sell the option. Often this will produce an enhanced yield. Remember also, we can put in an order to sell the option GTC above the current bid and ask. If the stock moves (even intra-day), we could get the higher price. Sometimes it pays to be patient.

CUT TO THE CHASE

Sometimes, you just don't want to take the time and explain the whole formula to your broker. Just tell him you are looking for stocks wherein the next month's call options are 8 to 10% of the stock price.

> **POINT:** If you buy a stock and sell the option for 8% of the stock price, your rate of return will be 16% if you use margin. You only have to put up half of the cash to buy, so you double your profits. Look for a high option premium compared to the stock price. Of course they change all of the time, but this exercise will help you see potential plays right now—if one exists.

Here is a list of some of the covered call stocks in my portfolio. For this writing we looked at a typical, but totally arbitrary window in time. There were eight trading days remaining in June and 28 trading days remaining in July when the trading department took this data from Bloomberg. If this window had been one week earlier, the June premiums would be significantly better.

STOCK	SYMBOL	PRICE	MO	STRIKE	OPTION BID	ASK
Cerner	CERN	$19³/₈	June	$20	$1¹¹/₁₆	$1⁷/₈
Corporation			July	20	2¹⁵/₁₆	3¹/₈
Picturetel	PCTL	9	June	10	³/₈	¹/₂
Corporation			July	10	¹⁵/₁₆	1³/₁₆
Sequent Computer	SQNT	12¹/₄	June	12.50	⁹/₁₆	⁵/₈
Systems			July	12.50	1³/₈	1¹/₂
Summit	BEAM	21¹¹/₁₆	June	22.50	¹¹/₁₆	¹³/₁₆
Technology Inc.			July	22.50	2³/₁₆	2¹/₄
Premiere	PTEK	14	June	15	⁷/₁₆	⁹/₁₆
Technologies Inc.			July	15	1¹/₈	1³/₈
Cabletron Systems	CS	14⁵/₈	June	15	⁵/₈	³/₄
			July	15	1⁹/₁₆	1³/₄
Cambridge	CATP	17	June	17.50	¹¹/₁₆	¹⁵/₁₆
Technology Partners			July	17.50	2	2¹/₄

Let's go down this shopping list together:

CERN The June $20 calls create a 17.41% return for eight trading days ($1.6875 divided by $9.6875 on margin, multiplied by 1,000 for 10 contracts); add another $.625 if called out for a total return of 23.87% ($2.3125 divided by $9.6875 on margin, multiplied by 1,000); not bad!

The July $20 calls return 30.32% for 28 days ($2.9375 divided by $9.6875 on margin, multiplied by 1,000 for 10 contracts); add in another $.625 for the capital gain, if called out, for a total possible return of 36.77%; impressive!

PCTL The June $10 calls produce an 8.33% return for eight trading days ($.3750 divided by $4.50 on margin, multiplied by 1,000 for ten contracts); add another $1 if called out for a total return of 30.55% ($1.375 divided by $4.50 on margin, multiplied by 1,000); great!

The July $10 calls return 20.83% for 28 days ($.9375 divided by $4.50 on margin, multiplied by 1,000 for 10 contracts); add another $1,000 for the capital gain, if called out, for a total possible return of 43.05%.

SQNT The June $12.50 calls create a 9.18% return for eight trading days ($0.5625 divided by $6.125 on margin, multiplied by 1,000 for 10 contracts); add another one-quarter if called out for a total return of 13.26% ($0.8125 divided by $6.125 on margin, multiplied by 1,000).

The July $12.50 calls return 22.44% for 28 days ($1.375 divided by $6.125 on margin, multiplied by 1,000 for 10 contracts); add in another $250 for the capital gain, if called out, for a total possible return of 26.53%.

BEAM The June $22.50 calls create a 6.34% return for eight trading days ($.6875 divided by $10.84375 on margin, multiplied by 1,000 for 10 contracts); add another $.8125, if called out, for a total return of 13.83% ($1.50 divided by $10.84375 on margin, multiplied by 1,000).

The July $22.50 calls return 20.17% for 28 days ($2.1875 divided by $10.84375 on margin, multiplied by 1,000 for 10 contracts); add in another $812.50 for the capital gain, if called out, for a total possible return of 27.66%.

PTEK The June $15 calls create a 6.25% return for eight trading days ($0.4375 divided by $7 on margin, multiplied by 1,000 for 10 contracts); add another $1 if called out for a total return of 20.53% ($1.4375 divided by $7 on margin, multiplied by 1,000).

The July $15 calls return 16.07% for 28 days ($1.125 divided by $7 on margin, multiplied by 1,000 for 10 contracts); add in another $1,000 for the capital gain, if called out, for a total possible return of 30.35%.

CS The June $15 calls create a 5.83% return for eight trading days ($0.4375 divided by $7.5 on margin, multiplied by 1,000 for 10 contracts); add another $.375 if called out for a total return of 10.83% ($.8125 divided by $7.5 on margin, multiplied by 1,000).

The July $15 calls return 20.83% for 28 days ($1.5625 divided by $7.5 on margin, multiplied by 1,000 for 10 contracts); add in another $375 for the capital gain, if called out, for a total possible return of 20.83%.

CATP The June $17.50 calls create a 8.08% return for eight trading days ($0.6875 divided by $8.5 on margin, multiplied by 1,000 for 10 contracts); add another one-half if called out for a total return of 13.97% ($1.1875 divided by $8.50 on margin, multiplied by 1,000).

The July $15 calls return 23.52% for 28 days ($2 divided by $8.5 on margin, multiplied by 1,000 for 10 contracts); add in another $500 for the capital gain, if called out, for a total possible return of 29.41%.

This is what I mean by shopping. And don't think we have to buy the stock where it is or sell the options where they are. Most prices are fluid. This chart should get you thinking about the possibilities. Now, I want you to follow me through this next exercise.

LIKE A BUSINESS
If we turn writing covered calls into a business–generating cash flow constantly, several good things happen.

1. We get good at it. It is not that the task becomes easier, but that our ability to do it gets better.

2. We keep adding fuel to the fire. Take our cash flow, add it to the account, producing larger margin capabilities, and more actual cash to work with.

3. Our brokers get trained on what we're looking for, when to get in and out, new companies to explore (test the numbers), et cetera.

4. We might be able to quit doing other things (like a boring job) because we have more income and the ability to make more, especially if we have more time to devote to this endeavor.

LET'S THINK BIG

So look at the following example and assumptions. Let's think big. Say you have $100,000 to invest. If you don't, then build it up to this in the next year even with a smaller starting amount. Look at the following–big or small amounts of money still produce the same percentages.

ASSUMPTIONS	RUN THE NUMBERS
1. We'll sell calls for 75¢ about 10 times. In real life, getting $1 to $1.50 is more prevalent but I'm trying to tone down these numbers. What I do in real life is nothing short of remarkable. We actually sell in all 12 months; I'm using 10 months. Again, I'm doing this smaller number to downplay the real results.	1. 10,000 shares (100 contracts) at $75 = $7,500 x 10 = $75,000 income for the year. (Most people can retire on this amount.)
2. Getting called out. In real life we get called every month, or at least every other month. Here I'll use three months. Also, we get a capital gain between 75¢ and $2, usually above $1. It's hard to make this strategy look bad.	2. Capital gain of $1 x 10,000 shares every three months $10,000 x 4 times = $40,000 (for the year)
3. Dividends. Most of these companies don't pay dividends. In real life we'll receive between $2,000 to $3,000 on our $100,000 (double our $200,000, if done on margin). I'll put in $1,000 here.	3. Dividends = $1,000
4. If we can leave all of the original principal amount and all, or part of the profits to buy more stocks and write more calls, we could generate another $50,000 to $60,000 or so. I'll cut this one way back as it just gets to looking too good.	4. Let it compound. Use profits to do more deals–pull out a little to live on, make $20,000 from compounding. Total for the year: $136,000. Add second level, margin account, minus margin interest of $8,000 = $128,000. For the year $250,000– plus ($136,000 + $128,000 margin profits).

One hundred thousand dollars buys 10,000 shares of stock at $10. Some purchases may be $8, some $12. We'll buy the 10,000 shares in 10 different companies for the sake of diversity.

If you do it on margin, you have to subtract the margin interest and you now have $100,000 making about $250,000 per year. Did you catch the "total" aspect of this? Your $100,000 is invested wisely and runs like a business. I tried to cut back the numbers so you won't get too excited. This is a remarkable strategy. I was hesitant to do this exercise because while $250,000 plus per year looks good, this only represents a portion of what can really be done.

Other places I've mentioned doubling some of your money every two and a half to three and a half months. It's not only possible but has been done, and can be done by you if you'll apply the strategies mentioned in this book. If you blend with this covered call strategy other strategies and formulas, it gets even more exciting.

If you only have $10,000 it can produce about $25,000 per year. My students do this all the time. You should retire, almost immediately, by implementing the cash flow machine.

"I have made about $7,000 to $8,000 in one month writing covered calls. My wife was very skeptical, but she's a believer now."

—J. BRENT LEWIS

"I went to the one day class. I took the information and bought a stock, I wrote a covered call. My profits in just four weeks is $3,750, I only invested $7,500. I'm hooked!"

—MARK ELSTON

"In five minutes I calculated the premium on covered calls on stock I own and on an annual basis it comes to $175,950. At today's listed options quotations, I have never done this or any other strategy besides buy and hold before. This is truly unbelievable!"

—JAMES ELLIS

"My favorite strategies are buying options on stock split companies and I really like covered calls. After 28 years with a well known company my wife took early retirement. We rolled her money over to a brokerage firm on 9/14/98 and immediately did covered calls. Before retiring she was making around $1,000 per month on her 401(k) plan. In October 1998 she made $7,756 doing covered calls and in November she made $7,180 in covered calls. I have a IRA account that I cleaned up in October of this year and I make about $2,500 per month. On the last 12 plays I did options and I haven't lost one yet. My goal was to make $100,000 the first year on my wife's account. I amazed myself since 9/14/98 until now—1/99—she is over $52,000."

—LEE HAMILTON

10

COVERED CALLS
Cash Generating Strategies

THE MAIN purpose in doing covered calls is to build up cash flow on a monthly basis. Our main risk is an "opportunity lost" risk. Yes, we generate income, but we give up the upside. Keep this in mind as the explanation continues. If the stock is volatile, and remember, I like some rolling volatility, and it goes above the intended strike price, you can receive a substantially larger premium for selling the call than by selling the call too quickly. In our example in the last chapter, we purchased the stock at $9. The $10 call options when the stock was at $9 may be only 25¢. We had to wait for the stock to get to $9.50 or $9.75 to get the $1. (Remember, buy the stock on dips, sell the call on strength.) As the stock moves above $10, the option price also goes up.

Look at the first table on the following page for the $10 strike price. (Note: I am using a fictitious company. However, these numbers are not too far from reality on any given stock and option movement.)

STOCK PRICE	STRIKE PRICE	OPTION PRICE	NOTES
$9.00	$10.00	$0.25	
9.50	10.00	1.00	
10.25	10.00	1.50	
11.00	10.00	1.75	#1
12.00	10.00	2.25	
13.00	10.00	3.00	#2
14.00	10.00	4.00	

NOTES:

1. It will probably be this high if there is still plenty of time before the expiration date. $1.75 option–remember, $1 is now intrinsic value.

2. The option might start going "tick for tick" with the stock. See the Delta Formula section, on page 93, for more information on this.

Now look at the same chart for a $12.50 strike price:

STOCK PRICE	STRIKE PRICE	OPTION PRICE	NOTES
$ 9.00	$12.50	no bid	#3
9.50	12.50	$.125	
10.25	12.50	.25	
11.00	12.50	.75	
12.00	12.50	1.00	#4
13.00	12.50	1.75	
14.00	12.50	2.00	

NOTES:

3. Market makers are not willing to buy this option at any price. They just don't think it will hit $12.50. Since it is $9 at the present time, they probably have a point. There are no believers in the stock hitting $12.50 so there is "no bid."

4. As the stock gets closer to being "in the money," the option price really increases.

Remember, in all these examples we're selling, not buying, options. We can be patient and wait for an increase in the option premium to substantially enhance our rate of return. But also remember, one component of options is the time value. We have to carefully weigh out the timing of our sell point. If the time gets close to the expiration date the time value will quickly deteriorate.

Let's return to our scenario. If the stock runs up to $12 or so, we have choices: Sell the $10 calls or sell the $12.50 calls, or sell part of our position at the lower strike price and the balance at the higher strike price, or hold on and wait some more.

If we sell at the lower strike price, we pick up a larger premium. We dramatically increase our cash flow. However, if we sell at the higher strike price, we pick up a smaller premium now, but a substantially larger capital gain if we get called out.

Specifically, in our example, we received $2.25 for the premium ($10 strike price) and only a $1 capital gain ($10 minimum strike price). If we had sold the $12.50 call, we would have received only 75¢ but $3.50 on the capital gain. That's $3.25 versus $4.25. Sometimes the disparity is even larger. So you see, it's decision time—take the larger amount of cash now or wait for the stock to rise and get called out at the higher price. If we wait and if the stock goes up we receive a lot more, but it might not go up to the extent necessary to get called out.

A THOUGHT: If we don't want to get called out—say we want to keep the stock to write calls another day—then selling a way out of the money call may be just the trick.

The other play would be to divide them up. Sell 500 shares (five contracts) at one call price and 500 at another. Or sell 700 at one and 300 at the other. If you're uncertain, you may want to do what I do. When in doubt, get the larger premium now. You just don't know if it is going to reach the higher price. You know the old saying about "a bird in the hand..."

Our last choice would be to stay long in the stock without selling options. If there is a run up in the stock, we could participate in the increase. You'll see, when we get back to our example, that this should have been our choice. But hindsight is perfect and I'm happy with the money I received on this deal.

Back to our example. We sold five at $2.25 and five at 75¢. Then the phase three testing came out positive and the next day the stock was at $19. The next week or so we were called out of the $10 and the $12.50 calls. Let's look at the income now. We received an extra $500 on the $10 ($10 minus $9 = $1 x 500) and $1,750 on the $12.50 ($12.50 minus $9 = $3.50 x 500). Take a look now at all the income from our $4,500 investment. Also, remember we have the $4,500 back. We had 1,000 shares.

Two-week option premium (May)	$1,000
One month's option premium (June)	1,250
Next month's option premium (July)	
$10 strike	1,125
$12.50 strike	375
Called out at $10 (500 shares)	500
Called out at $12.50 (500 shares)	1,750
	$6,000

Not a bad eight-week return on $4,500. This was an exceptional one. We usually only make about one half this amount, but about one in every 10 to 12 deals turn out this good. We have to settle for a 20 to 30% monthly returns on the rest of them.

If we had held and sold at $19, we would have made $10,000 ($19 sell price minus $9 purchase price = $10 profit x 1,000 shares = $10,000). However, this would be all speculation. I'm perfectly happy with all my income checks.

I brought it up here to show you what we lost. Again, if you really think a stock is going to run up, you may not want to give away your upside by selling someone the right to buy the stock from you at a lower price.

Here is a more typical deal. Bethlehem Steel was at $14¼. I bought 1,000 shares and waited for the stock to get to $14½, then sold the next expiration date calls for $1. Let's look at the numbers. Stock outlay on margin–$7,125. Income of $1,000 = 14% return. The stock went to $15.50. We were called out and made another $750. Now our four-week return is 25%. Not spectacular, but not bad, month after month. I want you to see a calculation of the compounding effects of repeatedly doing this month after month. Look at the end of this chapter.

Also, look at the results. Are they worth it? If you can leave the money in the account and let it compound, you have an unparalleled dynamic at work. Investing in the stock market is not easy. It takes a certain discipline, attention to details, and risk taking that even I have a hard time with. It is, however, easy from the perspective of accessibility. You're just a phone call away.

I made my first fortune in real estate. Except for that first day in the cab, I learned more about financial matters in those years than any other time. Through all this, my heart was in education. I did the real estate so I could become a teacher. To be a great teacher you have to learn the art of persuasion, a lot of marketing techniques, and how to not only teach to give out information but to teach so as to modify behavior.

This process taught me one of the greatest tools of leverage. Leveraging by implementing and then repeating ideas. If we learn how to do real estate a certain way then that knowledge repeated persistently brings success. The stock market is no different. Find one (or a few) great ideas that you know and like doing and get on with it. Do it so you can retire. Do it part time on through retirement for extra income. Get to be an expert at it.

I once again bring up income. Our need for growth of assets will be different at different times of our lives. Our need for tax write-offs will change from year to year, but our need for income will be constant, and if it changes, it will always change in the direction of needing more. My seminars and workshops are designed to help build up this income.

BUY AND SELL RIGHT WITH A "BUY-WRITE"

One little known secret of enhancing your yield when writing covered calls is a "buy-write." This could increase your yield 10 to

20%. Once again, I am writing about two to four week returns so this could add another 20% or more annually to your rate of return.

The concept and process is really quite simple. The option market makers will allow you to place a combination order. You buy the stock and sell the options at the same time. This time, however, you're getting both at the best buy price (stock) and sell price (option) available. The stock purchase price will be close to the ask and the option sell price will also be close to the ask. If the stock has a bid of $9.25 and an ask of $9.50, and if the next month's option ($10 strike price) is 75¢ bid and $1 ask, you will buy the stock at $9.50 and sell the call for $1–all at the same time.

The only way to see how good this is, is to look at the normal way of completing the transaction. Normally we would place an order to buy the stock somewhere between the bid and the ask, say at $9³/₈. Or, we would place an order to buy the stock well below the bid, say $9 or $8.50 and hope to pick up the stock purchase on a serious dip in price.

Once purchased, we would wait to sell the call option. We wait for an increase in the call option price, usually accompanied by, or tied to an increase in the stock price. One problem with the process is doing it at the right time. You see, unless you are on the phone with your stockbroker, or unless he calls you, you won't find out about getting filled on your stock purchase for a day or so. If you are out of town it could be much longer. Yes, if your broker is willing, he can keep tabs of your purchase order, and if you've discussed what you want to sell the call for, he can put in the order to sell once the stock is purchased. The problem is that by the time the order is placed on selling the call option it could have risen, say from 75¢ to $1.25, and fallen back to 62.5¢. The prices move very quickly.

All of this waiting and uncertainty can be eliminated with a buy-write. Even if you don't make quite as much, your returns will be constant, you won't miss a fluctuation, and you can go to more movies.

Let's look at the rate of return of the last buy-write example.

Normally, you buy the stock at the ask and sell the call at the bid. Now you ask for a better deal, for example, getting both the stock and the option in the spread.

COLUMN A	COLUMN B
Non Buy-Write	Buy-Write
• Buy stock at $9.50 x 1,000 shares = $9,500 ÷ 2 (margin) = $4,750	• Buy stock at $9.50 or less x 1,000 shares = $9,500 ÷ 2 (margin) = $4,750
• Sell call for $0.75 x 1,000 shares = $750.	• Sell call for $1 or so x 1,000 shares = $1,000
• Rate of Return: $750 ÷ 4,750 = 15.79%	• Rate of Return: $1,000 ÷ 4,750 = 21.05%
• Not bad for 3 weeks. Getting called out generates another $0.50 x 1,000 shares or $500	• Better for same 3 weeks. Getting called out generates another $0.50 x 1,000 shares or $500
• Total Rate of Return: $1,250 ÷ 4,750 ($750 + $500) = 26.32%	• Total Rate of Return: $1,500 ÷ 4,750 ($1,000 + $500) = 31.58%

There is not always a 6% differential in the rate of return, but this is very common. If you can pick up between an additional 2 to 8% every few weeks that could be between 20 to 80% extra per year. Now, some people are happy with 6 to 14% annual returns. I hear fund managers bragging about 6% returns. The above figure represents an add-on or "gravy" return, onto the 300 to 500% basic premium income and capital gain income we are already receiving. "Exciting" is an understatement.

IMPLEMENTING THIS STRATEGY

A buy-write is easy to implement. When you call your broker, shop around for a stock which looks good, and one which has fairly good current premiums (ones you are happy with) then just tell your broker you want to do a buy-write. He will say, "okay," and it will be done in a few minutes. Remember you're "doing the deal" at the market so your orders will go through quite quickly.

Getting back to covered call writing. In the last two chapters and in the next two I present ways to consistently get 20% plus returns a month. It's just not that tough once you learn how. Think of this: if you can compound all the money, then every three months or so, you have doubled your money.

Lets start in June with $10,000. By September you will have $18,000 to $20,000 in your account. By January you will have $35,000 to $40,000. By summer you will have about $150,000 in the account. What a great personal independence this will be. Now $150,000 at even 10% (a third or less of what you've been making) will produce $15,000, and most Americans can live handsomely on this amount. What have you got to lose? Again, this can be done in an IRA (with only one-half the result). It is that acceptable.

The question is simple. In one year you will either be retired or not retired. If you continue to do it your way, where will you be? If you try my way, even though life has no guarantees, you have a fighting chance. And what if you "shoot for the stars and only hit the moon?" Even 10% of these results would be nothing short of remarkable.

GET OUT YOUR CALCULATOR

The following calculation ought to perk you up. We're going to start with a very small amount of money, leave it in the account, and really work it. This will take dedication and application of the principles mentioned in this book, and a little luck. We're going to let the money compound at 20%–*but monthly*!

We do it in real life, why not here. Let's give a few caveats, assumptions, and cautions. No matter how difficult this is, the results are worth it. Even if we only achieve one-half of these results, the results are still worth it.

1. Obviously we're not going to get exactly 20% returns each month. Some months will be 24%, some 28%, and some 14%. Again, I'm taking my numbers from real life. I just

looked at the last three that are on my desk as I wrote this section and those three covered call deals represented 22, 23, and 28%. But, there are no guarantees.

2. Because commissions and margin interest are so small, I will not use them in these calculations. Obviously, in real life, they have to be figured in, so it will take a week or two longer to reach our million bucks.

3. This is a major point, a big concession, if you will. I'm not going to calculate in the capital gains from getting called out. In the following scenario we're going to start with a small amount of money, buy stock, receive premiums for writing (selling) calls, let the money stay in the account to compound, and keep repeating the process.

In all of our previous examples we sold the stock.

1. The stock dips down and although we keep the premium, we have to wait for it to rise again before we sell another call or sell the stock.

2. Sometimes we get called out right away. Even in a few days. However, it usually takes two to eight weeks.

3. Sometimes the stock shows weakness and never recovers. We might have to unload at a loss. This has rarely happened because of the cautious approach we take when buying.

All in all, we make substantial money on these capital gains. Buying stock at $6.75; selling a $7.50 call for $1 when the stock hits $8; having it dip back to $7.25 before the expiration date (we keep the premium); then it rises to $9.25, we sell the $10 call for 75¢, and on the expiration date the stock is at $10.50 and we get called out at $10. That's a $3.25 capital gain! One thousand shares ($3,375 on margin) generates:

$1,000	first premium
750	second premium
3,250	capital gain
$5,000	total profits

Take away $250 to $400 in commissions and margin interest and still your $3,375 investment (which is now back in your account), has created a remarkable return.

Again, for this example we'll ignore getting called out. No capital gains will be used.

Even on months when our premium only generates a 14% return, getting called out could pull it up to 25 to 45%. Yes, this is a one-month return.

If we figured in the capital gain, the results of this exercise would dramatically increase, and since there is so much skepticism from our professionals (usually stockbrokers, financial planners, and definitely CPAs and attorneys), I'll tone it down. My real life numbers (and those of countless students who have attended my Wall Street Workshop™ and then applied these principles) would cause a coronary in most of these professionals.

4. I've already stated this, but we're going to leave the money in the account. We'll not only use the same money every month, but we'll use the profits. This is not the place to extol the virtues and magic of compounding–if you don't know how compounding works you've lived a very sheltered life. Interest on interest–profits from profits. It's wealth accumulation at its second best. Leverage is first. That's the point of blending all these together–synergistically, getting money to work hard. Control more assets, generate cash flow, and live happily ever after. Once again, that's two to three years away for most readers.

So, let's get to it. A friend had $1,300. He learned about writing covered calls. Let's apply here what he learned and what he did. July is the start month.

In July he put in $1,300. Taking that amount times (x) 1.2 = $1,560.

One (1) is the constant–we're leaving the money in the account–.2 is 20%, our rate of return from the premium. Let's move on.

Aug. $1,560 x 1.2   = $1,872
(Compounding at work: 20% on $1,560 = $1,872)
Sept.   = $2,246
Oct.   = $2,695
Nov.   = $3,235
Dec.   = $3,882
Jan.   = $4,658

Now it really starts getting interesting.

Feb.   = $5,590
Mar.   = $6,708
April   = $8,049
May   = $9,659
June   = $11,590

Look what he has at the end of one year. Take back out his original investment of $1,300 and he still has a profit of over $10,000.

Now if you have $10,000 (or $13,000) to get started, you'll have over $100,000 in one year! If you have $100,000 you'll have over $1,000,000. A Million Bucks!

Now on to a couple other points.

1. If you start with $1,300, you're three years from being a millionaire and the process is so safe and easy you can do it in an IRA. (IRAs can't use margin without extra accounting problems. Since they functionally can't use margin, it will take twice as long–six years. A good point though: no tax on the profits.)

2. Once you've made this much money, you're probably worn out. To accomplish this, it will take 15 to 30 minutes a day or two to four hours two times a month to make it happen. Let's say you want to cut back and not work as hard. Even if you make 10% instead of 20% returns from now on it will generate $100,000 (plus or minus) a month. Let me repeat that. That's $100,000 *per month*, all from $1,300 put to work three years ago.

One final thought. This is what I've done in real life, plus now I have a legion of students on this same path. It's exciting, and if you're not excited, you need to check your pulse rate. Indeed, check and see if you have a pulse.

11

COVERED CALLS
EFFECTIVE PROCESSING TECHNIQUES

WE WRITE covered calls to generate income. We can create a lot of income in the 18 to 30% monthly range, or a small amount in the 8 to 20% range. Three factors need to exist and then be used for successful covered call cash flow generation. There need not be a long treatise on them. However, when writing covered calls, a good working knowledge of these three is a must.

These three factors are:

1. Margin account trading
2. Some volatility
3. The $5 to $25 price range

The successful blending of these three will allow you to accelerate your profits and minimize your downside. Once you understand the function of each one, you should not only see how they work together, but also how they benefit each other. Indeed, they are sine qua non to the 20% per month process.

I keep using 20%. Why? It is what I shoot for. A 20% increase each month of actual new cash hitting your account; then leaving that money in the account and using the whole sum (original principal and new profits) for investment the next month, makes it possible to double your money every three to four months. Sometimes it's better, sometimes not so great.

MARGIN TRADING

Start with margin trades made on the initial purchase of the base stock. Let it be clear, you don't have to trade on margin to write a call on your stock. However, if you want to accelerate your profits—to enhance your cash flow—you need to do it.

Briefly let's explore trading on margin. It is a form of leverage. Actually it uses debt to purchase some of the stock. This time, though, you're not getting a loan from the bank, but from your broker. He is more familiar with stocks, he can set the criteria for the collateral, et cetera.

Some real numbers might come in handy. Take $5,000, put it in a brokerage account, and you immediately have margin trading capability (buying power) of $10,000 worth of marginable securities. Where are you getting the other $5,000 to spend on $10,000 worth of stock? The broker will loan it to you. What does the broker get out of this? Two things:

1. More commission, because he has now sold more stock.

2. Interest on the outstanding loan balance. The interest rate is usually tied to an amount over the prime. Each broker is not only different in the amount of the rate, but also different in how they "fluctuate" the rate up and down.

The brokers also get happy customers. Now remember, they control the terms—as most lenders do. They say what they will use as collateral. They obviously don't like "penny stocks," but some can't even give a technical definition of a penny stock—one not listed on an exchange. They don't like low trading volume stock and companies in bankruptcy.

You may even have a stock that falls out of favor. Yesterday it was fine, today they're calling and asking you to bring in more cash on securities—you've had a "margin call."

A few more points:

1. Your stockbroker will recalculate the margin portion of your account every night. If your stocks have moved up in value, your buying power increases. You, in fact, may now buy more marginable stock with the increase in collateral. Conversely, if your stocks go down in value, you lose buying power and, as mentioned before, may have to make additional deposits.

A WORD TO THE WISE: Don't use all your buying power. Leave a cushion. You might need that buffer.

2. I've constantly used 50% margin since that is normal or usual, especially for new accounts with not too much cash. But once you have more money in your account, or have your account with one firm for a long time, your broker will often allow a higher percentage of debt. You might get to 30% margin capability. This means you'd have to put in $3,000 for an additional purchase of $10,000 of stock. If I used the 30/70% calculation, our yields in our covered call examples would be substantially higher. In this book though, I'll just continue touse 50%.

3. Options are not marginable until you have a larger account, more experience, et cetera, and you have a broker who allows options to be purchased with margin money. Even then, he or she will only make loans on certain options. Most readers of this book are a long way from this.

Now it's time to return to increasing yields with margin trades. If you can buy $20,000 worth of stock for $10,000 and receive an $800 call premium, you have a 16% yield instead of 8%. Look at the following illustrations:

MARGIN	NON MARGIN
Stock $9	Stock $9

MARGIN

Stock $9

- Purchase 1,000 shares = $9,000

- Divide by 2 (margin) = $4,500 (cash needed)

- Sell call for $1 ($1 x 1,000 shares = $1,000)

- Rate of return: $1,000 ÷ $4,500 = 22%

- This is the return if you are not called out. But if called out, you make an additional $1,000 ($10 sell price minus $9 purchase price = $1 x 1,000 shares = $1,000). Capital gain = $2,000

- New rate of return: $2,000 ÷ $4,500 = 44%. That's 44% for less than four weeks.

NON MARGIN

Stock $9

- Purchase 1,000 shares = $9,000

- Put up all cash

- Sell call for $1 = $1,000 ($1 x 1,000 shares = $1,000)

- Rate of return: $1,000 divided by $9,000 = 11%

- Again, this is the yield if you are not called out. But if called out you make an additional $1,000 ($10 sell price minus $9 purchase price = $1 x 1,000 shares = $1,000).

- Add $1,000 call premium + $1,000 capital gain = $2,000

- New rate of return: $2,000 ÷ $9,000 = 22%

- Most people would be ecstatic with a 22% return. But look to the left and see which is better.

I know, I know, I can hear you say, "You didn't calculate the margin interest." Remember, don't trip over pennies on your way to dollars. I'll figure in margin interest here for you. You'll realize how minuscule it is and hopefully you'll never worry about it again. Run the numbers: $4,500 x 8% = $360 (annual interest). Divide by 12 (for each month) and you have a monthly interest expense of $30. So you only make $1,970 instead of $2,000. Who cares, and with commission thrown in you have a 42 to 43% one month return instead of 44%. Do you see why I ignore these two items for most of my calculations?

In summary of the main point: to get the higher returns you need margin leverage. It allows a small amount of money to do double duty. Most real estate investors would never consider paying full price for a property and then put up the whole price in cash. You try to get the best deal with the smallest down payment possible. Obviously, the other side of the leverage coin is debt and I've already stated my concern and strategies so this doesn't get abused. The wise use of margin trading makes excellent returns possible.

VOLATILITY

Interestingly enough, most stock market investors hide from stocks with "mood swings." Not me. I thrive on them. It seems professionals only want stocks which go straight up, and while I'm not advocating stocks that go straight down, I am after stocks that move between certain prices–and ideally those with an upward trend.

Some readers, and likewise some of the attendees at my live workshops, may think this fits other models or formulas offered elsewhere in this book. For example, at the live events my staff or I work with 13 different stock market cash-flow strategies. We constantly are asked, "But I thought you said you buy calls."

Then we have to say, "Yes, in the option stock split strategies, that is true, but we're now talking about a completely different formula–with new angles, techniques, et cetera."People are constantly taking the "general" and making it "specific," or the "specific" and making it "general." Or they take a specific set of formulas and try to make them work elsewhere.

Writing covered calls is a specific cash-flow strategy. It has its own specific place, function and formula. We can measure our success each month. And I mean measure it to the *penny*. We generate actual income–cash hitting our account. It can be mailed to our house or left in the account. This cash generating strategy is difficult for some people to understand. I'm not surprised with all the brainwashing put out by the old, stodgy firms on Wall Street. People get their account statement and see that their $20,800 investment one day has a value of $20,940 and two days later is back down to $20,808. They're out of control and not too infrequently feeling helpless.

Stop it! Get control! Don't let someone sell you a bill of goods which doesn't generate cash for you, especially at first. Build up your cash flow–get your money to work as hard as you work (or harder) and you'll be able to buy all the boring investments you want. Just get the cash flow machine built and running, keep it greased, and it will churn out big bucks!

Two Types Of Income
Writing calls generates two kinds of income:

1. Money from the premium for selling the call. This hits the account the next trading day and would then be available for other uses.

2. Money from the capital gain. If you buy a stock for $9 and sell it for $10 or $12.50, you have that amount as a capital gain. This money would hit your account three days after the sell date. Usually in covered call writing, the capital gain will be three days after the Monday following the expiration date (third Friday) of the month in which you've agreed to sell your stock.

Yes, you could lose if the stock goes down and you sell, but that capital loss would be mitigated by any premiums you've received. Remember, you get to keep the premium for selling the call whether you sell the stock or not, and whether you sell it for a profit or not.

Okay, with that behind us, let's get back to the volatility issue. The way to enhance the yield is to get a large premium–especially in comparison to the price we pay for the stock. We buy the stock on weakness and sell the call on strength. Look at the chart on the following page. You see the stock goes from around $7 to $11and then down to around $6.Look at the bottom resistance line around the $11 strike price.The stock has been there twice.

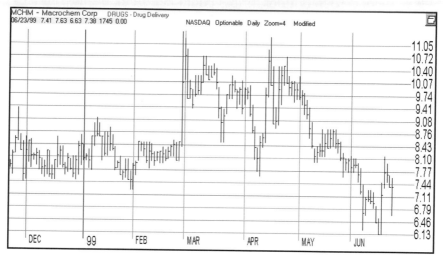

Now, while you're thinking about "buying low and selling high," look at the following diagram:

STOCK PRICE	STRIKE PRICE	OPTION PRICE
$7.75	$10.00	no bid
8.50	10.00	$.25
9.00	10.00	.50
9.50	10.00	1.00
10.00	10.00	1.25
11.00	10.00	1.50
11.00	12.50	.05
11.50	12.50	.75
12.25	12.50	1.00
13.00	12.50	1.25

Remember from the chapter on options: When there is a small movement in the stock, there is a magnified movement in the option. In this case we're not buying, we're selling the call options.

If we use a little patience, by looking at the chart we'll realize, or at least hope, the stock will rise, and we can sell the option at a higher price.

A lot of this comes down to timing. If time is running out on the value of certain options, prices could fall dramatically. But let's say we're still three to four weeks before next month's expiration day. The stock is at $9. We buy it and try to sell the option. Today we can get 25¢. This is not a great return. If we're selling the calls on 1,000 shares, that would be $250 (minus commissions) divided by $4,500 ($9 x 1,000 shares divided by 2 = $4,500), and it's only a 5.5% return. If we were called out (sell at $10), we'd pick up an additional $1,000 and we'd have a nice return. That, however, is a lot of "ifs." We just don't know if the stock will get above $10 before the expiration date.

Let's wait. We can monitor the stock and the option movement and sell it for 75¢ or $1, if and when it gets up there. We could also place our order to sell the option (GTC) now at a substantially higher price. Tell your broker you want to place an order to sell the (month) $10 call on XYZ stock for $1. You can always cancel your order and sell the option at a lower or higher price or just go ahead and sell the stock, or whatever. By leaving the order in for 60 days (GTC) we can:

1. Quit worrying about it and go to a movie.
2. Sell the option on an uptick in the stock price even on intraday moves.

The stock could move up so rapidly that you might want to sell the option at the next higher strike price. Let's explore this possibility.

The stock went up over the $10 strike price and we sold the call, making a nice premium. It fell back below $10 and we didn't get called out. Then it ran up to $11 and close to $12. We could sell the $10 call for a hefty premium because it's so far in the money. We would be selling for intrinsic value. Let's say the $10 call is going for $2.25. That would generate another $2,250. But think, we could sell the stock for $12 and get a $2 extra capital gain. The point is to show intrinsic value. The premium is my way to go. If you sell the stock you are done with it. If you sell the premium, pick up the $2.25 ($2,250) and you still own the stock. If the stock slides back down to under $10 (or maybe slightly above) we won't get called out, and we have the stock to generate another premium.

There is another choice. Look at the $12.50 calls. Obviously the premium won't be as much, since the stock is still out of the money. If we sell for $1 we will take in the premium and have the potential for a higher capital gain.

What should we do? The question has a pretty simple answer. Here is the rationale for each choice.

Sell the $10 call for $2.25

1. If the stock seldom goes above $12 to $13 but has most of its movement around $8 to $11, there is the likelihood it won't go above $12.50. We would be better off to take the "bird in the hand"–the $2,250.

2. How much time is left? If there is still plenty of time to get above $12.50, maybe waiting is better. We can also wait before we sell the $12.50. We just might be able to pick up $1.50 to $2 if it swings way up.

3. Do we need more cash now? Remember, selling calls generates cash in one day. You get either $2,250 or $1,000. When in doubt take the cash.

Sell the $12.50 call for $1.

1. If the stock has consistently been above $12.50, either recently or frequently, then the $12.50 call may be the way to go. Yes, you lose some of the premium income now ($1,250) but you just might pick up an additional capital gain of $2,250.

2. If there still are a few weeks before the expiration date and if there is a lot of good news coming out, maybe it will be enough to drive up the stock price.

3. If you don't think the stock will go below $10 and if you want to keep the stock to fight another day, then sell the $12.50 call for $1 (or wait for a little more).

The third choice would be to do some of each. Sell five contracts for the larger premium and five contracts hoping for the larger capital gain.

PRICE RANGE

The third factor, while easy to understand, presents a conundrum. One of the keys to covered call writing–and this is from the vantage point of my years of experience–is to buy stock low and sell the call when the stock price gets close to the next higher strike price, or at least moves up some. The call premium received will be much higher than the premium for writing a call on a stock a good distance from the next strike price.

Look at the following and I think you'll get the point.

STOCK PRICE	STRIKE PRICE	OPTION PRICE
$6.00	$5.00	$1.25
6.50	5.00	1.75
7.00	5.00	2.25
7.00	7.50	.50
7.50	7.50	.75
8.00	7.50	1.00
9.00	7.50	1.25
9.50	7.50	2.25
9.50	10.00	.75
48.00	50.00	.75
49.00	50.00	1.00
51.00	50.00	1.75
98.00	100.00	1.00
99.00	100.00	1.50
101.00	100.00	2.00

We can learn several lessons from this diagram. Before we get to the specifics let's review out of the money, at the money, and in the money. Understanding these three terms is very important for determining when to sell the call option. Our goal is two-fold:

1. Sell the option for as high a price as we can.

2. Get called out and capture as much capital gain as possible.

The preceding section on volatility gives the road map. This section will tell you how and when to follow the covered call route and get larger premiums.

Out Of The Money Calls

When the stock price is below the strike price, the stock is said to be out of the money. A $9 stock is out of the money by $1 on a $10 strike price. You can buy a call on this $10 strike price and make money if the stock goes up. You can make money two ways with this call. First, you can make it by locking in a stock price of $10. If the stock goes above that you can make money by buying and selling the stock (or just holding onto the stock). Your profits would be determined by calculating your capital gain or loss and subtracting the cost you paid for the option. Second, you could also make money (or lose) by selling the option in a timely manner.

I used the example of buying calls to prove a point. Remember, though, in writing calls we are selling, and by selling we:

1. Generate income.

2. Agree to sell at a certain price.

I make most of my profits by buying stocks slightly out of the money and waiting a short time to sell the option and receive the premium.

At The Money

When the stock price is the same as the strike price, the stock is at the money. For covered call writing, this is important only to the extent that we purchased the stock below the strike price and hope to sell the option when it gets close to being at the money, or better yet, in the money.

IN THE MONEY

When the stock price is above (more than) the strike price, the stock is in the money. A stock with a price of $11.50 is in the money by $1.50 on a $10 strike price, but $1 out of the money on a $12.50 strike price.

Options are broken into two different values. One is intrinsic value and the other is time value (extrinsic). You can find a more exhaustive explanation on this in the chapter on options. It is sufficient to say here, when we sell an option on a stock that is in the money, we're receiving money (premium) for that which is ours. One way we can make a lot of money is by selling an in the money call option, and then having the stock not stay above the strike price (or having it dip below the strike price) so we are not called out. We get to keep the large premium and we get to keep the stock. I'll explain this further as an additional "overdrive strategy" in the next chapter.

Let's sell a call on a stock we purchased in the money and see what happens.

We purchase a stock for $16. This is different than the "buy low" strategy. The stock may even be at its new high (or some sort of peak). The call premium on the $15 strike price is really great– say $1.75. Wow, look at the numbers on the following page:

NOT CALLED OUT	CALLED OUT
• Stock $16 x 1,000 = $16,000	• Same until we get called out. If the stock stays above $15, we will get called out and lose $1 per share or $1,000.
• Divide by 2 (margin) = $8,000	
• Sell $15 call for $1.75 $1.75 x 1,000 = $1,750	• New rate of return $750 ÷ $8,000 = 9.38%
• Rate of return: $1,750 ÷ $8,000 = 21.88%	
• For us to avoid getting called out and keep the whole $1,750, the stock would have to drop below $15 or at least close to $15.	

Look at this comparison. Even if you get called out you have a monthly return of 9.38%.

I'll use the expression "give back" once again to explain the process in terms most can understand. If you buy a stock for $16 and agree to sell it for $15, and then actually sell it (get called out) at $15, you have to give back $1 of your profits. Express it this way, as a give back, or as a $1 capital loss. Either way you've reduced your profits.

I don't want to bad mouth this type of play very much because it's a great way to make money. I'll reiterate; when you sell a call in the money, you're selling part of the intrinsic value (the amount that the stock is in the money) but, the bottom line is, you generate a large premium income. If the stock goes down and you can keep the premium, you make a nice return.

As I said before, though I do make money this way, most of my profits have been from buying stocks out of the money. Let's go directly to the inside scoop. Here it is, if you really want dynamic profits, follow the next example:

We buy a stock at $9.50. It's not only volatile, but moving quite rapidly. Even while we contemplate selling the option at the $10 strike price, it pops up to $11. You phone and the options are $1.50 because there is still plenty of time before the expiration date. Before you get your order in on the option at $1.50, the $10 options are selling for $2, and you get $2,000 cash on a $4,750 investment and potentially another 50¢ per share or $500 (50¢ x 1,000) if you get called out at $10.

I have made this exact play many times and have even had this happen: The stock dropped back to $9.25 before the expiration date. I kept the $2,000 and still owned the stock. I then put in an order to sell the option for the next month's play at $1.75 and 10days later the stock bounced up and I got it.

Another consideration, and one which may be helpful if you can't make up your mind, is to hold your position longer. Back to the same scenario. You are gathering prices on the $10 strike price. The stock is at $11, then $11.50. Yes, you can get the $2, but on checking the $12.50 strike price you learn that the option could be sold for $1. You give up $1 ($1,000) now and instead pick up the chance to sell your stock at $12.50.

Some considerations:

1. If the stock price is at a peak, and barring extraordinary earnings or news, I'd probably sell the $10 calls and pick up the extra premium.

2. If the stock has hit $13 to $15 recently or frequently in the past, I'd probably go for the $12.50 strike price.

3. When in doubt, take cash now. Once again, "A bird in the hand..."

Another strategy is to divide and conquer. You have 1,000 shares. That's 10 contracts. Sell five contracts at the $10 strike price and pick up the $2 for $1,000. Then sell five contracts at the $12.50 strike price and hope you get called. You will pocket a $3.50 capital gain ($12.50 minus $9 = $3.50) or $1,750. You could do six one

way, four the other, or seven and three. You could sell five contracts (options) and sell the balance of your stock outright. You
could do any combination which makes sense to you. Sometimes
a nice blend gives you the best of both worlds–more cash flow
now and a chance at high returns later.

THE LOWER RANGES

I've gone through all of this to give you a feel for the fluctuation in option prices, at or close to the strike price. If you look at
the previous diagram you'll see 50¢ to $1.75 options are very com-
mon on the next month at the next higher strike price.

If you can buy a stock at $9 and sell a $10 strike price call
option for 75¢, why would you buy a stock for $99 and sell the
$100 strike price for 75¢? You can buy 10 times as many stocks at
this lower price.

Now, don't misunderstand, if you purchase higher priced
stocks and write options three to five months out you can get some
nice returns, but you have to hold onto the stock for that longer
period of time.

I've had my best results in the $5 to $20 range. I still find some
in the $20 to $30 range, but rarely. I'll even get more specific: Most
covered calls I do are in the $9 to $12 range. Why? Because there
just aren't that many marginable and optionable stocks in the $4 to
$10 range. Stick to the stocks in this lower range for maximum
returns.

INOSCULATION OF THESE THREE

To now see how powerful each of these three factors is indi-
vidually, let's look at what they bring to the table. We'll do so in a
problem/solution format. I think you'll also see how they enhance
each other–how synergistic they are. Again they are: margin trading, some volatility, and lower-priced stock.

We need margin buying power for leverage. We're using other
people's money. It lets us double our profits. Volatility, especially
on a stock we can chart and see distinctive highs and lows, allows
us to buy the stock low and sell the option high. Once in a while
we find a stock we can do repeatedly–month after month, or at

least every few months. Lower priced stocks allow greater gains because we're not tying up large amounts of cash. Again $1,000 buys 10 $100 stocks but 100 $10 stocks. Caution: If you only have $1,000 to get started you may want to buy stocks even lower, say in the $4 to $6 range and then write the $5 calls. Why? The commission will eat up most of your profits on small purchases. We need to purchase larger blocks so the commission is not such a large part of the purchase price. $5,000 will buy 500 shares—or five contracts. This is the reason why I always use 1,000 shares in all of my examples.

SUMMARY

We all need more cash flow—by selling options, we get it. We all want to limit our downside. Again, we have a winner. We don't need to employ all three of these factors all the time, as this whole process still engenders success even if a couple of pistons aren't working, but the successful application of these three, blended together, produces many happy returns.

12

COVERED CALLS
OVERDRIVE STRATEGIES AND FORMULAS

EVERY GAME in every sport, every technique for managing money and every business strategy has inherent in it the components for improvement. How well one taps into and uses those components determines the difference between amateurs and professionals. Covered call writing is no exception: What I have learned from my actual experiences, and by thinking through and applying different principles, has substantially changed my returns. "Getting good" at this process will also enhance your cash flow.

We'll explore several of these formulas and the variations of established techniques. To me, the underlying point of everything I've mentioned so far in regards to not only covered call writing, but almost all other strategies and formulas in this book has been to build up cash flow. Not growth, even though that is important, and certainly not tax write-offs, which is important to the extent it helps us build our "net" cash flow. I'm talking about cash that actually flows into the account.

If there is a way to make the checks larger, or get checks in on a more regular basis, or to avoid losses, or to get higher capital gains—then I want to look for and find it.

Even while I'm writing this book, I'm thinking of and trying several different strategies. I continue to read books and talk to some of the sharpest people in the field of investing. I won't write about these new ideas, or twists on old ideas here, as I only write about what I actually do. I do incorporate these new tried and proven formulas in the live Wall Street Workshops™ around the country. I would suggest you come once for the basics–and actually do the deals–but then come back often for continued processing of these profitable strategies.

Our theme at these live events is to create our own cash flow "Bar-B-Que" (BBQ)–Bigger, Better, Quicker. Let me borrow a few of those live seminar ideas for this book and let's get on to enhancing your cash flow.

OVERDRIVE TECHNIQUE #1

This strategy will not make as much money as the ones coming up, but it is useful and proves a point. It's designed to get more cash into your account–quicker. However, it involves going naked on the stock and most readers will not be able to do this at first. Keep it in the back of your mind and use it when appropriate.

A scenario would be in order. It is May 20th. You buy 1,000 shares of XYZ Corporation for $9. You place an order to sell the June 17th (expiration date) $10 call for 75¢. On May 25 the order is hit and you receive $750. The stock flounders and stays right around $9. You're confident the stock won't go above $10 before the expiration date. About June 8th to the 10th you check on the July $10 calls and you can get $1 right now. If you sell the option for the cash flow, you will receive $1,000 tomorrow, and yes, you get to keep the $750 received previously. The risk is, you have now sold another option, guaranteeing to someone that you will sell them 1,000 shares at $10. For the next nine days you're not covered on these shares. You are still covered on the first batch of 1,000 shares. If the stock goes up to $12 and if you have to buy it and sell at $10, you would create a slight loss. I say slight because you did pick up the $1 (or $1,000).

Why do this? If you think the stock will not rise above $10 before the June expiration date, you sell for quicker cash flow.

Now, some other thoughts:

1. If the stock really is staying around the $9 range, instead of just selling the July $10 call for $1, place an order to sell it at a higher price, say $1.25 or $2.25. Then if the stock bounces up you will get the much nicer premium.

2. Take a look at the July $7.50 call option. If the stock is staying substantially under $10, maybe a larger premium on the next strike price down would be in order. Let's say the option is $2. It's mostly intrinsic as the stock is around $9 or so. Now, let's look at the results if the stock stays around $9 and you get called out at $7.50.

Stock sold at	$7.50
Purchased at	$9.00
Capital loss	$1.50 or $1,500
But	

Received June $10.00 call $1	$750.00
Received July $7.50 call	$2,000.00
Premiums totaling	$2,750.00
Minus capital loss	$1,500.00
Net profit (minus commissions)	$1,250.00

Not bad money. I also brought this up here to continue to deal with the problem of stocks going down. There are so many naysayers. Well, be one, but be a profitable naysayer.

Also you could sell the $10 call and buy the $12.50 call creating a $2.50 bear call spread. You sell for $1 and buy the $12.50 calls for 25¢. That's a net of $750. If the stock stays below $10 you get to keep the $750. If it flies, you could lose a little. (See *Safety 1st Investing* for more on spreads, in this case bear call spreads.)

OVERDRIVE TECHNIQUE #2

The next strategy won't knock your socks off, but it is valuable and will definitely help you make money. It is a strategy I use called "cleaning house." Another way to express it would be "get what you can get."

Let's revisit several techniques and parts of formulas previously covered. We buy stock and want to write a call. We're really busy
shopping around and placing orders. You will be busy on the
Monday after the third Friday. Why? Because you find out what
cash you will take in for selling the stock, and what stock you have
left over. In short, you have to know what you have to work with.
There are two considerations:

1. How much stock is left in the account? Sometimes you just
    don't know. For example, if you've written the $20 call and
    the stock is at $20.25 you may or may not get called out.
    You might get called out of 400 of 1,000 shares. Once the
    report is in to your broker, you can find out how much
    stock you have to sell or work with, or use to sell more
    calls.

2. How much cash is now available? This is obvious from
    how many shares you had "called away" from you. What is
    not obvious is the affect this new cash will have on your
    margin account. Once you know this you can start looking
    for more stocks for the next month.

Before I go on, let me deal with this "next month" topic. I know
I've mentioned this before, but we all get so much bad advice it's
important to give you enough ammunition to counter all the igno-
rance out there. Specifically what will happen is your broker will
just look for the biggest premium he or she can find—even if it's
three months out?

Once in a while I'll write calls eight to nine weeks out, but very
rarely. I'd rather get a smaller premium for a shorter period of time
(and hopefully get called out). After all, the next month is still
there. You can get the next month's premium after this month's
calls expire.

This "take what you can get now" approach is a nice introduction to this Overdrive Technique #2. When we buy the stock and
then go for the biggest premium we can get, or when we've had
the stock for several months (writing calls each month) and now
go to sell the next month's call, we usually have to exercise a lot of
patience and wait. We place an order to sell the call for $1. It's cur-

rently 25¢–we're waiting for an uptick in the stock in a timely manner to get the $1 call premium.

Now, however, it's a week or maybe 10 days before the expiration date. The stock has not performed like we hoped. The call option didn't get up to $1. It did get to 75¢ but it's currently 50¢. Should we:

1. Go ahead and sell the call?
2. Continue to wait (after all we still have a week or so)?
3. Sell the next month's call (same strike price) for, say, $1 or so?
4. Sell the stock for whatever we can get?
5. Ignore it and go to a movie?

So here's what I do: I go to a movie. I then sell the call for whatever I can get. In this example it's 50¢ or $500 (minus commissions). I also look at purchasing more stock after checking the charts. Think about it–if it's volatile but hanging near its low range, maybe it's time to buy some more.

Do you see why we have to look at our account during this period? Getting something is better than nothing. Then we hope the stock bumps up and we get called out, or at least rises some before we write the call for next month.

Keep your hand on the gearshift as we move into our next overdrive technique. You'll see the cash flow really start to come in with this one.

OVERDRIVE TECHNIQUE #3

This technique works best on highly volatile stocks. If the stock moves quickly, it helps too. Here is the scenario. We've bought the stock and sold a nice call for $1.25. Now the stock dips way down, there's still plenty of time before the expiration date, and we want to see if we can play it again.

Actual Numbers: The stock was at $13.50 when we bought it in January. (At this time the February $15 call option was 37.5¢.) When it hits $14.75 we sell the call for $1.25. But in two days it's back to $13.25 and the option is 25¢. We buy the call back. I say back, but what we're actually doing is just buying a call. Now think about this: We have sold the call (the right for someone to buy the stock from us at $15) and we have now purchased the right to buy the same number of shares for $15.

To your broker's computer it's a wash. We have in fact covered a call with a call. This means our stock is free and clear (an old real estate term) for whatever we want to do: sell it, or wait for another movement and sell another call.

Let's do this transaction again:

Stock purchase $13.50 x 1,000   = $13,500
Margin purchase (divide by) 2   = $6,750
Sell $15 call for $1.25   = $1,250
Rate of return ($1,250 divided by $6,750) =   18.52%
Buy back call at 25¢   = $250
(Plus commissions)

New rate of return
($1,000 divided by $6,750)   =   14.81%
($1,250 minus $250 = $1,000)
Next transaction on upswing:
Sell call again for $1 or $1,000   = $1,000

New rate of return $2,000 ÷ $6,750   =   29.63%
($1,000 from first premium + $1,000 from second premium)

If we get called out, we make another $1,500
($15 minus $13.50 = $1.50 x 1,000 shares)

Our new rate of return is 51.82% for four weeks. Annualized, this is a 621.84% return.

The most I've done in one month is two premiums, but one month I missed the third transaction (before the expiration date) by just a few days.

PUT IT TO WORK
Here's how to put this to work. If there is still plenty of time before the expiration date (a chance for the stock to roll again), it

goes like this: when you sell the call option, place an order to buy the same option at a substantially lower price. Again there has to be plenty of time, say three to four weeks, or it is not worth it. Why spend the money to buy an option if the one you've sold is going to expire anyway (as there is little time left for enough movement in the stock for the stock to increase to the strike price)?

This is a powerful cash generator. You already own the stock. You've collected one premium and now it's time to collect another.

Do you want to have some fun? If you take the $1,000,000 calculation (at the end of the last chapter) which I'm sure most of you are skeptical about anyway, and throw in a few of the "double dips" every now and then–generating even greater returns–it will not only be fun, but time to retire–nicely.

Let's keep the car heated up and show you another "big time" cash flow strategy.

OVERDRIVE TECHNIQUE #4

You've heard that most things in life come down to timing. This next strategy is not a matter of timing, but of reverse timing.

All throughout these pages you read "buy low, sell high" or "buy the stock on dips, sell the call on strength." Look at the chart below:

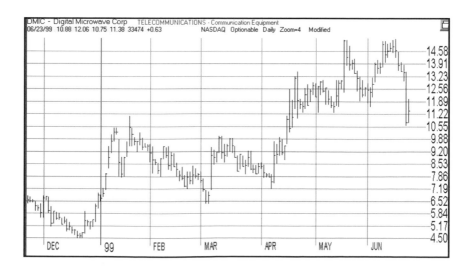

You see the stock moving between $7 and $15. Let's say you hear about this stock when it's around $11. The $10 call (next month) could be sold for $2. The $12.50 strike price option could be sold for $1. These are both excellent premiums. One (the $10) would generate huge cash now, but you run the risk of having to give back part of your profit if you get called out. The other ($12.50) has a smaller premium but you pick up an additional capital gain of $1.50 ($1,500) if you get called out.

So, here is our play: We sell the call without owning the stock, then we'll buy the stock when it dips down to $8 or $8.50. You can see that buying the stock at $8 and selling the $10 call (picking up the $2 premium, or $2,000) or even selling out at $10 would be a lot more profitable than buying the stock for $12.

Here's a possible play that will really enhance your profits. Only do this when the charts look like the stock is at its peak. Recent history says it will go back down. How much or how fast can't be guaranteed. Getting and keeping the premium with small downside risk and some upside potential is the plan. If you don't get called out and keep the stock to sell a call another day, then so much the better.

Let's look at each one and then, without the aid of flipping a coin, try to figure out which one to do.

It's the same, buy low, and sell high strategy, but in reverse. This time we sell the call and then buy the stock later. I know I'm being redundant, but some of your brokers won't let you do this at first. You can't sell uncovered calls until you jump through a few hoops.

The comparison:

1. We sell the $10 call for $2. The stock is at $11. When the stock dips to $8 or $8.50 we buy the stock. Now we're covered. If we get called out at $10 we make a little or break even, but we get to keep the $2, or $2,000. Two more points:

   a. If you sell the call without buying the stock you are naked. You make $200 or $2,000 or $20,000 depending on how many contracts you sell. Your rate of return at this point is "infinite" as you can not divide by zero ($2,000 divided by 0 = infinite). How many can you do?

b. You still have to tie up cash in your account. Why? Because you have the obligation to sell the stock if you get called out. Your broker will want you to have enough cash in the account to cover this contingency. If you have plenty of cash (money market funds), you'll be okay, but if you don't have that much in the account your broker will make you deposit enough cash to cover your position. In this example it would be $20,000 or $10,000 on margin. Most will let you use the premium received to offset this amount. Remember, you have the obligation to sell the stock. If you think the stock will only get down to $10.50 to $11.00 you will get called out. You may want to consider plan two.

2. Sell the $12.50 call for $1 and get $1,000. You obviously have captured more upside potential and might sell at a profit, but if the stock dips down (once again, the chart says it will) you get to keep the premium and you get to keep the stock.

If you think it will go below $10, the first play is best. If it's going to stay above $10, the second play is best. See how hard it is to decide? Get the coin.

Sell high then buy low is a phenomenal way to double and triple your profits–and possibly pick up an infinite rate of return along the way.

If you're capable of trading this way, get good and check the stock's history. Study its current status and direction and add this to your quiver of cash flow arrows.

13

OPTIONS ON STOCK SPLITS

MY FAVORITE strategy changes from time to time. Sometimes the catalyst for change is that I make a ton of money on a particular play, or several consecutive plays. Sometimes the catalyst is the ease of doing things a certain way–usually dictated by how busy I am in other areas of my life. Once in a while a favorite strategy pops to the forefront because it's new and exciting. One thing is for certain though: each favorite generates steady, almost predictable cash flow.

My staff and I teach 13 different cash-flow strategies at the Wall Street Workshop™. Some of these are covered in this book–not with the same vivacity of actually doing deals, but at least covered. My three favorite ways of making money have several things in common.

1. They are definitely about cash flow–actual money hitting the account.

2. They generate cash quickly–usually every two to six weeks.

3. They lend themselves to duplication. My motto is: "Don't do anything which can't be duplicated," sung to the tune of "I'd rather lose money and know how I lost it, than make money and not know how I made it." But not for long.

4. They are easy to understand–I love teaching and usually do repeatedly that which most of my students and I, this former cab driver, can do.

5. The downside risk is mitigated: the risk is lessened either by the inherent nature of the strategy, or by all the cautions I've built into the particular way I use the formulas.

6. Some can be done in a "tax free environment." This is difficult for some to understand. Some people have heard of tax free investments, like a municipal bond, but most have not heard of a tax free entity which makes all forms of investing tax free (Keogh Plans, IRAs, SEP IRAs, 401(k)s, and the best, a Corporate Pension Plan).

7. The strategies and formulas almost become self-perpetuating.

At the time of this writing, my fourth favorite way of generating cash is rolling stock. Even though this was my favorite and first real income strategy, and even though I use it all the time, it has slipped to fourth. My third favorite method is writing covered calls. You can tell how much I like it by the serious quantity of information on it in this book. My second favorite method is to buy call options on companies announcing a stock split. That is what this chapter is all about. You'll have to go to *Stock Market Miracles* and *Safety 1st Investing* for my favorite strategy: selling puts and its kissing cousin bull put spreads.

Actually, this stock split strategy is two different strategies blended together to produce quite remarkable results. We get the best of both worlds, which synergistically really heats up the cash flow.

Let's look at each strategy separately. They are options and stock splits. We've covered options extensively elsewhere but a quick review and a highlight of pertinent information would be in order.

STOCK OPTIONS
1. Gives the owner (purchaser) the right (not the obligation) to buy or sell a stock on or before a certain date, at a specific price, called the strike price.

2. A call is an option with the right to buy. A put is the right to sell.

3. Options are fixed time investments. They are inherently risky because they expire. However, one can only lose the amount or cost of the obligation and still have incredible unlimited upside potential.

4. Only 15 to 20% of all options ever get exercised. There are a lot of gamblers who lose their bets. One loses money when the underlying stock doesn't perform as expected and the option goes down in value, or becomes worthless.

5. One can make money two ways on call options if the stock goes up:

   a. He/she can buy the stock at a guaranteed lower price– if the stock is above the strike price–then hold or sell the stock.

   b. He/she can sell the option at a higher price. This is what my plan is all about. I don't buy options to buy the stock, I buy options to make a profit by selling the options at a higher price.

6. There are certain formulas one can use to minimize risk– they indicate to me that I should not buy a certain option. I'll mention these briefly as we move on, and it is because of my desire to not lose money that I've found this strategy of investing. You'll see these ideas come to light as you keep reading.

Let's cover the other side of the equation.

STOCK SPLITS

There are many reasons why companies announce a stock split, or a stock for dividend. Before we get into why they do stock splits, let's talk about the mechanics of splits and some other interesting information.

QRS company has finally become really profitable. The stock has climbed from $30 a share (where it had been for three years) to $60 a share. The company is now highly profitable with a lot of cash on hand. There are 24 million shares outstanding. The Board of Directors meet and decide to do a two-for-one stock split. If they currently have enough authorized stock, each shareholder's shares become diluted by a factor of 50%. There are now 48 million shares outstanding and each share is now worth $30. The capitalization of the company is still the same–it's divided now by 24 million more shares, or 48 million total shares.

This stock split will be reflected in your brokerage account by new shares on the day after the pay date or, in other words, the ex-dividend date.

> *A QUICK POINT*: On normal dividend distributions, you have to purchase the stock, which takes three days to hit your account, before the owner of record date. The day afterward is called the ex-dividend date. The stock should be in your account if you purchase it on time and then, and only then, do you get the dividend. The dividend is actually paid on the pay date. If it's a large cash dividend, perhaps a return of capital to the shareholders, or if the dividend is stock or a stock split, the ex-dividend day becomes the day after the pay date.

Think of this in theory, whether you buy 100 shares today at $60 or 200 shares tomorrow at $30, it's the same. I said "in theory" because in real life the stock may bounce up or down on the ex-date. That is one point of this chapter and we will get to the formula shortly, but a few more ideas on the ex-dividend date are warranted.

Typically, "ex-dividend" means that date upon which if you do something you don't get credit–you're "ex-ed out." With the special dividends on stock splits, it really is the day after the pay date–but you get the effect anyway. Your 100 shares become 200 shares whether you buy them before or after. I'm constantly asking my brokers, "What's the ex-date?" because that's the day that the new shares hit your account.

STOCK FOR DIVIDENDS

Whether a company announces a stock split or a stock for dividend, it effectively means the same thing.

For example, one company recently announced a 25% stock dividend. That means for every share you own you'll receive a quarter share of new stock. The next day, the news wire said the same company was doing a 5:4 stock split. It's the same thing. For every share you get a quarter share, so it would take four shares to get one new full share. If you have four shares you'll now have five. If the company had 20 million outstanding shares it now has 25 million. If the stock was at $20 and you had 100 shares (or $2,000 of value) you now have one 125 shares at $16 (or $2,000 of value).

There can be 2:1 splits, 3:2, 5:4, and even 10:1. Conversely, there can be 1:10 reverse stock splits. I usually avoid these, as they have the opposite effect of what I am looking for. I really like 3:1– they are common enough to act on. The 5:1 or 10:1 splits are very rare. Most companies announce 2:1 splits, but I really get excited when I can find an optionable stock heading towards a 3:1 split.

WHY DO THEY SPLIT?

Just imagine the Board of Directors meeting. The stock has risen substantially and they have lots of cash. They notice that as the price has risen, the volume (number of shares) trading has decreased. The stock has become pricey. They want the "average Joe" to buy the stock. They do the split to get their stock afford-able again.

At the same meeting they decide on, and then announce later, an increase in the dividend over the last quarter, and even over the same period last year. They adjourn and sometimes things go crazy. Why? Because so much good news is hitting the airwaves all at once. Many times the stock price jumps up because of the vol-ume of stock–purchasing by people trying to purchase the stock to capture the increased dividend, or to just strengthen their portfo-lio position in this profitable company.

Now to the main point. There is a tendency, once a company does a stock split, for the stock to regain "lost ground." It may take two or three years, but think of that: If a $100 stock becomes two shares at $50 and you purchased it at that price, and one to two years later it is flirting with $100 again, you have doubled your money. What if, as a play, you purchased 10 such stocks? One doesn't go anywhere; seven double in a year or so; one doubles in six months; and one doubles in a year and the stock splits again. Wow! It's great. Now, it's going to get much better, indeed, much much better, as you apply enhanced cash flow methods to this strategy.

Other points to consider:

1. I've read recently that 90% of the time when a company announces a stock split, they also announce an increase in the dividend. I don't know where or how the writer came up with the 90%, but from real life I can't deny it. Almost every company I've looked at recently has done so. The announcement of an increase in the dividend usually has a positive effect on the stock price.

2. My brokers are telling me constantly, "Wade, you can't play stock splits in and of themselves." I want to shout, "Why not—show me a company that has done a stock split which one year later (or two) is trading down?"

NOTE: This is a remarkable challenge and so important I've interjected this note. We'll get back to point #2 in a moment. For years I've challenged brokers and other professionals to find a company which, two years after the stock split, is trading below the price before the stock split. They have found some from time to time. One mentioned Compaq Computer. It, however, came back up later. Are there dips and bumps in the road up to or above the original price? Of course. Do they always shoot right back up? No.

For every stock they find which slipped down, I can show 50 that have gone up. One of my students did a whole survey. He took the 2:1 splits—not the 3:1 or the 3:2s; he took buy prices at the time of the stock announcement and sell prices on the day of the split (usually a three to six week time period), which I have not necessarily recommended, and still on 102 stocks, over a several-month period, 94 had gone up. Your rate of return on all these stocks (had you done them all—including the ones that went down a little or stayed the same) would have been 229%.

Before I move on, did you catch what he did? He sold right away. Most of the dramatic increase is over the several months after the stock has actually split!

I have achieved similar results on numerous stocks. I've actually had dramatically better results because of leveraged control using options. We'll get to those later, but for now, back to the conversation with the stockbroker.

2. (Continued) Because of their biases I have to be patient. I say, "You know I've heard LMN Corporation is really profitable. How's their stock doing?" They check it out and start giving me all kinds of information, then they say, "Oh, by the way, they've announced a stock split." Then I ask, "I wonder if it's optionable?" And we're off to the races.

3. Not all stocks are optionable. However, if they are optionable, meaning there are listed options for buying and selling, then the stock is also marginable. The play here, as you will see, is not in the stock but in the option. This is only important if you are planning to purchase the stock, say for covered call writing.

4. If the stock is in the $5 to $20 range, it may be a nice play for covered call writing. There usually is a downtick then several upticks and quite a bit of volatility.

5. Small stocks worry me only to the extent that there is low trading volume. I usually stick with the larger issues.

6. By investing in the option, and not investing in the stock we do not receive the dividend. I bring this up here because I've mentioned the increase in dividend. We would have to own the stock to obtain the dividend. It's only important to the option play because it affects the price of the stock and the price of the stock usually affects the price of the option.

THE OPTION PLAY

Here's the strategy—so simple and yet so powerful. We're going to buy options on the stock around the time the company announces a stock split. Why? The answer is twofold. Be careful of the time of the actual announcement unless you're in early with your sell point already known.

1. We get to leverage our money. We control a large amount of stock with a relative small amount of money. We generate cash quickly, as there is usually an up movement in the stock. Sometimes, however, the stock price goes up then backs off a little. This gives us a chance to buy and sell the option several times.

2. We've minimized our downside risk. You cannot imagine how much I hate losing money. If I make $16,000 on several plays in a day and lose $800 on one, I'll worry and fret about the $800 for weeks. I have many built-in defense mechanisms to avoid losses. I feel bad for the people who come to my live events and want a "throw caution to the wind approach." They want unbridled risks and I can't deliver. I'm a "meter drop" kind of guy. Those sane, safe, and comfortable 20 to 40% monthly returns are good enough for me.

Again, I build in safeguards. I employ my five strategies rule, wherein, when buying options, I try to double my money on the option. If I don't think I can do this, I usually avoid the option play. I know I miss some good deals, but I avoid losers. I check the Delta formula. When in doubt, I verify news and then after gathering all this information I use my gut feelings to proceed or not to proceed.

However, when it comes to options on stock splits, most of these concerns melt away if you really know how to play them. Rarely do these options go down (over the long term) if you purchased them correctly in the first place. Most of the safeguards are built in. Also note: I sell a lot of puts on stocks going through splits. However, many stocks go down in value the day of the split, or within a few weeks.

Think about what I've just written, and ask yourself this, "Why am I still sitting here reading this book? I need to be on the phone collecting news and buying options on these stocks. At least, I should start paper trading these."

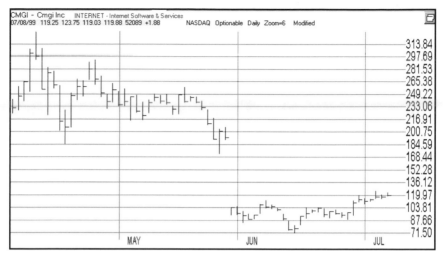

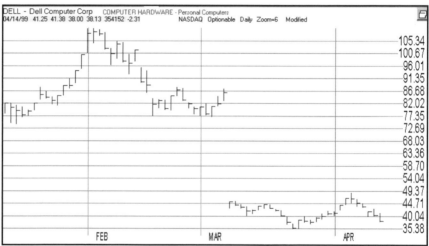

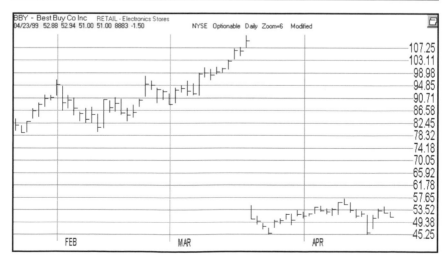

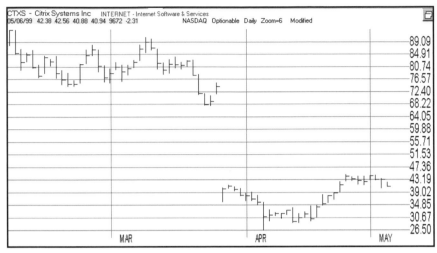

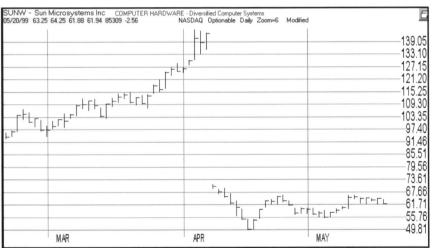

With options, we use the best of both worlds. We have a small amount of cash working in one or several deals. We have really minimized any risk and we have tapped into a play with tremendous upside potential.

Remember that a small movement in the stock usually generates a magnified movement in the option. Let's look at an example.

A computer company's stock has risen to nearly $80 a share. They just announced a 3:1 stock split. The next day, they also announce an increase in the quarterly dividend. Within 14 seconds of learning this (see how to find these in the next chapter) we call and place an order to buy options on the stock. It's now March 10. The ex-date for the stock split is April 12.

The April $80 calls are $4.50; all time value–all extrinsic value. The April $85 calls are $2.50. Now let's check the longer term for the options. The July $80s are $8.50 and the $85s are $5. They (the options market) have a July $90 call, and it's going for $3.

There are two plays–two strategies: a long-term strategy and a short-term strategy. We'll get to those (in detail) shortly, but you'll see a little of these methods here. These options might move fast. The stock is already up to $81½ on the news. The $80 call was $4.50 and is now $5.50. If we purchased these, $1.50 is intrinsic value as the stock is $81.50 on an $80 strike price, and $4 is time value (or the extra premium we pay). We buy 10 contracts and spend $5,500. The stock closes at $82 for the day and our options are $5.50 x $6–bid and ask. We haven't made anything yet, but we could at least get out and get what we paid for them.

We also put in an order to purchase another three contracts of the same month and same strike price for $4. It may never get down there, but if it does, even on an intraday dip, we'll pick up some more. Remember we still have plenty of time before the stock actually splits.

Now, about selling the option. This is a tough decision.

1. Do we hold on and watch and monitor the stock (and option) constantly?

2. Do we place the order to sell the option now, at say $9 to $11? Double our money and get out?

3. Do we also look for more buying opportunities?

In this example I'm going to do a combination; place the order to sell at a really high price–$15. I'd be more than happy to sell at that price, but I'm also going to watch it closely. If it starts to roll, I'll get out earlier. (Remember to cancel the order to sell the option at $15 if you sell earlier).

That's what happened. The stock went to $86 in a few days. When it hit $87 on March 28, I sold the April calls for $9.50. A nice $4 profit ($4,000). The stock then dipped back to $84 and I repurchased 10 contracts (April $80 call) for $6 and the May $85 call for $4. On April 4, the stock hit $90, and I sold the April $80 call for $11. Another $5,000 profit. A day later when the stock hit $91.50 I sold the May $95 call for $8, another $4,000 profit. Then the stocks dipped back to $89 and so on and so on.

Let's look at the mechanics of what actually happens to the option when the stock does the split. Usually, the stock will try to regain lost ground. This is really important to the option also. Let me show you what happened with Intel (INTC) awhile back when the stock split. The stock was in the high $120s. They announced a 2:1 stock split effective April 11. The additional shares, if you actually owned the stock would be in your account April 12.

Doubling and tripling your money can be done in a matter of days. Also, if you're willing to really get involved and watch the stock and option movements, you could repeatedly make these returns until the play is over. It's over, from a rapid, get-in get-out standpoint when the news has played out. There is usually dramatic movement (from a percentage point of view) in the first few days after the announcement. Often it's an upward movement. Then the stock backs off, right before the split there is a nice up movement, and right after the split has actually been reflected there is usually a down movement.

Be very careful on the announcement. If you're not in before the announcement or within seconds, you should probably wait a few days. Don't chase the options. You will get burned. And don't,

I repeat *do not* place market orders on these options. Place limit orders so you're not caught paying an excessive price.

Remember, when I say big it might only be a dollar or two. Wasn't that, however, the point of buying options? A $2 move on an $80 stock is peanuts, but when our $4 option becomes worth $5, "big" is an okay word to describe this movement.

As I said when I started this chapter, currently this is my second favorite strategy. We have the best of all worlds (except being able to do this in an IRA or other tax-free vehicle). Do you want to have some fun? Compound $10,000 by doubling it every two to four weeks—do this for a few months and you'll see how mind-boggling this becomes. But enough of this big talk. You need to take $500 to $2,000 and do your first play. Get more cash hitting your account. So put down this book and get going.

"Just by reading Wade's book *WSMM*, I was able to change my account to margin and options. On my first four option plays on stock split companies I netted $38,000. Thanks Wade and Staff."

—EDUARDO LLAGUNO

"I did my first stock split trade with Wade. I purchased 275 shares at $17.75, sold 600 shares at $8.00, and the final 225 shares at $11.00 that was 50% return in two weeks"

—JEREM E. GUTZMAN

"Using your strategies, we've done some fantastic deals. On December 17, I did a call option with Cisco and sold it on the 18th for a nice profit of $906.50, or a 25% return on my money after one day. But, Wade, it gets better! Following your Stock Split Strategy number four, I played the January 4 amazon.com split. That option play bought me in $8,148.00 or a return of 138%! That's $13,779.50 in 13 working days—over $1,000 per day!"

—DAVID J. HEPP

"Before ever entering Wade's Wall Street Workshop™, while prepping for the workshop (Zero to Zillions™ and *Wall Street Money Machine*) I followed his strategies and made

$233,000 in one month playing stock split options. Thanks Wade for making me aware of how to play the market that was kept a secret from a regular person."

—CAMERON K. LIU

14

OPTIONS ON STOCK SPLITS
CASH FLOW ENCHANCEMENT TECHNIQUES

My live seminars produce a variety of questions. When it comes to teaching the section on stock splits, and more importantly options on stocks going through a stock split, people are emphatic in their desire to try to do this without a broker. I don't understand this. I guess they want to do everything on their own. Maybe it's possible, but unless they are willing to spend hundreds of dollars a month on computer/news systems, they need to rely on someone who already has this available.

Even if you hear about a stock split, the movement is so volatile and so quick, the different option plays (short term or long term, straight wait or rolling) need to be discussed with someone who has current prices. There's not a right play or wrong play, but several potential plays. You need to discuss these variations, and I mean really discuss the possibilities. Yes, we have options on options. Don't go running to your stock market dictionary as I'm talking about opportunities on options. You can't do this with a day-old copy of *The Wall Street Journal.* You can't do it with certain news services, because the information is old. You can't do this with certain brokers because:

1. Some don't specialize in options.

2. Some don't have good news retrieval services.

3. Some are hard to reach.

4. Some don't even know how to do this (but they won't tell you that).

5. Online services are slow with poor fills. (Really be careful with electronic, or e-trading.)

NOTE: I use several brokers because I need a variety of choices and I need up-to-date information.

If all looks good, you surely can't place an order unless you have the services available and/or you have your broker on the phone who can act quickly.

SOME MECHANICS OF THE DEAL

Let's once again look at what we're trying to do. Using leverage (option investing), we are tying up a large amount of stock with a small dollar amount. We're going to buy options on a stock going through a stock split so we can take advantage of an upswing in the stock, generate extra cash, get out, and get on to the next deal. All the time we minimize our risk, because most of these stocks will start right up once the announcement is made, and if not immediately, usually shortly after the split has taken place.

Yes, you can get involved several places along the way. Here are some possibilities.

1. Before the announcement. These are not hard to find.

2. Right when the company first announces the split. Don't chase options on the announcement until the price settles down.

3. A few days after the announcement.

    a. Especially if there is more good news coming out.

    b. If the stock dips back down. This is a common scenario: the stock is at $40. They announce a split. The stock goes up $3 the first day, $2 the second and then backs off $4 the third day. Now if you bought the stock or the option the first day you might have to wait it out. You could also buy some more. What you definitely should do is look at the charts and see the history of weakness and strength. Yes, I know the split announcement changes everything, but at least you will start the tracking process. The next several weeks could be quite erratic. Look for short-term movements. Remember, buy on dips, and sell on strength.

4. Anytime along the way—when you think there is still plenty of upside.

5. On dips—once again look at the charts and check out the ups and downs. You'll be amazed at some of these stocks. Here's an example. The stock of ABC Company is $135. They announce a 2:1 split. The stock, over the next few days, goes to $140, then $142. It backs off to $137 but a week later it is up to $143. This happens in four to five days. What can we do? Well, if we've purchased the stock, we usually wait it out. All the movement just mentioned happens in the four weeks before the stock actually splits. This rapid movement could have a dramatic impact on your psyche. It's up—you're up. It's down—you're down. However, you could become a player here and take advantage of these swings. Either by selling, then re-buying the stock or by playing the options.

Let's do that. Upon the announcement we look at several options and then buy the $140 calls (three months out) for $12.50. We could have purchased the $135 calls for $14.50. I'll explain some of this rationale in the next chapter. The stock now moves up to $140. Our call options are worth $14. When the stock hits $144 they're worth $16. We sell for a nice profit.

A few days later, when the stock backs off to $137, the $140 calls are $13. We also check the $145 calls and they are going for $10. $1,000 will buy one contract, $10,000 will buy 10 contracts. Remember, there is still plenty of time before the actual split and also plenty of time between the time the stock splits and the expiration date of the options. We could also look further out. Eight months from now the $150 options are $8. That is a long time and a lot can happen. I do this a lot. I like the extra time for these stocks to go back up. In our current example, if the stock split 2:1 and the split happens when the stock is at $144 you now have two shares at $77 each. Eight months later the stock is at $105 and our $8 option on the $150 call (strike price) is now 20 option contracts on a $75 strike price. The options split when the stocks split. Our basis is $4 because our cost basis also splits. Think of this, we purchased 10 contracts to buy the stock at $150. We now have 20 contracts to buy the stock for $75. The expiration date stays the same. We own options that now have a lot of upside potential.

Check it out, the stock is $77, there is still time before the expiration date, it could still go up more. Our options were $8, now they move up to $12, then $20, then hopefully more. Remember the strike price is $75. We can sell now or a little later and make a nice profit. The stock play is good, the option play is great.

Other potential plays:

1. You could have placed your order to sell at the higher price.

2. You could just watch it from time to time. Remember that you have plenty of time on this long-term play.

3. You could roll the option as the stock rolls. With this in mind let's get back to our pre-split example.

The stock hit $143 and we sold the option we purchased at $8 (now $4 after the split) for $12. Now place an order to buy the same option again for say, $10. It's in the computer. If the stock dips (which it might not ever do again) we'll pick it up. If we do let's place an order to sell it at $16 or $18. If we sell it at this higher price, then let's try to buy it again at the lower price. We have repeated this process three to five times on different companies. It's very exciting. Especially when you think that behind this play is a stock that's splitting. The fundamentals for this type of play are intact. We can jump back in, get out, back in, then out.

If all goes well, a $8,000 initial investment can generate $4,000 to $7,000 profits in a few weeks. Anyone who has played options knows this is done all of the time. It is the naysayers who don't get it. When I say "it" I mean "it" from a knowledge point of view, but also from a cash perspective. They have no cash in their accounts. I hope you make the money. Leave the pessimism to others.

"After reading *WSMM* we tried 2 plays–a rolling stock on Dell–I made $600 in 3 days. Stock Splits–holding Wal-Mart–I am hoping to cash in on close to a $6,000 increase in less than a month. Thanks for the info! I don't know if I would have really understood what I was doing if I hadn't have read the book. Thank you!"

–YVETTE A. MABE

"Financial Clinic, WSMM and update are very helpful. Repetitive learning is very good I made 160% on my money on technique Wade shared at Wade Cook Live. I bought AOL Calls at $3¼ they doubled, the stock split and went up another $1.00 all this in three days. Thank you Wade!"

–ROBERT STINE

S.O.S.

As I've said before, buying options on stock split companies minimizes risks and lets you make huge returns in a short period of time. Once you understand the strategy in general terms, it's time to get down to the nitty gritty stuff that really helps you excel.

There are two ways to play this strategy: short-term options and long-term options–and then variations on these. In the short-term play we're going to buy options with a strike price close to the current stock price and get out quickly with a profit. In the long-term play we buy options with a strike price one to two brackets above the current price of the stock, but out for six months. There is a lot of money to be made both ways. If the options move against us on the short-term play we've got to be prepared to eat our losses early and get out before we lose it all.

THE SHORT TERM PLAY

There usually is a lot of volatility when a company first announces a stock split. People want to jump in, then the news cools down, and then they announce an increase in the dividend. Sometimes this announcement drives the stock up, sometimes down.

Right when you think everything couldn't get better, some other company files a lawsuit. Sometimes the company announces new products, or other expansion plans. Remember the Board of Directors has just met and many things, both positive and negative, could be in the works.

But the main news—and therefore, the play at hand—is the stock split. All these other things are important, but somebody show me why this stock split could not and should not be a play in and of itself.

The volatility or the quick shoot up of the stock price could mean some nice profits in a few days or at least in a few weeks. Here's what we do. Let's say a stock is at $50. The company announces a 2:1 split, effective in four weeks. We immediately check on the $50 strike price, and perhaps the $55. The stock is already at $51. We also buy the option with an expiration date slightly past the ex-date. (Sometimes in two weeks or so, sometimes five to seven weeks because there may not be options written the next expiration date out, as it's the wrong month's cycle).

We want to capture the short-term bump and also be poised to get out when we've made a nice profit and get ready to get back in on weakness (if we still have enough time). We also want there to be enough time for the stock to actually split. To repeat, the ex-dividend date should be before the expiration date on the option. Let's put some dates with our numbers. It's now October 3. The stock is going to split on November 10, we look at the November 20th expiration date. We check out December. The $50 calls are $4.75 and the $55 calls are $2.50. Which one should we buy? The stock is at $51 and moving fast. Yes, it may back off in a day or so. You have to do some reasoning—but very quickly.

1. If the stock continues up to say $60 before the ex-date it will split to two shares at $30. If so, you will now have the option to buy the stock at $25 (if you had purchased the option on the $50 calls). Remember, the options and the basis also split.

2. If you purchase the $50 calls and the stock is at $51, one dollar of your option money is actually buying some of the

stock or intrinsic value. The other $3.75 is the extra premium you're paying to buy time and tie up the stock. Conversely, if you purchase the $55 call option, the $2.50 is all time premium. The option is out of the money.

3. Here's the crux of the question: should you spend an extra $2.25 ($4.75 minus $2.50 = $2.25) and pick up a strike price $5 lower? The answer is usually yes.

I like to purchase these short term, slightly in-the-money options. You have some insurance wherein some of your money is actually buying part of the stock. I also like the $55 play, since it costs less money.

Here's what I do in real life. If I have enough money in my account at that time, and if I really like this company, I purchase some of both—say 10 calls at $50 ($4.75 or $4,750) and 20 calls at $55 ($2.25 or $4,500). Just think, we have around eight weeks for something to happen.

THE LONG TERM PLAY

Much of what I'll write here on the option play on stock splits is about the same as the short-term play, except that we're going to buy the call options out further. We'll give ourselves even more time. We may even want to consider LEAPS®, if they are available, and buy out one to two years.

Let's use our same example. The $50 stock has options in January of next year going for $9.75 on the $50 calls and $7.50 on the $55s. Yes you're paying $4.50 more ($4.75 + $4.50 = $9.25), but you're buying another 12 months. I like this because it's good backup insurance.

Now, don't think that I'm going to hold onto these options until January of the next year. That is not my intention at all. I'm going to get out when the news has played out—in a month or two. Or, I'm going to get in and out several times as the stock (and options) roll up and down. The extra premium just buys me a little peace of mind. If it is a slow mover, I've bought the extra time. If it dips down, and I go underwater, I can wait it out. Most quick turn money and bigger profits, however, are made on the shorter-term plays as the options move more.

Sometimes I buy a few of the long-term options as a back up for the short-term play. I've rarely lost money, even on the short-term options, but the few times I have, I more than made up for the losses by the profits on the long term options.

You see, I do both. Then I add some more on top. When the company announced the split there were not any $60 calls being written. The stock hits $57 and now they start writing higher strike prices. At first the short-term options are only $2 and the long-term $60 calls are $4. Later, if I still see potential, I may jump in on the $65 calls, which after the split will become the $32.50 calls. There are many odd option strike prices on stock split companies. They will expire eventually and then the standard option strike prices take over.

WHAT TO DO WITH YOUR PROFITS

You can see that if the stock keeps climbing up and new options are written, you have a host of potential plays: long term, short term, at the strike price, or close to it. But think. If the stock is getting close to $60, your $50 options are very profitable. You may be able to sell the ones you purchased for $4.75 for $9 to $11.

Let me show you what I do.

1. I get out of some and keep a few contracts for the ride. I'm profitable and now have a free ride.

2. I sell all or some of the options, and if I still like the company, I'll jump back in at a slightly higher strike price. This is a major strategy, so let's take out the tent and camp awhile. Remember our main play here–play the run up in the stock price once a company announces a stock split. And remember, my main concern is to invest so as not to lose money.

Keep all these in mind as we reason together about this add-on strategy. We can sell our options, take the cash, and run when we are profitable. We can also jump back in any time we want. This simply means we can buy more options.

We have more choices:

1. Buy the option on dips in the stock price when the options are lower. This could be options on the same strike price as the one we just sold. If the stock (and hence the options) are rolling up and down, this could be quite profitable and you may be able to repeat this several times.

2. Buy options on the next one or two strike prices up. They will be less expensive and therefore tie up less of your cash—in this case, less of your profits.

3. Sell puts and do bull put spreads—using much of the same reasoning as herein mentioned.

Let's delve into this second strategy. I have covered the first one elsewhere (rolling options on volatile stocks).

Here's the scenario. The company's stock was $88 when they made the stock split announcement. It popped up to $92 on the first day. It's May 2nd and the ex-dividend date is June 20th. We check the May $95 calls and they are going for $4. There would need to be a quick rise to make some money, and there was. The stock went to $98, then $100, and then $102 in just a few days. I put in an order to sell the $95 calls for $12. It got up to $11.50 then backed off. On May 6th I sold the $95 calls for $10. It backed off a little more and we jumped back in at $8.

I will tell you what I was thinking, then I will finish up with what some students did. I started looking at the $100 calls and the $120 calls. At that time, the $120 calls were the highest ones being written. I bought these when the stock was between $96 and $98. I bought them further out. The company had LEAPS® available in January—7 and 19 months away. The $100 calls were $13.50 and the $120 calls were $4.50. I bought 10 contracts of each.

I also took some of my profits from selling the May $95 calls and purchased the $135 calls when they became available. When I did so, the stock had risen to about $106—so the invisible "they" (the market makers) start listing more expensive calls. I paid $4.50 for these also.

Back to my students. They re-purchased the same options (May) for $8 and sold them a week later for $15 to $16. They had more guts than I did. Once again, I am too conservative and I will probably never make "zillions" of dollars in the stock market. I take enough risks. Some of my students take more. Now, in this case, I really don't think I would have lost money getting involved at $8, but I did feel my money could be better spent elsewhere. You will see what I mean as we continue.

Here is what I owned:

10 contracts	January $100 calls	Basis $13.50
10 contracts	January $120 calls	Basis $4.50
10 contracts	January $135 calls	Basis $4.50

The stock split on schedule. It was at $114, and the next day it was at $57, but two shares. Remember, when the stock splits, the options split.

Here is what I then had:

20 contracts	January $50 calls	Basis $6.75
20 contracts	January $50 calls	Basis $2.25
20 contracts	January $67.50 calls	Basis $2.25

You have to ask yourself: "Would I rather own an option for $135 or two for $67.50? What if the stock heads back up because this company is highly profitable? What if, within days, it is over $60 and within two weeks it is approaching $75?" Before the split, several analysts said this was a $150 stock. Obviously, that is a pre-split projection and they gave it a year to get to that range. This all happened so fast. I figured it would not go much higher, at least in the short term. I decided to bail.

The January $100 calls were going for $18. No kidding. I sold some for $18 and some for $21. Yes, these are the ones I purchased for $6.25. Not a bad five-week return. I sold the $120 calls for $9 and $11. I sold half of the $135 calls for $8 and held on to the rest for a free ride. Free? Hah! I made a huge profit on the ones I sold and it was like having the $67.50 options and getting paid to own them.

A few months later, after several dips and bounces, I jumped back in on the April (eight months out) $75 calls for $6. Think of this. The stock is in the high $60s. It has just done a stock split and

I have eight months for a $69 stock to get to $75 or above. The analysts said it was a $150 (pre-split), now, post split, that would be a $75 stock. At the time of this writing (a few months later) they are still around $8 to $9. They have been all over the map—from $5 to $11. I could have gotten in and out several times but now that I am president of a publicly traded company, I have a very busy schedule. Plus, I have a family to raise and a horse farm to attend to. I am bringing all this up as a back door approach to let you know you don't have to get in on every play and, as I have learned watching the *Karate Kid*, you need balance—wax on, wax off.

Here is the jumping back in point. As the stock starts to head back up—and if you think it will continue to rise—you can buy options at the next higher strike price. Now, let's think about that. Why a higher strike price? Well for one thing, they are cheaper. Back to just part of our example: we purchased an option for $2.25, we sold it for $8. We take $2 and buy an option on the same stock at a $10 higher strike price. We keep $6 profit and do what we want with it. We are still involved in the stock (even though it's the option) and hopefully will see another increase.

> **ANOTHER POINT:** If I have a chance to buy a different stock that is just heading into the stock split process, I will probably do that. The chance for profits are greater than investing in a stock that has already played out.

SUMMARY

I hope you see by the preceding example that you have many chances to get involved, and when you do, you have repeated short-term opportunities and many long-term opportunities. If I can't make up my mind, I usually do both. Play the short-term option with a strike price close to the current price of the stock, and the long-term play wherein the strike price is two or three strike prices above the current price of the stock.

Why close in on the short-term play? We want to own the option close to at the money, possibly slightly in the money. Then, a small movement in the stock is usually reflected quickly and sometimes like a mirror of the stock. For example, buy a $4 option on an $85 call when the stock is at $86. If the stock goes to $87, the option might go to $5, $88 and the option is at $6, and so on—

small movements, big profits. Plus, there is a little insurance if the stock dips a little as we purchased an in-the-money option.

Why higher strike prices on the long-term play? Because they are cheaper. Yes, we are buying options way out—say four to eight months, and because there is so much time the in-the-money or at-the-money options will be quite expensive. For example, if the stock is $86, the $85 call in four to six months might be going for $10. The $80 (in the money) call is going for $14. The $90 call is $6 and the $95 call is $4. You see, you can get in cheaper. Yes, you have more risk, as the stock (and now your option) has a long way to go, but you have paid a premium to buy this extra time. This is the time value to the premium, but it has time to work. Also, this is a stock split company and it will probably have an upward trend. You have plenty of time for it to play out.

I have continued to use a "divide and conquer" strategy. Let's use it here. If you feel good about the short-term possibility but like the security of the longer time, do both. Buy five contracts of the $85's (next month) and five contracts of the $95's (in six months). One more thing: Sometimes the longer-term options haven't moved up on the news. Make sure you check them out. Many times the short-term options are $4 (like our last example on the $85 call) and options six to eight months out at the $85 strike price are $4.75. That's a small extra premium to buy another six months.

Now, just because you have done this doesn't mean you have to wait the entire six months. If the stock runs up to $92 in a week or so, that $4 call could be worth $8 to $10. You could sell and jump back in—repeating the process. The possibilities are endless and very exciting. This is an easy strategy to implement because it's easy to master and easy to build up cash quickly. It's also very forgiving of dips as you have purchased the longer-term options, like an insurance policy.

15

THE LAST CHAPTER

LET'S GO back and make another stock market comparison to my days of driving a taxi. Learn from what I did back then. Compare the investments that you are going to make with passengers who are getting in and out of your cab. This is fun for me as I think about all of those people that I dealt with as passengers. Quite a few people use a taxi regularly as an alternate source of transportation. People I met constantly needed to go for doctors' appointments or to hospitals. They were usually on welfare or were older or handicapped people. Many of them had vouchers and other forms of payment. (We could turn these in and use them as cash.)

If they liked me as a cab driver, they'd call up and ask for me by name. Some days I would arrive at work and there would be 13 or 14 runs already lined up for me. I would squeeze in other runs by picking up fares at the bus station, airport, et cetera. You can build up a solid business this way, with the assurance of making a lot of money with your "set" passengers.

Let me compare this to rolling stocks, in which certain stocks are used repeatedly. You give the same stocks a ride over and over again, like set passengers. Another type of passenger is the high roller, window dressing passenger. These are the big-name companies in my financial cab. Another type of passenger is one that tips a lot, even though the runs may be short. These are the stocks that I use for quick turns. Even though the amount of money I am going to make is minimized, in terms of capital gains, the dividends are quite large. Other passengers–the writing covered call types–provide more income.

This comparison, obviously, can only go so far because in a taxi you can only have one passenger. In a brokerage account you can have many passengers. You can have stocks you are buying just for income and other stocks and investments in your portfolio you use for tax deductions. You can have other stocks that you are hoping will go up, like bottom fishing stocks, those "homeless" stocks out there trading under $1, which you are hoping will turn around and trade for $10 or $100 some day. I guess in the stock market you don't have a taxi, you have a bus, and you are the driver putting a lot of these different passengers on board. Each one solves a problem. Each one has a purpose. Each one adds to your total return. Remember, we are going for income, growth and tax write-offs, and hope to be getting all of them at the same time.

INOSCULATION OF CASH-FLOW STRATEGIES

Each one of the strategies used in this book work well by themselves. They work much better when synergistically coupled with other strategies. I'd like to say that I thought of this blending process, but most of this has come from my students.

As I explained the rolling stock process, I would frequently have previous students, my alumni, say that they were doing rolling options on my rolling stocks. This chapter is about successfully blending, or weaving–inosculating–these techniques. They taught me much more. While giving several examples, I'll briefly explore the cash flow enhancement techniques in conjunction with the use of the various entities.

ROLLING OPTIONS

I'll explain two uses of this format–each is very powerful.

1. Rolling options on rolling stock: when you roll stock that is optionable (usually over $5) then a substitute play would

be to purchase options on the stock instead of the stock itself. I've done this often, so let me give an example. The stock was rolling between $5 and $8. It was doing it frequently and relatively quickly–about every two to three months. Then it dipped down to $5 to $5.50. When it got close to $5, I would buy the $7.50 strike price option. They were cheap, usually 25¢ to 37.5¢. Now, I knew the stock very seldom hit $8 and for quite a while it rarely got to $7. No matter. As it moved up to $6 and $6.50, my 25¢ option became worth $1.50 and sometimes $2. I would sell and make a nice profit; 25¢ calculated into 20 contracts equals $500 (25¢ x 2,000 shares = $500). If I sold them for $1.50, I'd make about $2,500 in profit ($1.50 - 25¢ = $1.25 x 2,000 = $2,500).

2. Rolling options on stock splits. Stock split news is good. Usually it's followed by news of an increase in the dividend payout. Sometimes the stock shoots right up and then backs off. The time between the announced and actual pay date is usually four to eight weeks and can be a very volatile time. I've covered this in more detail in chapter 13, but I'll briefly mention the strategy here.

The stock is at $80. A stock split is announced. The $80 calls are $4 and the $85 calls are $2. The stock moves up to $84 and the $80 calls could be sold for $7.50 and the $85 calls for $4. We sell and make a profit. A few days later the stock slides back a bit to $82. The $80 calls could now be purchased for $5 and the $85 calls for $3. The stock goes up to $87 in a week or so and we sell the $5 options for $9 and the $3 options for $6. It dips again and we play it again.

Additional thoughts:

1. We can place a (GTC) order to buy at certain prices. If the option dips down we'll pick them up at the lower price. We can also put in GTC orders to sell.

2. The stocks sometimes continue to roll or at least show some volatility after the split. Keep watching them and stay in the game until the lights go out.

OTHER BLENDS

1. Margin makes everything more profitable if you're careful.

2. Do most high cash-flow trading in a tax free account.

3. When you have a good covered call stock, there are a couple of ways you could play it. Say, for example, the stock is rolling between $8 and $12. You could buy the stock at $8, wait for the stock to get up around $10, and then sell the $10 call option.

Another trade may be pure option play. When the stock is trading around $8, the $10 call two or three months out would be only 50¢ or so. You could just buy the option, wait for the stock to get close to or above $10, and then sell it for a profit.

4. Use a Nevada Corporation, and set up a brokerage account in a state with no income tax.

5. Use Section 29 Energy Credits (on stock also purchased on margin) and Section 42 tax credits to wipe out taxes owed by you or your corporation.

6. Keep trying to get your stock purchases on margin. Risky? Yes, but, oh so profitable, if you use caution.

7. Find good covered call stocks (to buy in your corporation) which pay dividends–sell the calls after you've held them for over 45 days to claim the 70% dividend exclusion.

8. Ride the range either in:

   a. options

   b. covered calls, or

   c. the stock itself

   with margin on turnarounds and spin-offs, stocks which have a high potential for growth. Play the rocky road and continually capture profits.

9. Actively use a variety of brokers and information sources to keep you up on what's going on.

10. Get on W.I.N.™ and find out what my Team Wall Street and I are doing. We'll help you find and use these different strategies. (For more information go to my website at www.wadecook.com.)

Let me share with you my stance on tax write–offs. Many times after I do a radio show and walk out of the studio, there is someone there to meet me who has some incredible plan for me on how to get out of paying income taxes. I could become a "sovereign citizen," a "patriot," or whatever. I have heard several different angles on getting out of paying income taxes. I decided a long time ago, because of my high profile, that I did not want to get involved with these kinds of ideas. It is not that I do not sympathize with them or even agree with them from time to time, it is just that I have always been told these stories by people who seem to be dead broke. They are always fighting the IRS to save that last little bit of money.

A lot of people who come to my seminars are making hundreds of thousands of dollars a year and still paying very little in taxes. Why? Because the investments that they purchase, such as apartment complexes, are the very investments that are producing tax write-offs. Their investments are more than likely going up in value. Even if they are not producing cash flow now, they are sure to produce a net cash flow some time in the future.

Even more enticing is that these profits are offset by deductions, some so large that these "paper losses" even offset other income. Often they reduce their income almost down to zero: real profits, paper losses. The very investments that get people wealthy are also the ones that help them to fight the IRS legally, and this is the path that I have chosen to walk down.

ENGINE–NEW–ITY

We are always looking for cutting edge information, the inside track, the thing that will get us in on a deal in the earliest possible stages. That has been the heartbeat of W.I.N.™–getting information out on strategies that we use about as fast as we can. "ITY" to me means Increase The Yield.

Once again, while your need for tax write–offs will change from year to year, and your need for growth will rise and fall, the need for income will always increase. Invest in assets that will produce income so that you can purchase more assets now which will produce more income to purchase more assets and so on. This means that when you get ready for retirement or you are ready to send your kids to college, you will have income from your investments to draw on. The greatest concern of mine when I am thinking of an investment is how much it will make me. Refer to my game called Friday–how much can you make by Friday? *Cash flow is king!*

Beat The Market With Knowledge

This simple cab driver has ways of beating the returns that typical Wall Street financial advisors are getting for their clients, especially those brought in by "pension fund" administrators.

When I look at what professional administrators make for their clients, the funds they are managing, and hear them bragging because they are getting a 3 to 4% return on their money, it just sickens me. People can get those kinds of returns by buying simple CDs.

To accumulate wealth rapidly, you need to get involved in handling the investment directly. Do the rolling stock strategy, covered calls, and any number of other things to enhance the value of your assets. In short, beat the market with knowledge. You will get better results by knowledge and trusting your hunches than by trusting anyone else around you.

Also, there is no substitute for research. I am constantly looking for new companies and often refer to research done by a lot of other people. I also like getting conflicting opinions about other companies. This way I can make my own decisions based on my own desires and hunches at the time.

Get information by calling the companies or talking with your stockbrokers, but also get it by keeping your ear to the ground. For example, several years ago my wife wanted to go to a crafts store in Paradise Valley, where we were living. I got tired of waiting for her, so I went inside. I could not believe my eyes. There were seven to eight cash registers across the front of the store, all busy. The aisles were packed with people, and I saw several store employees helping customers. It was jam-packed and this was not any particularly special time of the year.

This store, called Michael's, is one of those I wish I had invested in, but didn't. The stock at that time was around $5 a share. I checked it recently. It was around $40 a share. By keeping your ear to the ground, you can find companies expanding and creating new marketing images and products. This gives you the inside track.

SUMMARY

The point of all you see written here is to help you build up your cash flow. Remember, there are three reasons for investing, three benefits in owning a particular asset. They are: 1) cash flow or income, 2) tax write-offs and/or tax credits, and 3) equity appreciation or growth in the value of an investment.

What is the engine that runs the company you are thinking about investing in? What is the pressure behind it or the big secret that makes the stock go up or down or pay a bigger dividend to you? That is what this is all about–finding the right company.

I hope, more than anything, that you find a strategy herein and make it personal to you–get to be an expert. Then you will realize the power and peace that come from perpetual monthly income. Maybe, you'll find enough freedom from financial anxiety to go after the truly peaceful aspects of life which are obviously not found on Wall Street. May your enhanced income help you be a better you. Do well so you can do more good.

GLOSSARY

A

ALL OR NONE An additional option you have when placing a buy or a sell order, which tells your broker to either, fill the order in its entirety or to fill none at all. The customer will not accept a partial execution. For example, if you tell your broker to sell 2,000 shares of XYZ Corporation but he or she can only find a buyer or buyer for 1,000 shares, and then the broker should sell none of your shares at all.

AMERICAN STOCK EXCHANGE (AMEX) The American Stock Exchange (see: Stock Exchange) is the second largest U.S. stock exchange. It is based in New York City and sometimes called "the curb."

ASK The current price for which a security may be bought (purchased).

AT THE CLOSE The last price a stock security trades for, when the market stops trading for the day.

AT THE MONEY An option where the strike (exercise) price is exactly equal to the trading price of the underlying security.

AT THE OPEN The price a stock security trades for, when the market starts trading for the day.

B

BEAR MARKET Term describing a long-run, downward-moving securities market.

BETA Measures the volatility of a share of stock. A high beta stock, for example, will rise more in value than the stock market average on a day when shares in general are rising. And it will fall more sharply than the average on a day when shares are falling. The Standard & Poor's Composite Index of 500 Stocks, an index that represents large-company stocks, has a beta of one.

BID The current price at which a security can be sold.

BLUE CHIPS Stocks that have a capitalization value of more than $2 billion. Blue chips are typically held for long term capital appreciation.

BOOK VALUE A company's total assets minus intangible assets and liabilities such as debt. A company's book value might be more or less than the market value of the company.

BOTTOM FISHING A strategy of buying low-cost stocks in the hopes of them rising in value. Low-cost stocks can refer to two different types of stocks. The first are new companies to the exchanges that are low valued with many unknowns and a potential for capital appreciation. The second type are stocks that have been high in the past and fallen for poor performance reasons. They have some news that will turn the company north again. The second type of stock are also known as turn-around candidates.

BULL SPREAD The purchase of one call or put and the sale of a higher strike price call or put. As the name implies, this is a bullish strategy.

BUYING POWER The dollar amount of securities that a client can purchase using only the account balance and without depositing additional equity.

C

CALENDAR SPREAD When you buy a longer term option and sell a short term option against the long term option. It is similar to a covered call except you use an option to cover instead of buying the stock.

CALL An option contract giving the owner the right (not the obligation) to buy 100 shares of stock at a strike price on or before the expiration date.

CALL PRICE The price paid (usually a premium over the par value of the issue) for stocks or bonds redeemed prior to maturity of the issue.

CALL SPREAD The result of an investor buying a call on a particular security and writing a call with a different expiration date, different exercise price or both on the same security.

CASH ACCOUNT An account in which a client is required to pay in full for securities purchased by a specific date from the trade date.

CLEANING HOUSE Cleaning out short term options prior to expiration.

COMMISSION The fee an investor pays a broker for buying or selling securities.

COST BASIS Original price of an asset, used in determining capital gains. For example if you bought Novell (NOVL) at $9^{1}/_{2}$ and sold the May $10 call for $1, then your cost basis in the stock becomes $9^{1}/_{2}$ - $1 = $8^{1}/_{2}$.

COVER Can be either futures purchased to offset a short position or being "long actuals" when shorting futures.

COVERED CALLS A stock strategy in which you own a stock and write (sell) a call at the next strike price above the current stock value. (Also the Chicago Board of Options Exchange has an excellent explanation of the Covered Call Strategy.)

COVERED CALL WRITER An investor who writes a call and owns some other asset that guarantees the ability to perform if the out is exercised.

Current Yield The price of a stock dividend in relation to the value of the stock. A $10 stock that pays a 50¢ dividend for the year has a 5% yield.

D

Day High The highest price that a security has traded at during the day.

Day Low The lowest price that a security has traded at during the day.

Day Order The stock or option order that is good for today only.

Dead Cat Bounce is a stock that has fallen in one to three days by 50% or more on bad news like earnings, failed FDA test or losing a major customer. We typically play the stock to go up a little after the slam. These are also referred to as Slams.

Delta Formula The percent an option changes in relation to the underlying security. For example, if an option has a delta of 50% and the underlying stock increases by $1 you would expect the option to increase by 50¢. Put options have a negative delta because when the underlying security goes up, the option value will fall. Most full service brokers have access to a delta screen and can give you the data. A software program called "Trade Station" also has delta information.

Discount Broker A broker that provides less investment help but will take orders for your account at a discount price in comparison to full service brokers.

Divergence When two readings are not moving generally together when they would be expected to do so. For example, if the DJIA moves up a lot but the S&P 500 moves very little or even declines, a divergence is created. Divergence's can signify turning points in the market. At a major market low, the "blue chip" stocks tend to move up first as investors become willing to purchase quality. Hence the S&P 500 may be advancing while the NYSE composite is moving very little. Divergences, like everything else, are not 100% reliable. But they do provide yellow or red alerts, and the bigger the divergence, the stronger the signal. Divergence and breadth are related concepts.

DIVIDENDS The amount of money paid to shareholders to distribute some of the profits.

DOW JONES INDUSTRIAL AVERAGE The best known U.S. index of stocks. It contains 30 blue chip stocks that trade on the New York Stock Exchange. The Dow, as it is called, is a barometer of how shares of the largest U.S. companies are performing. There are thousands of investment indexes around the world for stocks, bonds, currencies, and commodities. This is probably the most famous stock index in the world. When most people ask how the market is doing, they usually are referring to this index. The companies in the index are changed occasionally by Dow Jones to try to reflect the largest cross section of United States large industrial companies as possible. The most recent change was early in 1997 when four companies were taken off the list and replaced by four other companies.

D.U.C.K Dipping Undervalued Calls. Trend lines are essential to determine if it is a DUCk or not.

E

EARNINGS PER SHARE (EPS) A company's profit divided by its number of shares. If a company earned $2 million in one year had two million shares of stock outstanding, its EPS would be $1 per share.

EQUITY The market value of securities less any debt incurred. Also funds provided to a business by the sale of stock.

EX-DIVIDEND The interval between the announcement and the payment of the next dividend. The buyer of shares when they are quoted ex-dividend is not entitled to receive a declared dividend.

F

Full Service Broker   A broker that provides advice and recommendations and works for a major brokerage house.

Fundamental Analysis   The analysis of the financial side of a company to decide on an investment strategy. Common Fundamental Analysis includes Earnings, Sales, Debt, Dividends, and Profit Margin.

G

Good-Till-Canceled Order (GTC)   An order to set a specific buy or sell price and which will be good until you cancel it. The broker's computer will remember it. They expire 60 to 90 days after being placed depending on your broker.

H

Hedge   A securities transaction which reduces the risk on an existing investment position.

I

Indicators   Charting techniques that use price volume and momentum to predict future movement in a stock. Indicators are used when performing technical analysis on an investment decision.

Insiders   The directors and senior officers of a corporation—in effect those who have access to inside information about a company. An insider also is someone who owns more than 10% of the voting shares of a company.

Insider Trading   The buying or selling of securities by directors and senior officers of a corporation.

In The Money   For a call option, it means that the current market value of the underlying interest is above the exercise price of the option. A put option is said to be in-the-money if the current market value of the underlying interest is below the exercise price of the option.

INITIAL MARGIN REQUIREMENT The amount of equity a brokerage customer must deposit when making a new purchase in a margin account.

INITIAL PUBLIC OFFERING (IPO) A company "going public," in other words selling its stock to the public for the first time.

INTERNET BROKER A brokerage house that has Internet investment service available online

INTRINSIC VALUE The amount, if any, by which an option is in the money.

L

LEAPS® (LONG-TERM EQUITY ANTICIPATION SECURITIES) Long-term equity options traded on U. S. exchanges and over the counter. Instead of expiring in two near-term and two farther out months as most equity options do, LEAPS® expire in two or three years, giving the buyer a longer time for his strategy to come to fruition.

LIMIT ORDER An order to buy or sell an equity at a specific price. The order will not be filled unless it can be filled at the specified price or better.

LONG Either owning the security on which an option is written or a person's position as the writer of an option.

M

MARGIN Allows investors to buy securities by borrowing money from a broker. The margin is the difference between the market value of a stock and the loan a broker makes.

MARGIN ACCOUNT An account in which a brokerage firm lends a client part of the purchase price of securities.

MARGIN CALL A demand for a client to deposit money or securities when a purchase is made in excess of the value of the margin account.

Market Cap The company's market capitalization. If a company has 10 million shares and the company's shares are selling for $10, the market cap is $100 million.

Market Maker A warehouser of stock willing to accept the risk of holding securities to facilitate trading in a particular security or securities.

Market Order An order to buy or sell a security at the current trading price.

Market Value The price at which an investor will buy or sell each share of common stock or each bond at a given time.

Momentum The price change of a security for a fixed period of time. It measures the rate of changes in price as opposed to price itself. When momentum changes from negative to positive, it is a buy signal. When momentum changes from positive to negative, it is a sell signal.

Monthly Income Preferred Securities (MIPS) Preferred stocks which pay monthly dividends.

Moving Average Takes the closing price of a stock for a set amount time to indicate the direction that the stock appears to be moving. Once a stock starts moving in a particular direction it tends to gain strength and doesn't reverse easily. This indicator helps reduce the daily fluctuations in a stock's price so that a smooth trend line can be seen. The Moving Average is an excellent technique to filter out the market noise and uncovering trends.

Mutual Funds Pools of money managed by a company. They offer investors a variety of goals, depending on the fund and its investment charter. Some funds, for example, seek to generate income on a regular basis. Others seek to preserve an investor's money. Still others seek to invest in companies that are growing at a rapid pace. Funds can impose a sales charge, or load, on investors when they buy or sell shares. Many funds these days are no load and impose no sales charge.

N

NAKED PUTS A term referring to selling a put. It is naked even if you own the stock. Selling naked puts is considered a bullish move, meaning that you expect the stock to go up. It also can be a way to buy stock at a wholesale price. Most brokers have their own requirements as to who they will allow to sell puts.

NET CHANGE The difference between a day's last trade and the previous day's last trade.

NET-DEBIT Your total cost basis in the stock after applying the money from selling the option. So, if you bought stock at $10 and sold the call for $1, your net debit would be $9. When you ask to do a buy-write, you specify a net debit, or the target cost basis when the trade is done. Most brokers will just look to current bid-ask figures and say yes or no to the request. A good broker will try and work you into the spread on both the stock purchase and the option sale to get the best net debit they can.

Getting the "ask" for both the option and stock, is tough to do unless you have some things in your favor. You will have the best luck if you have: 1) Large amounts of money in the account ($20 to $50K). 2) A broker who is aggressive and willing to shop around. 3) A broker who is willing to work closely with the trading desk and possibly trade favors at times. 4) A large trade, so you can get the net-debit you want. (If you can go in the spread both buying the stock and selling the call, you can get closer to the "ask-ask" trades net-debit figure.) 5) It also helps if your broker is the market maker in the stock. Getting the ask-ask (or its net-debit equivalent) maybe the target, but not getting it doesn't mean its a bad trade. The bottom line is what is your net on the trade?

NET PROFIT The difference between the total price you paid for a security, with the brokerage commission you paid, and the current value. It will show either a profit or a loss.

NUMBER OF SHARES The number of stock shares that a company has outstanding.

NEWS-DRIVEN The volatile movement of a particular stock due to some news, not by any intrinsic value to the company.

O

Open   The price at which a security opens the trading day. Generally, the opening price reflects the previous day's close—unless extraordinary news or demand to buy or sell have occurred before the market opens.

Open Interest   The total number of option contracts outstanding for that specific option at the close of market.

Open Order   An order to buy or sell a security by an individual investor. That open order stays active until it is completed or the investor cancels it.

Option   The right to buy or sell a specified amount of a security (stocks, bonds, futures contracts, et cetera) at a specified price on or before a specific date (American style options). We don't advise putting all your money in options, but rather only 5 to 10% of your risk capital should be in options at any given time.

There are two different types of options, cash settled options and physical delivery options. Cash settled options refer to puts and calls on the index options like the S&P 500 (SPX) or the S&P 100 (OEX). Physical delivery options are written on specific stocks and may be exercised or bought and sold for cash. Cash settled options are more expensive.

Out of The Money   When the exercise price of a call is above the current market value of the underlying interest, or if the exercise price of a put is below the current market value of the underlying interest.

Over The Counter (OTC)   A security that is not listed or traded on a recognized exchange.

P

Pay Date   The date that a company pays a dividend or stock split out, which is usually the day before the ex-dividend date. In stock splits, we use the pay date for the "duck tail play" in which we buy a call one to two days before a split (pay date) and then sell the call one to two days after the split.

PAPER TRADING Doing make-believe trades on paper as if you had really done them. This can be a great way to refine your trading skills.

P/E A stock's price-to-earnings ratio: the share price divided by earnings per share for the company's most recent four quarters. A projected P/E divides the share price by estimated earnings per share for the coming four quarters. P/E ratios are helpful when comparing stocks in their same industry or group. For example if Intel has a P/E ratio of 25 and AMD has a P/E ratio of 203, then Intel is at a better value.

PEAK When a stock rises in value quickly due to hype, good earnings, or good news, they typically have extremely high P/E ratios and are extremely over valued. We watch those stocks that are peaking for potential slams.

PERCENT CHANGE A calculation of the change in the price of a security from the previous trading day's closing price.

PORTFOLIO Where the equities you own are held.

PREMIUM The value of an option on an exchange. This represents the cost if you are a buyer or cash in if you are a seller.

PRICE GAP Occurs when a stock opens in the morning at a price either higher or lower than the closing price the day before. This usually happens when some news affecting the value of the stock is announced after the market closes. A simple example: Company XYZ closes Monday at $20. After the market closes, company ABC announces that they are planning to purchase XYZ for $30. The stock will open the next morning very close to $30. You will not be able to purchase the stock at the lower previous closing price.

PRICE SPREAD A spread involving the purchase and sale of two options on the same stock with the same expiration date, but with different exercise prices.

PUT An option contract that gives the owner the right to sell a specified number of shares of stock at a specified price on or before a specific date. Usually you buy a put if you think the stock is going down, with the intention of selling it when it increases in value. Usually you sell a put on a stock if you think it is going up, with the intention of letting the option expire worthless and you getting to keep the entire premium. Puts also are powerful hedges in such strategies as covered calls, giving you protection if the underlying stock plummets. The Chicago Board of Options Exchange has an excellent article on using puts for hedges.

PUT SPREAD An investment in which an investor purchases one put on a particular stock and sells another put on the same stock but with different expiration date, exercise price or both.

R

RANGE RIDER A stock that is gradually rising to a higher range with various smaller lows and highs over a period of time.

REAL-TIME Stock, bond, option, or futures quote that reports the most current price available when a security changes hands. A delayed quote shows a security's price 15 minutes and sometimes 20 minutes after a trade takes place.

RECORD DATE The date that a stock must be in your account for you to receive a dividend. The record date has nothing to do with how we trade stock splits.

REFLECTED TODAY The stock will show up at the split price on the market on that day. In other words, you will see the change in your brokerage account on this day.

RESISTANCE LEVELS Levels that the stock seems to rebound off of. They can best be seen using trend lines. For example an advance to a price, say 45, which is repeatedly followed by a pullback to lower prices is said to be a resistance level of 45. The notion is that there are buyers who purchased at 45 and have watched a deterioration into a loss position. They are now waiting to get out even. Or there are sellers who consider 45 overvalued and want to take their profits. One strategy is to attempt to purchase near support and take profits near resistance. Another is to wait for an "upside breakout" where the stock penetrates a previous resistance level. Purchase on anticipation of a further upmove.

RETURN ON EQUITY Measures the return, expressed as a percentage, earned on a company's common stock investment for a specific period. It is calculated by common stock equity, or a company's net worth, into net income. The calculation is performed after preferred stock dividends and before common stock dividends. The figure shows investors how effectively their money is being used by managers.

REVERSE STOCK SPLIT An increase in the stock's par value by reducing the number of shares outstanding.

ROLLING STOCK A stock that fluctuates between its high and low price points for long periods of time and whose history makes it seem to be predictable. We typically like rolling stocks that roll at least 50¢ or more.

S

SECURITIES & EXCHANGE COMMISSION (SEC) is a federal agency that regulates the U.S. financial markets. (Web address is http://www.sec.gov.)

SECURITY A piece of paper proving ownership of stocks, bonds, and other investments.

SETTLEMENT DATE When an investor must pay for the purchase of shares by the third business day after he or she buys securities in U.S. financial markets. And an investor must deliver an investment that he or she has sold by the third business day after the transaction.

SHAREHOLDERS' EQUITY A company's total assets minus total liabilities. A company's net worth is the same thing.

SHORT A condition resulting from selling an option and not owning the related securities.

SHORT INTEREST The total number of shares of a security that investors have sold short–borrowed, then sold in the hope that the security will fall in value. An investor then buys back the shares and pockets the difference as profit.

SHORT SALE Happens when many speculators sell a stock short and then the stock begins to increase. As the stock price rises, the short sellers scramble to cover their short positions. This drives the price up quickly and good returns can be made in a day. See the chart on Iomega (IOM) in July and August of 1996 for an example.

SHORT STRADDLE The position established by writing a call and a put on the same stock with the same strike price and expiration date.

SLAMS A stock that has fallen in one to three days by 50% or more on bad news like earnings, failed FDA test or loosing a major customer. We typically play the stock to go up a little after the slam. These are also referred to as Dead Cat Bounces.

SPIN-OFF When an independent company is created from an existing part of the company by selling or distributing new shares in the so-called spin-off.

SPREAD The gap between bid and ask prices of a stock or other security. There is also a number of strategies used that make use of different spreads between calls, puts and the underlying stock.

STOCK EXCHANGE is a place where securities are traded. There are three main U.S. stock exchanges. AMEX is the American Stock Exchange. NASDAQ is the National Association of Securities Dealers. NYSE is the New York Stock Exchange.

STOCK SPLIT A reduction in the par value of stock caused by the issuance of additional stock. There are a number of different strategies you can use with stock splits.

If you are interested in hearing of stock splits at the time of the announcement, a good idea is to be in close contact with your stockbroker. They are usually the first to hear of these announcements. You can also actively listen to or subscribe to news agencies that commonly report such things.

It seems that some market makers have increased option premiums for large companies about to split. They know that there can be an increase in volume around a split. One possible way around this is to buy your options an extra week ahead of a large split.

STOCK TICKER A lettered symbol assigned to securities and mutual funds that trade on U.S. financial exchanges.

STOP LOSS ORDER A brokerage order that executes a trade if your equity falls to a predetermined value. This is to limit a loss on a specific equity investment.

STRADDLE Either a long or short position in a call and a put on the same security with the same expiration date and exercise price.

STRANGLE The combination of a put and a call where both options are out of the money. A strangle can be profitable only if the market is highly volatile and makes a major move in either direction.

STRIKE PRICE The price at which the underlying security will be sold if the option buyer exercises his/her right in the contract.

Market makers will inflate or decrease option prices sometimes based on such things as volume of contracts or their perception of strike price direction. It sometimes has no relation to stock price, especially out of the money options. Once the option is in the money, they tend to follow the stock much closer. Sometimes it helps to get quotes on options further out in time and compare prices. For example: option X for May is $1, and the option price for July is $1³/₄. The May option is probably inflated, and for only $³/₄ more you can buy two months more of time. Time value on most options averages about $³/₄ per month. (This is a rough estimate and definitely not set in stone)

SUPPORT LEVELS Levels that the stock seems rebound off of. They can best be seen using trend lines. Suppose a stock drops to a price, say $25, and rebounds, and that this happens a few more times. Then $25 is considered a support level. The concept is that there are buyers waiting to buy at that price. Imagine someone who had planned to purchase and his broker talked him out of it. After seeing the price rise, he swears he's not going to let the stock get away from him again. One strategy is to attempt to purchase near support and take profits near resistance. Another is to wait for an "upside breakout" where the stock penetrates a previous resistance's level. Purchase on anticipation of a further upmove. The support level (and subsequent support levels after rises) can provide information for use in setting stops.

T

TECHNICAL ANALYSIS The use of price and volume charts and indicators to make trading decisions. Technical analysis attempts to use past stock price and volume information to predict future price movements. It also attempts to time the markets. You should consider delaying purchase of stocks whose chart patterns look bad, no matter how good the fundamentals. Equities Analytics has a good tutorial on a wide variety of technical indicators.

TICK A change in the price of a security, either up or down—as in uptick or downtick. ("-" denotes down, "+" denotes up)

TICKER SYMBOL A trading symbol used by a company to identify itself on a stock exchange.

TIME VALUE The premium of the option in addition to its intrinsic value.

TRADING HALT Sometimes the SEC or one of the markets stops the trading of a security. Trading of a stock, bond, option or future contract can be halted by an exchange while news is being broadcast about the security, or if the market drops a great number of points suddenly.

TREND LINES Lines used to display the direction that a stock is moving. We focus on changes in trend to make trading decisions.

TURNAROUND COMPANIES Stocks that have been high in the past and fallen for poor performance reasons. They have some news that will turn the company north again. These are one type of bottom fishing stock.

U

UPSIDE BREAKOUT Happens if a stock has traded in a narrow range for some time (i.e. built a base) and then advances above the resistance level, this is said to be an "upside breakout." Breakouts are suspect if they do not occur on high volume (compared to average daily volume). Some traders use a "buy stop" which calls for purchase when a stock rises above a certain price. The opposite of an upside breakout is called "penetration of support" or "breakdown."

V

VALUE The current price of the security multiplied by the number of shares you own. If you own 1,000 shares of Intel, and the shares are selling for $95, the value is $95,000.

VALUE STOCK A stock perceived by the marketplace to be undervalued based on criteria such as its price-to-earnings ratio, price-to-book ratio, dividend yield, et cetera.

VOLATILE When the market or security tends to vary often and wildly in prices.

VOLATILITY Can be figured as an indicator by using the annualized standard deviation of the logarithm of returns.

VOLUME The daily number of shares of a security that changes hands between a buyer and a seller in a specific period. It can be used as an indicator to confirm the direction of the trend.

When the price plot has the same pattern as the volume goes–high price with high volume, low price with low volume–then the market will have the same trend as before.

When the price plot has the opposite pattern as the volume goes–low price with high volume, high price with low volume–then the market will have the opposite trend as before.

W

WALL STREET   The common name for the financial district at the lower end of Manhattan in New York City, where the New York and American Stock Exchanges and numerous brokerage firms are headquartered.

1

A LETTER FROM WADE COOK

THE FOLLOWING is a letter (advertisement) I sent to people at about the time this book was near completion. I wanted to share with you information about the Wall Street Workshop™ and could think of no better way than to include a copy of the letter here. My life is dynamic. Things are always changing, so to find out current schedules, tuition and dates—plus an update of topics covered at the event, please call 1–800–872–7411. Tuition and schedule are subject to change without notice.

"I feel very grateful that I became aware of Wade Cook Seminars through a friend and my brother-in-law early in 1998. Prior to that time my investing experience was mainly through no-load mutual funds making about 10 to 15% per year. Now, using my favorite strategy of selling puts, I've been making more than that per month. In fact, I made considerably more money in the last two months than I made in a whole year from my previous employer as a purchasing agent. One of my trades that stands out is when I sold a Feb 145 put on America Online 10 contracts for $13\frac{1}{4}$ ($13,250) and bought these back seven days later for $2\frac{1}{8}$ ($2,125) which is a net profit of $11,125, minus commissions.

I am now investing full-time at home and loving it. I am able to spend more time with my family and donate more money to my church. Thank you Wade Cook Seminars for helping to make possible this positive change in our lives"

—DON G.

Dear Friend,

My name is Wade Cook. I made a fortune in real estate and then wrote a book about it, *Real Estate Money Machine*. Since then I've traveled to 43 states, been interviewed on over 1,600 radio and TV talk shows, and have spoken to millions of people. My theme has been cash flow and retiring rich.

That first book changed the way thousands of people handled real estate. *Real Estate Money Machine* (and 23 other books I've written) has been successful, and my seminar career has been super successful. I then put some of my profits into the stock market with dismal results, but after years of trying and exploring, I designed a few ways of making money–actually making really great money. I'd like to invite you to come and spend a few days at the Wall Street Workshop™ with my excellent instructors so you, too, can employ these cash-flow stock techniques.

Let me use that last sentence to tell you what my style of investing entails. There are three reasons and benefits to investing: cash flow, tax write-offs, and growth. The most important is cash flow. Your need for tax write-offs and growth will change from year to year. Your need for income will always increase. Also, if you learn how to create a large cash flow you can buy all the boring investments you want–later.

When I die I want my tombstone to say Wade "Cash Flow" Cook. Now, the income I'm talking about is perpetual: month after month. It's not an increase in your portfolio value, but actual cash hitting your account, a check in your mailbox.

To help you understand what I really mean by cash flow, read what some of my students are doing."

"Today we made $230,079–January 12, 1999. We made it on CMGI. A tech stock. In fact, on January 11th, we made $47,855, and on January 7th, we made $46,644. We've made $372,725 in just the opening days of this month. That does not mean we have never lost money. Oh Boy! Have we lost. But we've never lost a dime when we followed the rules as taught at the Wall Street Workshop™. It was only when human nature took over and we got "greedy," that we ever lost anything. It was only when we got careless. Mostly though, we were on the straight and narrow, as the old saying goes."

–Joseph Dietrich

"My wife and I attended the Wall Street Workshop™ in New Orleans October 22 through 24 in 1997. This was probably the worst time for us to get in, being so "green." After an intense three months ongoing learning curve and some errors on my part I am happy to report our last week's trades. Now we are really getting excited!

AMFM, post split duck, 1/29/98, four contract of the April $35 calls at $2.75; $1,100 out. Sold 2/4/98 at $4.625; $1,850 in, $750 gain, 68% return in four days.

CPQ, post split duck, 2/3/98, three contracts of the April $30 calls at $3.25; $975 out. Sold 2/4/98 at $5.50, $1,650 in, $675 gain, 69% return in just one day!

Thanks so much Wade and staff, we certainly needed this confidence builder."

–Stan and Sue Carver

As you can see, the amount of money that you can make is as varied as the strategies I teach. Some people go for it all and score big, but most are consistently making money every day, week, or month. That's what builds wealth. Not getting rich quick, but getting rich steady.

Let's reason together: if you have your own business and you don't show up, how long will it last without you? (Across the board in America, it's 2½ weeks.) If you work for someone else, and you don't go to work, when does your income stop? You've heard of income producing assets, and for most people they are it.

They are the only income-producing assets they have, and if their asset doesn't show up for work, there's no income.

Question: Can you have income without assets? No, someone or something has to be producing the income. Next question: Can you have assets without income? Yes, and far too many of you have far too many of these—assets with no income.

From the beginning of my financial educational career, some 19 years ago, I've been successfully helping people build up a group of assets which produces the income they need to live on: income which will let them spend more time with the kids or grandkids, income to go fishing, income to go back and take worthwhile classes, income to live the life they really want to live.

I love teaching, and so do my Team Wall Street instructors. These instructors, handpicked, are part of my investment "mastermind" group. Several years ago I started sharing some of my stock market insights at my real estate seminars and my asset protection and entity structuring events. This led to a full-scale stock market seminar. We call it the "Wall Street Workshop™."

The tuition is cheap compared to the money you'll make. It truly is a great value. Don't come if you want us to sell you investments. We don't do that. We teach unique, yet powerful cash-flow formulas. We treat the stock market like a business. We teach you how to get consistent one-month returns of 20 to 40%. This last statement is no joke. Many people are very pleasantly surprised when they come and make those returns right in class.

The Wall Street Workshop™ is a two-day event. It is not a seminar, but a roll-up-your-sleeves and "do the deals" workshop. Team Wall Street instructors will use newspapers, charting services, brokers on the phone, et cetera. to not only tell you how to make money, but show you how to do it, and then watch over you while you do it yourself. Our format is unique in this world of "money making" events. We call it "experiential learning." You learn best by doing. We teach a formula, then we implement it. We make money in class. You, as an attendee, use the phones in the hallway (or cellular phones), call your brokers, and make deals also. At least do paper or practice trades. It is education at its powerful best. Read what our students learn and do:

"April '97 I attended the Wall Street Workshop™ in Cherry Hill, NJ. I did lots of studying before and after attending class (your book and tapes). I had $10,000 to invest at the time of the class. I followed the advice in the book and tapes and found a broker and opened an account under my business name. W.I.N.™ has been a great help to me. I opened an IRA account with $23,000, bring my total $$$ to invest to $33,000. I've followed your principles and have made a total of $16,000 profit as of November 30th. My in-laws have been very sick recently and I had to choose between working or doing what I had to do for them. Naturally I did what I wanted and had to do. Money has been very tight. Thank God I took your classes and did what I did. The profit I made is paying the bills. Thank you."

—Burt Sklaroff

"Our very first trade was Microsoft. We bought on December 4, 1998 five contracts for the April 1999 $130 calls at $10. We sold these calls on January 20, 1999 for $37.88 for a gain of 271% in 47 days, happy time! Since that time we have made 18 plays for a total profit of $32,000 after commissions. We particularly like covered calls. If you do your research thoroughly they are really a "no brainer."

My wife and I are retired. This additional income will dramatically increase our ability to do what ever we desire. In fact, we are planning a one-month vacation in the South of France this spring."

—Jerry Keyes

"My wife and I worked hard for 13 years building a business from scratch. Our objective was to create a nice lifestyle and build for retirement. We had a goal of having one million dollars in securities and cash for retirement. Along the way we had a nice lifestyle with a six-figure income. Our goal of one million dollars in cash and securities was reached in June 1998 when we sold our business.

Along the way we dealt with two stockbrokers. Both did very poorly with our funds. My wife and I were very concerned, as it looked like we would not both be able to retire and maintain our lifestyle even with a million dollars to work with. That could be depressing couldn't it? Then I heard an advertisement for one of the Wade Cook free seminars and called the toll free number. I practically wore the tape I was sent out listening to it. Then I read *Wall Street Money Machine* twice the week before I attended the seminar. The next Monday, January 11th, I started reinvesting our funds and selling covered calls. To date, we have received over $43,000 in premium income. That is in just one month. We no longer are worried about our retirement income. I have set a date for retirement, July 3, 1999, my 58th birthday."

—KEN ROVSCH

A common comment we receive is that the money they made more than paid for the tuition.

"I read the *Wall Street Money Machine* in January of 1998. I made 22% the first month, literally with very little knowledge of stock trading. We made 23% in one trade in one day. Thanks!"

—BOBBY MEADOWS

"I began reading Wade's *Wall Street Money Machine* early in February of 1998. I then opened a brokerage account on 2/18/98 and made two plays make $3,200 on a $4,000 investment in four days."

—BRUCE BARILAR

It would be easy for me to say how wonderful this seminar is and how much money you can make by attending the Wall Street Workshop™, but as you have just read my students are the ones telling you how much this seminar has meant to them. Sometimes they do it by throwing out dollar amounts and percentages, but I feel the ones that are more important are usually about realized goals and dreams. They are about freedom, true freedom of choice or being in a position to help a family member or friend who may find themselves in a bad situation.

The major point is this: If you spend your money for this invaluable information (less with tuition discounts—see end of letter) and make all of it back plus some, or even half of it, in just two days (starting with as little as a few thousand dollars to invest), then how much more will you make over the next year? This is the first event that could cost you $100,000 or more to *not* attend.

"Dallas was 25 years old with a wife and a new baby. He had been laid off from his job from corporate downsizing. He had $6,000 to his name. He had been reading *Wall Street Money Machine* and from there attended the Financial Clinic in Orlando, FL. He decided to try investing in options using the stock split strategies he learned. In a month he was able to bring $6,000 to $30,000—and that was before he attended the workshop! Then he wen to the Workshop and was able to soar from there. The last I heard he had brought the $30,000 to $60,000 and was very pleased that his wife and he were now able to both stay home and raise their new baby. What would it have cost Dallas if he had not learned and the applied Wade's strategies?"

—Dyan

"Another person who has been successful is my younger 23-year old son-in-law. He was a university student newly married to my daughter and anxious to learn a way to augment his income to support his new little family that included my first darling little granddaughter. He, Jeff, attended a Wall Street Workshop™ but had no money for trading at the time. His father gave him $1,000 and my husband and I added to that. Being the ambitious, self-confident individual that he was, Jeff started trading options with most of his money, totally contrary to what he had been taught in the Wall Street Workshop™. He quickly lost most of his money and had only $500 left. This sobered him considerably and he decided that if he was going to follow his dreams he needed to do things the "Wade Cook way." This time Jeff was trading as he had been taught and in just two months his $500 had grown into $7,000!

—Bonnie Granger

You see everytime I turn around I receive letters and emails with some awesome stories of success. The reason I put so many testimonials in is so you won't have to take my word alone about how wonderful the Wall Street Workshop™ really is. It truly is a life changing experience.

The Wall Street Workshop™ is heavy-duty; there is no namby-pamby, wishy-washy information taught here. We teach and implement industrial-strength strategies.

Strategies that have been proven to make money. Now, before I get into these strategies, let me stress to you how risky the stock market is. This is an entity that can change in a heartbeat and take away everything you have invested, but it can also reward you like nothing else. Let me ask you some questions. Is fighting a fire risky? How about flying an airplane? Here, try this one; being a police officer. All of these professions are very risky and could result in your death. So what do these men and women do to lower the risk? Learn. That's right, they get educated. They learn everything that they can about fires, planes and law enforcement they can. The education never stops. And as they learn they practice what they learn until they feel confident that they can handle anything their job throws at them.

This is how you should treat the stock market. That is why I have developed the Wall Street Workshop™. By attending you will be getting the education you need to eliminate a lot of the risk involved. At the workshop you will be encouraged to Simutrade™, also known as paper trading. This is when you are trading in the market but instead of using real money you write it down on paper or use monopoly money. And when you are getting the results you want from each trade every time, then you start using real money. This may take a few weeks or a few months. However long it takes will save you thousands of dollars you might lose by trading before you are knowledgeable or confident enough to make money.

The Wall Street Workshop™ will teach you the same strategies that I use to make thousands of dollars each month and keep the risk at a minimum. And you know what? These methods are tried and proven and some are easy enough to do in an IRA.

Take a few minutes to look over the following list of strategies and topics covered at the Wall Street Workshop™. You will see that we cover the ABCs of investing.

The Wall Street Workshop™ is an ever-evolving event that changes to meet the needs of our students and the stock market. Here is a list of topics currently being taught at the workshop:

GETTING STARTED
- Five step process to wealth
- Strategies of engagement

BUILDING A GREAT PORTFOLIO
- Stock purchase basics
- Two types of analysis

ROLLING STOCK
- Two rules about rolling stocks

OPTIONS
- Call options
- Put options

STOCK SPLITS
- Basic and straight stock plays

WRITING COVERED CALLS
- The three rules of writing covered calls
- The five power strategies

SELLING PUTS
- Buying at wholesale
- Margin requirements
- Tandem plays
- And more

PEAKS AND SLAMS
- Definitions of Peaks and Slams
- How to find them

BARGAIN HUNTING—NEW ISSUES
- How to find
- When to buy

Bargain Hunting—Turnarounds
- Why down?
- Why up?

Bargain Hunting—Spin-offs
- Advantages
- How to find

Bargain Hunting—Penny Stocks

Range Riders
- How to play Range Riders

Rolling Options
- Explanations
- Examples

Balancing Strategies
- Balancing a portfolio
- Balancing strategies
- Now what do I do
- My four step plan

There is no way this short letter can do justice to what the workshop really is; I can't begin to tell you how powerful this event is. Just think: two days of learning and implementing these "profit-charged" cash-flow formulas. You'll see example after example of deals that work. You'll work the formulas. You'll learn how to double some of your money every $2^1/_2$ to 4 months. We do it all the time.

I'd like to say that the Wall Street Workshop™ is the greatest event of its kind—it's number one; *but* when I look around, no one is in second place. There is, simply put, no other format like it. We've taken the best cash-flow enhancement strategies and put them to work. Here's what you won't get at the event:

- You won't hear about mutual funds—too boring.
- You won't be sold investments; you get to keep all the profits you earn.

- You won't be bored–this is a jam-packed, "do the deals" action workshop.

You can't afford to miss this event. Even if I charged $25,000 you'd still get your money's worth and more. I have a "meter drop" personality from my taxi-driving days. It has served me well in real estate and the stock market (make a killing at small, repetitive transactions), so I'll continue to use it in my educational events. I've kept the price low so more people can get exposed to these income generating strategies.

> "The Wall Street Workshop™ experience has allowed me to have a lifestyle I want and live the way that I want to live with the time I spend working totally up to me. I have no boss but myself. I have no limitations but my own. What a wonderful gift I have myself when I decided to learn something new and put my money for the classes and my energy behind strategies that were all new. Thank you, Wade, for making all the strategies available and in a language and format I could understand."
>
> *—Virginia Haas*

You have to ask yourself these questions, "If I don't go to the Wall Street Workshop™, where can I learn to take $20,000 and have it generate $5,000 to $7,000 income per *month*?"

- Where can I learn these cash flow methods?
- Who else will teach me how to power up my IRA or pension plans to get 10% to 20% monthly returns–actual cash?
- Where will I go to learn to double some of my money every $2^1/_2$ to 4 months?
- Who else is teaching?
  - Options on stock split companies
  - Covered call writing
  - Rolling stocks
  - Rolling options
  - Spreads
  - Balancing strategies

This Wall Street Workshop™ is dynamic, powerful, comprehensive, innovative, yet safe and sane. You'll be angry with your stockbroker for not showing you these "easy-to-implement" formulas and strategies. To prove my point about most stockbrokers, read the following testimonials from some brokers who actually attended the workshop.

"I am writing to you to let you know that there is one more broker completely sold on your strategies. The Wall Street Workshop™ was more than I expected. I went to the Boston Workshop last week. If I could sum it up in one word, it would be explosion! I was really impressed in how your instructors pulled out all the stops and let us have it, so to speak, as far as the detailed formulas. These are literally life changing strategies. I know that I can never look at investing in the same light again.

Thank you for all that you have done for me, as well as my business! You really are for real!"

—KEVIN SULLIVAN

"My name is Bryan Meares and I have to tell you how my life has changed due to your seminars. Last July my granddad bought your book *Wall Street Money Machine* and was excited with joy with what could be done in the stock market. So he challenged my cousin and me to go with him to your seminars. At the time my life seemed worthless to me. After we went to your seminars I started to think of the possibilities of profit in the market. As a result my cousin and I have now become masters in the stock market. I am only 22 and have not finished college, but I am making more money than most professional brokers.

Now I feel that I have found my destiny, making money! As I started to become more involved in the market I shared with my dad, a well-known preacher, the returns I was making on the money my granddad gave me and my cousin to invest. After he saw what I made in the first two months he was constantly encouraging me to stay at it.

As it all turns out, my cousin and I are in the process of getting our investment advisor license and series seven license. My granddad tells us that we have the chance of a lifetime and will be years ahead of most brokers. Now our accountant's firm wants us to be the ones to invest all the money for our pastor's pension plan.

—*Bryan Meares*

"As a former stockbroker and current commodity broker, everything I ever wanted to do to help people make money in the markets was here. This is a dream come trues for me and I can never truly explain how much of an impact was made on me today."

—*Richard Milhomme*

All of this for a small price. I want every dollar you pay my company to come back to you tenfold. We're geared up for success. We want to share all we do with you.

"I came in here completely ignorant about the stock market. This really opened my eyes to the possibilities and made me feel like even I could make significant amounts of money. It also was made clear to me that I have to work for my money through education. This is not an overnight get-rich-quick scheme. It is a legitimate form of making money."

—*Beth Messina*

"Well, if I learned one thing from the workshop is was about getting in on stock splits. I have been watching DELL and I thought all signs were go. Yes it was taking a position and standing strong. Yesterday, I bought May $120 calls on DELL at $8½. By doing that I was giving myself some time, even if there was no split and earnings fell shy. DELL is a good company. So I felt I had covered my angles. Well, this morning my 120s were at $12¾.

Isn't that around 12,500% annualized? What a kick. While that is good I still must remain emotionless. I just renewed my W.I.N.™ subscription. Keep churnin' and earnin'.

Side Note: That Wade Cook is a crazy man, but I like his style. People still look at me like I am a nut. Well, you have got to take some initiative and go for it. I just recently graduated a year ago. I am now a full-time trader. I have taken $100,000 and in two months and ten days made around $36,000. Wade Cook was the start and ya' know I received one of his tapes one day in the mail. I still don't know who sent it or why. Serendipity or what?"

—SHAWN REED

You have read what the Wall Street Workshop™ is all about. You have read testimonials from students. Not just testimonials about how much money people are making, but how much this workshop has changed their lives. When you really think about what "financial freedom" is, it is the ability to be in control of your life; doing what you want to do when you want and still be able to meet your financial obligations. Let's face it, our bills will never go away and our needs are always increasing. Not to mention our want list. Each of us can use more cash flow.

Of all the financial stepping stones in life, this workshop is a must. You'll make more, you'll keep more, and you'll enhance your wealth and your cash flow. We never promise what we can't deliver and we always deliver more than we promise.

Hope to see you soon.

Sincerely Yours,

Wade B Cook

p.s. Seats sell out fast so call today at 1-800-872-7411. Ask the sales representative for the next Wall Street Workshop™ in your area. Also be sure to find out what specials, if any, we are offering.

"This seminar enhanced my knowledge from the tapes and books. I have made approximately $8,000 since starting with Wade's strategies and following them to the letter. I lost $7,000 in the month of February by not following Wade's formulas. The market is a very expensive teacher. This seminar will make me hundreds of thousands in the next year. See you at the Next Step and beyond..."

—ERIC STIMACH

"Wade Cook's strategies are comprehensive to turn any movement in the marketplace into profit. The strategies are well designed to profit the participants with small to very large portfolios. The seminar is profitable as well as motivating to realize the dream."

–AMRISH PATEL

Call 1–800–872–7411 for dates, cities, and seating. Space is very limited, so call right away and check out our guarantee.

Our simply powerful money back guarantee:

- Three trades
- Three months
- 300% annualized return

The approach we take to help our students is unique. Team Wall Street™ will identify at least three transactions of ours during your Wall Street Workshop™, or within three months thereafter, which produce a 300% annualized return using the techniques we teach. For example, a $1,000 option premium made on a $4,000 stock in a covered call strategy for one month would be a 25% return. Annualized, that would be 300% and would qualify as one of the three trades.

Transactions are listed on W.I.N.™ Our obligation is to show you these transactions. We will prove that our techniques *can* be successful. We have yet to fail to meet our money back promise! The burden is on us. If we fail to show you at least three trades within the three months that qualify, we will refund your tuition.

2

ENTITY STRUCTURING

YOU HAVE no doubt heard of estate planning and financial planning. That is the old way of looking at your financial life. What I do and what I teach is entity planning–actually using different entities to structure your affairs, thereby reducing your taxes, lessening exposure to risks and liabilities, preparing for a great retirement, and then making sure your family or church receives everything you've worked so hard to build up. The following is given here to help you structure your affairs wisely.

Entity structuring is quite simple, yet the ramifications of wise entity structuring are quite dynamic and far-reaching. The result is not only a diversity of investments and business interests, but also a diversity of entities owning or controlling those same investments. Let's preview each possible entity:

CORPORATION
The backbone of your family liability protection–a workhorse that adds so much to all the other entities.

1. It is perpetual–it does not end
2. Different classes of stock can be issued

3. Different voting rights can be applied to different shares

4. The officers are protected from liability for their business decisions

5. Shareholders have no personal liability

6. It has incredible tax advantages:

   a. Works with a pension plan

   b. Can have fiscal year end different from December 31

   c. Can make forgivable loan

   d. Can have deductible investments

   e. Operates multiple businesses

   f. Can be established in Nevada to take advantage of laws there

   g. Can deduct travel for business–for attending meetings, et cetera

   h. Can be "S" or "C" corporation and receive tax benefits

7. It protects assets

8. It is an estate planning tool like no other

9. It can own stock in other corporations or units in Limited Partnerships

LIVING TRUST
The umbrella entity

1. Helps avoid probate–saves time, money, exposure

2. Provides for estate planning

3. Used properly, it can reduce estate taxes

4. Allows for stepped-up basis to avoid capital gains taxes

5. Provides for smooth transition of business enterprise

6. Allows you to provide for children and grandchildren or charities

PENSION PLAN
Work hard–retire rich

1. Provides a tax haven

2. Like a forced savings plan

3. Donations are tax deductible

4. Investments grow tax-free until distributed

5. Provides asset protection

6. Borrowing money allowed for certain items

7. Combination of plans allows for maximum contribution– up to $30,000 in defined contribution plans

8. "Self-Trusteed"–you control everything

LIMITED PARTNERSHIP
A different entity for different purposes

1. Good for families with large asset base

2. Several at one time can control separate investments

3. Works nicely with the corporate structure

4. Allows maximum and effective use of the gift giving rules

5. Difficult for creditors to get at assets

6. Can own stock in corporations or units in other partnerships

7. Can be used in conjunction with corporation for maximum tax benefits, i.e., Corporation as General Partner

8. Distribution is considered "unearned income" and is not subject to social security taxes

9. Discount valuation takes advantage of gifting laws

CHARITABLE REMAINDER TRUST
Deductions and many benefits later

1. Donate assets to charity, receive substantial deductions without losing the benefit of the donated assets

2. Special rule allows for "Pension Type" aspect–draws out substantial income later

3. Protects family interests

4. Lessens your "taxable estate" and saves money

Many of you need three or four of these different entities. They work together, not alone. The audio seminars in my *Financial Fortress* course will teach you how to integrate and use the various entities.

Because of the different nature or function of each particular entity, they overlap well and work with each other to provide you with maximum benefits. I'll give one typical example here. You'll be able to follow along as you read the points after the diagram.

AN INTEGRATION OF ENTITIES

Let's look at entity structuring for the Lincoln family: Dave, Marcie, and their three children. Dave has a manufacturing company, which is growing quite rapidly and takes a lot of his time. It's worth about $700,000, owns about $110,000 worth of equipment, and produced about $180,000 in net profits this year. However, it is a high–risk business and he is constantly worried about lawsuits.

Marcie has a type-setting business. She works part-time and has one other part-time employee. Her business is a sole proprietorship with $40,000 worth of equipment. She nets about $25,000 a year.

Their home is worth $280,000 with an $80,000 mortgage. They have no formal retirement plan, but do have $8,500 in IRAs. They own a cabin in the mountains worth $40,000. They have stock investments of $45,000 in their personal name. They have a duplex (free and clear) worth $140,000 and two other rental houses with combined equities of $80,000.

Dave's brother has a software company worth $300,000. Dave's share is 35% or $105,000 because he put up $40,000 to help found the business. He draws no money now but expects some in a few years.

This year the Lincolns will pay about $45,000 in taxes. You can see they:

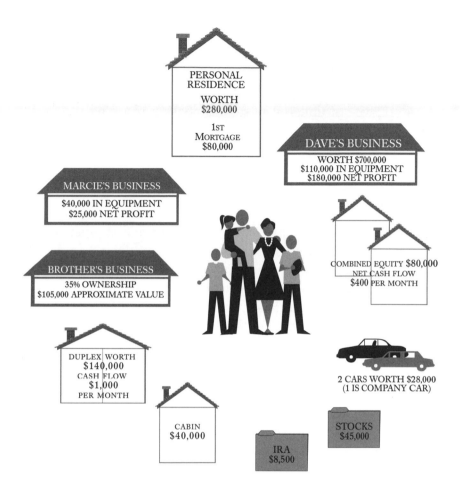

1. Have no serious lawsuit protection strategies (only liability insurance)

    a. One lawsuit could ruin everything

    b. Liability for the brother's debts is possible

2. Have no serious tax planning vehicles

    a. Some into IRA

    b. Sole proprietorship

       • No diversion of funds–year end, et cetera

       • No corporate brackets

       • All income to one bracket

       • Could use CRT

3. Have no estate planning vehicles

   a. No stock splitting

   b. No Living Trust

   c. No Charitable Remainder Trust

4. Have not undertaken serious pension planning

   a. No Keogh or, better yet, corporate pension plan

   b. No tax deductions

   c. No tax-free growth

   d. No control

If you are seeing an analysis like this for the first time, don't let it confuse you. Stick with it and you'll see the logic behind each move. Also, don't expect your CPA or financial planner to understand this. They're locked into their old, ineffective strategies. It will take you a half hour, maybe one full hour, to grasp all the ramifications of integrating entities. But it will take them weeks because they have to undo so much wrong information that's been fed into their brains for 20 years.

Remember, we're not here for quick fixes or bandaids. We are taking a "holistic" approach to complete wealth enhancement, entity integration, tax strategies, retirement planning and estate structuring. You'll take an integral role in setting this up.

I once met a couple with 12 children. I asked them how they kept track of all their names. They looked at me like I was crazy. They rattled them off so fast I barely caught one. Likewise, this will be your family of entities. You know them by what they do, by their functions. You can have nicknames for each entity, like TOP for Technical Optional Products, Inc. You'll love seeing your growth, keeping tax money working for you and retirement accounts building–all protected and ready to meet any contingency.

The list and diagrams on the next few pages show Dave and Marcie Lincoln's entity integration:

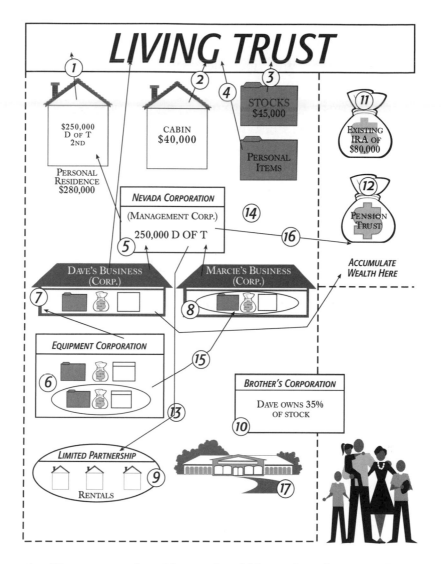

1. Your personal residence should be assigned to your Living Trust

    a. Unless you're really susceptible to lawsuits (then perhaps a Family Limited Partnership is better)

    b. Residence goes to stepped up basis if one spouse dies and the other spouse sells property. But that's not all; all property, stock, units, rentals, or other investments go to stepped up basis if owned in Living Trust

    c. Equity should be encumbered (See 14)

2. Cabin–Put in Living Trust

3. Stocks–Put in Living Trust

   a. Assign either individual stocks or whole brokerage account to Living Trust

   b. Possibly divvy up to other corporations
      - Trade stock–public for private
      - If dividends are taken–take advantage of 70% exclusion rule

4. Personal Items–Assign to Schedule A of Living Trust

5. Management Corporation–Nevada

   a. Move money–deduct–to "no tax" state

   b. Could own property, but should not own too much,this is a "cash flow" entity

   c. Manage other corporations–by contract

   d. General partner for Limited Partnership

   e. Put lien on personal residence to encumber equity

   f. If you do #5, try to make name like a bank, i.e. Capital Funding Corporation

   g. Put money into corporate pension plan

6. Use Corporation for Equipment Leasing

   a. Buy, hold, lease equipment to corporation

   b. Corporations lease or rent

   c. Use proper forms–UCC, et cetera

   d. No interaction with public other than through your entities

   e. Asset protection

7. Big Corporation

   a. Divvy up stock, to children or others

   b. Do asset freeze on parent's preferred stock

   c. Pay management company–Nevada

   d. Don't own equipment, lease from Equipment Corporation

   e. Consider even putting land (building) in separate Limited Partnership

f. Try to establish as many "independent contractors" as possible instead of employees

g. Pay money to pension fund (or see 5g)

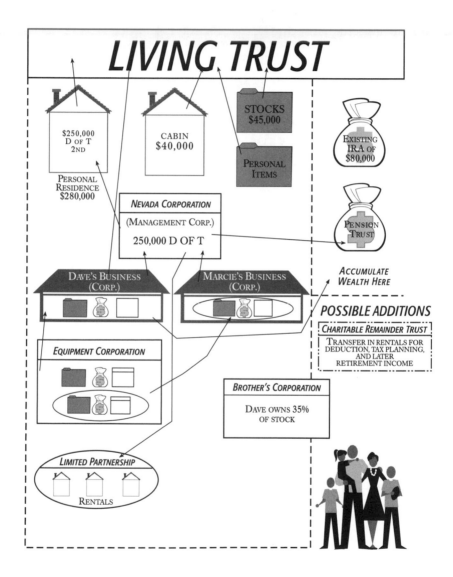

8. Corporation (Nevada)–Typesetting

a. Avoid personal liability

b. Tax structure–fiscal year end, asset freeze, lower brackets

    c. Lease equipment from equipment cororation

    d. Pay money to management corporation (or keep, if lower bracket)

    e. Possibly have own pension fund

9. Limited Partnership

    a. Own existing rentals

    b. Let corporation be general partner–avoid personal liability

    c. Initially issue all assets to Dave and Marcie (Living Trust Schedule A)

    d. Gift $20,000 in units per year to each child ($10,000 from each spouse), or hold in trust for them

10. Brother's Business

    a. Should be corporation for all the above reasons. Dave and Marcie avoid liability as shareholders

    b. Dave's percentage of ownership assigned to other entities–Living Trust is a good bet. Could be assigned to other corporations or directly to children

11. IRA

    a. Keep separate

    b. Review beneficiary payout (see if different combinations work)

    c. Keep adding more

12. Pension Account

    a. Set up and contribute as much as possible (30% of employee salary, up to $30,000 per year)

    b. Include employer–consider 401(k) of Corporation 7 (Dave's Business)

    c. Get investment with high growth-diversify later

13. Management Corporation to be general partner of Family Limited Partnership

14. Lien

    a. Dave and Marcie have too much equity–a big target

b. Trade stock for a mortgage. Record it so there is no equity available

15. Equipment Corporation leases equipment to Primary Corporation

   a. It earns money

   b. Pay money to children to avoid dividend (double taxation) treatment.

16. Pay (contribute) money to pension funds

   a. Fully deductible–great tax savings

17. Own land, but keep building as separate entity– Corporation leases building from Partnership

NOTE: If the primary corporation folds, the building is still controlled–the equipment is owned by the equipment corporation. The primary corporation has cash flow, but no substantial assets.

Because of the net profits and value of the entities (business assets), Dave and Marcie are strong candidates for Charitable Remainder Trust. Now review the previous diagram. (Note: Trusts cannot be put inside trusts.)

3

NEVADA CORPORATIONS

THE FOLLOWING section is an excerpt from *Brilliant Deductions*. To order a copy, call Wade Cook Seminars at 1-800-872-7411.

A new business generally chooses between three forms of business organization: sole proprietorship, partnership (general or limited), or incorporation. How do these three forms of organization compare?

LIABILITY FOR DEBTS, TAXES, ET CETERA.

When a person goes into business without any special arrangements, he or she is said to be involved in a sole proprietorship. The business is an extension of oneself for all legal and tax purposes. If the business earns money, that person is considered to have earned it all and is liable for taxes on all of it. If the business borrows money, it is no different than if he/she borrowed money personally. If the business is liable for injuring someone (as in the case where it sells a faulty product), the owner is personally responsible for the damage.

A partnership is similar to a sole proprietorship in that the two (or more) individuals who start the business are collectively liable for all taxes, debts or damages. It can be very difficult to keep tabs on one's partners, yet in a partnership each partner is legally his brother's keeper. (In the special case of a limited partnership, a limited partner is liable only to the extent of her/his investment in the business, but the limited partner has no management or voting rights of any kind and is completely at the mercy of the general partners, who are fully liable for all partnership taxes, debts or damages.)

When one forms a corporation, the corporation is deemed to be a complete separate entity from the person who formed it, owns it, or derives profit from it. It is subject to different types of taxation than individuals. Anyone owning a part of a corporation has limited liability; that is, an individual's responsibility for taxes, debts or damages of the corporation is limited to the amount invested in the stock (equity) of the corporation. A corporation could go bankrupt in the face of crushing financial burdens, and yet its owners could keep all of the money they derived from it over the years of its successful operation. Limitation of liability, without surrendering management control over the business, is one of the major advantages of incorporation.

In the sole proprietorship or partnership, tax-free contributions to pension plans are severely limited. All such pension plans are comparable to IRA plans for individual retirement except for the dollar amounts.

With a corporation, the business can establish a Qualified Plan, which allows a much greater tax-deductible yearly contribution. Such a pension plan could even be directed by the employee (who could be an owner) for whom the plan is established—a so-called "self–directed retirement program." The rapid accumulation of funds in a corporate pension plan is another major advantage of incorporation.

TAXES

Under the 1986 Tax Reform Act, the rate of corporate taxation, in most instances, is lower than the rate for individual taxation. Tax benefits are still another major reason to incorporate. Inasmuch as the corporation is a separate entity from its owners, it is possible for the corporation to provide very substantial benefits to its employees/owners and avoid taxation on money spent for such purposes, while the owners could avoid taxation on the benefits so provided.

A good accountant can use the combination of a corporation and its pension plan to save its owners substantial amounts of taxes in ways too numerous to mention in this limited space. Suffice it to say that incorporating is widely considered one of the most effective tax shelters in existence–and the *only* tax shelter available to most middle-class business people.

RAISING MONEY

Although a partnership or even a sole proprietorship might be a larger business than an individual corporation, the corporation nonetheless has certain advantages in doing business. The corporation can raise money much more effectively than a partnership or sole proprietorship. For example, a corporation can sell stock (equity in the company) or bonds (debt of the company) on any terms acceptable to a potential buyer (subject to the limitations of federal and state securities laws). In this manner, a corporation can raise money without having to gamble its future on bank loans or short-term debt. Such debt spells the end for most businesses which fail in America.

The process of "Going Public" (selling shares of the company to the public), is also available to a corporation, but not to a sole proprietorship or general partnership. While it would be difficult to explain the process in the space available, the process is extremely valuable to companies making the transition from small business to medium-size business (characterized by sales from $1 million to $10 million yearly). While many people who start businesses are not looking that far into the future, those with foresight are often rewarded.

NEVADA CORPORATIONS

The advantages to incorporating in Nevada are numerous. No other state can give you all the advantages that a Nevada Incorporation can.

No Corporate or Personal Income Tax

When your corporation earns money in Nevada, none of it goes to pay a tax bill to the state—and when the corporation distributes money to *you* as owner, none of your money goes to the Nevada tax collector. Only a handful of American states can still make that claim—and most of them are actively debating imposition of such taxes.

When you sell products throughout the United States (or even in more than one state), this tax advantage can mean lots of extra money in your corporation's coffers, and in your pocket. For example, a California Company is subject to substantial taxes on its earnings anywhere in the world! In New York, the level of taxation has helped drive over two million jobs out of the state in a twenty-year period. Can you afford headquarters in a state that will rob you blind—or perhaps even cause your business to fail?

The Most Liberal Securities Laws in America

If a corporation needs to raise money, there is no better state to be incorporated in than Nevada. Nevada securities regulators understand the needs of business in a way that securities officials of few other states do. Encouraging business expansion has been one of the state's highest priorities—and it has paid off with one of the most rapid business expansion rates of any state in America. Recent legislative changes have even made it possible for Nevada-based "high-tech" companies to borrow money for expansion and growth directly from municipalities, and up to $100 million has been made available. Furthermore, the relative wealth of Nevada's citizenry has made possible the expansion of one of America's strongest "penny stock" markets, private placement markets, etc.

If going public, pursuing mergers and acquisition, floating bonds or other issues is part of your corporation's plans or even dreams, Nevada is unbeatable.

The Broadest Corporate Powers Available

At one time, the State of Delaware was considered to have the best corporate laws in America, and businesses all over America flocked to incorporate in Delaware. Today, Nevada permits your corporation's directors to exercise a range of powers exceeded by no other state, including Delaware.

By the expedient of writing a grant of powers into your corporate Articles of Incorporation, your Board of Directors can exercise any and all powers permitted by the laws of Nevada—as they now exist, and as they are expanded in the future! The Board can simply vote to act as it sees fit—to sell the business, acquire another business, issue dividends in cash or stock or stock options, issue stock of any type or any class on any terms it likes, and so on.

ISSUE COMMON, PREFERRED, OR SPECIAL STOCK

Most states will permit you to issue Common (voting) stock, usually in only one class, and "Preferred" stock. Usually, all of the preferences accorded to "Preferred" stock must be spelled out in the Articles of Incorporation. Your corporate planning must be elaborate and extremely effective.

Not in Nevada! With a Nevada incorporation, you can have several classes of Common stock, several series of Preferred stock, and several classes of Special stock—and you don't even have to spell out the preferences of any class or series in the articles. You can leave all of those decisions, as need arises, to the Board of Directors.

For example, if you want to acquire another company with stock of your own corporation, and plan to "spin-off" the acquired company later on, you could issue Special stock to the owners of the acquired company with no voting powers, but with special rights to distributions of stock dividends in any spin-off created (or even in just the first spin-off created). Yes, your Board of Directors can make up the conditions as it goes along, as business and/or negotiating strategy demand. No other state gives you this kind of latitude.

PROTECTION OF DIRECTORS

Often, it would be desirable to include respected members of your community as Directors on your Board, but such people are usually unwilling to serve. Why? Because of the threat of stockholder suits against the members of the Board of Directors, which are common in many jurisdictions.

Nevada incorporation eliminates the threat of successful suits against distinguished Directors. Under Nevada law, unless such a Director was directly and personally involved in fraud that caused losses to the shareholders, she or he could not be successfully sued by shareholders. Few states offer this kind of Director protection.

LIMITED DISCLOSURES

You can incorporate in the State of Nevada by providing no more personal information than the proposed name(s) of your corporation and the names and addresses of your initial Directors. If you choose the broadest powers available to the Board and no more than 25 million shares of stock (with the most possible classes and freedom of action), you have no more decisions to make!

LOW COST

What would you expect to pay for all this, plus all preparation fees, resident agent fees, etc.? It all costs much, much less than you would think.

In short, these extensive benefits make incorporating in Nevada one of the best and most powerfully far reaching actions you can take. You need the type of protection and versatility only a Nevada Corporation can offer.

LOWER PERSONAL TAXES

There are many ways to receive money, but the trick is not to have to claim that money as income. One way to do that, especially if you are going to play the stock market, is to avoid owning stock in your own personal name. Stocks in the stock market should be owned in an IRA, some other type of retirement account, or a corporate account. I'll show you why.

If your corporation owns stock in the stock market and it receives a dividend, the corporation does not have to claim 70% of that dividend (whether it's a common stock dividend or preferred stock dividend). This is called the 70% exclusion rule. All you have to claim is 30%.

For example, let's say you build up a substantial portfolio in a corporate account over 10 or 15 years. You buy and sell some stock, you keep some and it grows in value. Maybe these shares are not paying any dividends today, but they will in the future. Then let's say you receive a $10,000 dividend check for one year. This is not unheard of if you have $100,000 to $200,000 worth of stock.

Now look at your tax brackets. The dividend payout adds to your income and jacks you up over $50,000 a year, or even over $75,000. You are in a 25% to 34% tax bracket, but as a corporation, all you claim is 30% of that, or $3,000. The other $7,000 is ignored. If, for instance, you're in a 15% tax bracket, you'll pay 15% of $3,000, or $450, as opposed to 15% of $10,000, which is $1,500. This corporate dividend exclusion is one of the better reasons for having a corporation.

THE 70% EXCLUSION RULE

Let's continue with another ramification of this example. You have taken in $1,000 in dividends. That money can go into your corporate checking account, or it can be used to pay bills or buy a new car. Your corporation has taken in the money, but it only has to claim 30% (or $300) of that money as income. The remaining 70% of the dividend income paid from one corporation to another is excluded from taxation.

You are probably thinking, "Why didn't my CPA tell me this?" I'm going to ask you that question too. At my seminars, I ask, "Why did you have to come here and learn this from a former cab driver? Why didn't your CPA tell you this?" Most people shout, "They just don't know." And that's true.

I want to isolate the small amount of money from the aforementioned example to prove a point. You've taken in a check from the XYZ Company for $1,000. All you have to claim is $300, even though you've taken in $1,000. You could pay out that $1,000 on expenses, so your books show $1,000 in expenses and $300 in income, and your bottom line is a $700 loss. Most of you are just taking in the $1,000, claiming the whole thing, and paying taxes on the entire amount.

I hope you see the value in this simple, yet powerful, investment strategy. Specifically, look at companies that are paying high dividends–but only worry about claiming 30% of it as income. You have to ask yourself, "Does Mobil Oil own stock in AT&T? Does AT&T own stock in IBM?" The answer is yes. They own stock in other companies. They have their own brokerage accounts because their tax preparers realize they can build up a substantial amount of income and only have to worry about claiming 30% of it.

If you like this 70% exclusion rule, you must realize that "S" corporations do not qualify for it. Only "C" corporations or regular, ordinary corporations can qualify. (For further explanation on the difference between "S" and "C" corporations, see the *Incorporation Handbook*. Call Wade Cook Seminars at 1–800–872–7411 to order your copy.)

4

SUGGESTED READING

SOME OF the magazines and newsletters I read and use to gather information from are listed here for your convenience.

- *BARRON'S*   *1-800-822-7229*
  200 Burnett Road
  Chicopee, Mass 01020

- *CREATIVE REAL ESTATE*   *(619) 756-1441*
  Drawer L
  Rancho Santa Fe, California 92067

    A must for everyone–whether you buy real estate or not. Mention me and they might give you a deal.

- *DICK DAVIS DIGEST*   *1-800-654-1514*
  P.O. Box 350630
  Ft. Lauderdale, FL 33335-0630

    I really like this newsletter.

- *EXPLANATIONS*   *1-800-706-2825*
  14675 Interurban Avenue South
  Seattle, WA 98168-4664

- *FINANCIAL WORLD*   *1-800-829-5916*
  1328 Broadway
  New York, NY 10001-2116

- *FORBES*   *1-800-888-9896*
  Box 10048
  Des Moines, Iowa 50309

     I like it. From a money point of view the back
  sections are really good.

- *INDIVIDUAL INVESTOR*   *1-888-616-7677*
  Subscription Fulfillment
  P.O. Box 37289
  Boone, IA 50037-0289

- *NATIONAL REVIEW*   *(815) 734-1232*
  150 East 35th Street
  New York, New York 10016

     My favorite. Mostly political. The section
  "Random Wealth" has good insights.

- *REASON*   *1-800-998-8989*
  Box 526
  Mount Morris, Illinois 61054

     More political than economic but still really
  good.

- *TAX UPDATE NEWSLETTER*
  81 Montgomery Street
  Scarsdale, New York 10583

     A must if you're serious about staying informed
  and cutting taxes.

- *The Economist*   *1-800-456-6086*
  Box 58524
  Boulder, Colorado 80322

    Written from an international slant. I love this magazine.

- *The Money Paper*   *1-914-381-5400*
  1010 Mamaroneck
  Mamaroneck, NY 10543

    This newsletter gives you the names of companies with a dividend reinvestment program. For a small fee, they will also sell you a single share from one of these companies.

- *The Wall Street Journal*   *1-800-221-1940*
  200 Burnett Road
  Chicopee, Massachusetts 01021

    Obviously a must for every serious investor and business owner. I particularly like the editorial section.

- *Worth*   *1-800-777-1851*
  P.O. Box 55420
  Boulder, CO 80322

5

AVAILABLE RESOURCES

THE FOLLOWING books, videos, and audiocassettes have been reviewed by the Wade Cook Seminars, Inc., Lighthouse Publishing Group, Inc., or Gold Leaf Press staff and are suggested as reading and resource material for continuing education to help with your financial planning, and real estate and stock market investments. Because new ideas and techniques come along and laws change, we're always updating our catalog.

To order a copy of our current catalog, please write or call us at:

Wade Cook Seminars, Inc.
14675 Interurban Avenue South
Seattle, Washington 98168-4664
1-800-872-7411

Or, visit us on our web sites at:

www.wadecook.com
www.lighthousebooks.com

Also, we would love to hear your comments on our products and services, as well as your testimonials on how these products have benefited you. We look forward to hearing from you!

AUDIOCASSETTES

13 FANTASTIC INCOME FORMULAS-A FREE CASSETTE
PRESENTED BY WADE B. COOK

Learn 13 cash flow formulas, some of which are taught in the Wall Street Workshop™. Learn to double some of your money in $2^1/_2$ to 4 months.

ZERO TO ZILLIONS
PRESENTED BY WADE B. COOK

A four-album, 16-cassette, powerful audio workshop on Wall Street-understanding the stock market game, playing it successfully, and retiring rich. Learn 11 powerful investment strategies to avoid pitfalls and losses. Learn to catch "day-trippers," how to "bottom fish," write covered calls, and to possibly double your money in one week on options on stock split companies. Wade "Meter Drop" Cook can teach you how he makes fantastic annual returns in his account. You then will have the information to try to follow suit. Each album comes with a workbook, and the entire workshop includes a free bonus video called "Dynamic Dollars," 90 minutes of instruction on how all the strategies can be integrated, giving actual examples of what kinds of returns are possible so you can get in there and play the market successfully. A must for every savvy, would-be investor.

POWER OF NEVADA CORPORATIONS-A FREE CASSETTE
PRESENTED BY WADE B. COOK

Nevada Corporations have secrecy, privacy, minimal taxes, no reciprocity with the IRS, and protection for shareholders, officers, and directors. This is a powerful seminar.

INCOME STREAMS-A FREE CASSETTE
PRESENTED BY WADE B. COOK

Learn to buy and sell real estate the Wade Cook way. This

informative cassette will instruct you in building and operating your own real estate money machine.

MONEY MACHINE I & II
PRESENTED BY WADE B. COOK

Learn the benefits of buying, and more importantly, selling real estate. Now the system for creating and maintaining a real estate money machine is available in audiocassette form. Money Machine I & II teach the step by step cash flow formulas that made Wade Cook and thousands like him millions of dollars.

MONEY MYSTERIES OF THE MILLIONAIRES-A FREE CASSETTE
PRESENTED BY WADE B. COOK

How to make money and keep it. This fantastic seminar shows you how to use Nevada Corporations, Living Trusts, Pension Plans, Charitable Remainder Trusts, and Family Limited Partnerships to protect your assets.

24 KARAT
PRESENTED BY WADE B. COOK

Learn how to protect your family's finances through anything–including Y2K! 24 Karat seminar on cassette teaches people how currency fluctuates and the safest currency to have. This seminar is packed with must-know information about your future.

UNLIMITED WEALTH AUDIO SET
PRESENTED BY WADE B. COOK

Unlimited Wealth is the "University of Money-Making Ideas" home study course that helps you improve your money's personality. The heart and soul of this seminar is to make more money, pay fewer taxes, and keep more for your retirement and family. This cassette series contains the great ideas from *Wealth 101* on tape, so you can listen to them whenever you want.

RETIREMENT PROSPERITY
PRESENTED BY WADE B. COOK

Take that IRA money now sitting idle and invest it in ways that generate you bigger, better, and quicker returns. This four audio-tape set walks you through a system of using a self directed IRA to create phenomenal profits, virtually tax-free! This is one of the most complete systems for IRA investing ever created.

THE FINANCIAL FORTRESS HOME STUDY COURSE
PRESENTED BY WADE B. COOK

This eight-part series is the last word in entity structuring. It goes far beyond mere financial planning or estate planning. It helps you structure your business and your affairs so that you can avoid the majority of taxes, retire rich, escape lawsuits, bequeath your assets to your heirs without government interference, and, in short-bomb proof your entire estate. There are six audiocassette seminars on tape, an entity structuring video, and a full kit of documents.

PAPER TIGERS AND PAPER CHASE
PRESENTED BY WADE B. COOK

Wade gives you a personal introduction to the art of buying and selling real estate. In this set of six cassettes, Wade shares his inside secrets to establishing a cash flow business with real estate investments. You will learn how to find discounted second mortgages, find second mortgage notes and make them better, as well as how you can get 40%-plus yields on your money. Learn the art of structuring your business to attract investors and bring in the income you desire through the use of family corporations, pension plans, and other legal entities. A manual is included.

When you buy Paper Tigers, you'll also receive Paper Chase for free. Paper Chase holds the most important tools you need to make deals happen. Wade created these powerful tapes as a handout tool you can lend to potential investors or homeowners to help educate them about how this amazing cash flow system works for them. It explains how you'll negotiate a lower interest rate if they make a larger payment. You will use this incredible tool over and over again.

HIGH PERFORMANCE BUSINESS STRATEGIES
BY WADE B. COOK

Your business cannot succeed without you. This course will help you become successful so your company can succeed. It is a combination of two previous courses, formerly entitled Turbo-Charge Your Business and High-Octane Business Strategies. For years, Wade Cook and his staff have listened to people's questions, and concerns. Because they know that problems are best solved by people who already know the ropes, Wade's staff wanted to help. They categorized the questions and came up with about 60 major areas of concern. Wade then went into the recording studio and dealt head on with these questions. What resulted is a comprehensive collection of knowledge to get you started quickly.

THE REAL ESTATE CASH FLOW SYSTEM
PRESENTED BY WADE B. COOK

This six-volume audiocassette set, originally sold separately, contains everything you'll ever need to begin investing in real estate immediately, do so successfully, handle all of the business aspects and retire sooner than you ever thought possible. Just look at all the tremendous information that can be yours.

BOOKS

WALL STREET MONEY MACHINE
BY WADE B. COOK

Appearing on the New York Times Business Best Sellers list for over one year, *Wall Street Money Machine* contains the best strategies for wealth enhancement and cash flow creation you'll find anywhere. Throughout this book, Wade Cook describes many of his favorite strategies for generating cash flow through the stock market: rolling stocks, proxy investing, covered calls, and many more. It's a great introduction for creating wealth using the Wade Cook formulas.

STOCK MARKET MIRACLES
BY WADE B. COOK

The anxiously-awaited partner to *Wall Street Money Machine*, this book is proven to be just as invaluable. *Stock Market Miracles* improves on some of the strategies from *Wall Street Money Machine*, as well as introducing new and valuable twists on our old favorites. This is a must read for anyone interested in making serious money in the stock market.

SAFETY 1ST INVESTING
BY WADE B. COOK

Over two decades of research and experience have culminated in Wade Cook's latest book, *Safety 1st Investing*. In it you will learn how to "preserve and grow your asset base as you build an ever-increasing income stream," by utilizing cash flow strategies designed for low risk with good cash flow, including: Writing In-The-Money Calls, Bull Call Spreads, Bull Put Spreads, Bear Put Spreads, Bear Call Spreads, Calendar Spreads, Index plays, and Index Spreads. Pick up a copy of *Safety 1st Investing* today and learn the latest Wade Cook cash flow strategies!

BULLS & BEARS (FORMERLY TITLED BEAR MARKET BALONEY)
BY WADE B. COOK

A timelier book wouldn't be possible. Wade's predictions came true while the book was at press! Don't miss this insightful look into what makes bull and bear markets and how to make exponential returns in any market.

ON TRACK INVESTING
BY DAVID R. HEBERT

On Track Investing is the instruction book for novice stock market investors or anyone wanting to practice investment strategies without risking actual cash. Combined with your personal game plan, the Simutrade™ System helps you originate good trades, perfect your timing, and check your open trades against your personal criteria. There are Simutrade™ Worksheets and step by step guides for 10 strategies. *On Track Investing* helps you develop a step by step map of what exactly you're going to do and how you're going to accomplish it.

ROLLING STOCKS
BY GREGORY WITT

Rolling Stocks shows you the simplest and most powerful strategy for profiting from the ups and downs of the stock market. You'll learn how to find rolling stocks, get in smoothly at the right price, and time your exit. You will recognize the patterns of rolling stocks and how to make the most money from these strategies. Apply rolling stocks principles to improve your trading options and fortify your portfolio.

SLEEPING LIKE A BABY
BY JOHN C. HUDELSON

Perhaps the most predominant reason people don't invest in the stock market is fear. *Sleeping Like A Baby* removes the fear from investing and gives you the confidence and knowledge to invest wisely, safely, and profitably.

You'll learn how to build a high quality portfolio and plan for your future and let your investments follow. Begin to invest as early as possible, and use proper asset allocation and diversification to reduce risk.

MAKING A LIVING IN THE STOCK MARKET
BY BOB ELDRIDGE

In simplistic, easy to understand terms and presentation, Bob Eldridge will show you how you can change your job and your life by making a living in the stock market. This powerful book is full of real life examples of profitable trades. Pages full of charts, diagrams, and tables help the reader understand how these strategies are implemented.

If you live for your job, have little or no money at the end of each paycheck, and have forgotten your dreams in days gone past, this book is for you. In *Making A Living In The Stock Market*, you can learn how to make money with cash generating strategies including: channeling stock prices, covered calls, selling naked puts, selling naked calls, call (debit) spread, and stock splits.

101 WAYS TO BUY REAL ESTATE WITHOUT CASH
BY WADE B. COOK

Wade Cook has personally achieved success after success in real estate. Now, *101 Ways To Buy Real Estate Without Cash* fills the gap left by other authors who have given all the ingredients but not the whole recipe for real estate investing. This is the book for the investor who wants innovative and practical methods for buying real estate with little or no money down.

Cook's Book On Creative Real Estate
By Wade B. Cook

Make your real estate buying experiences profitable and fun. *Cook's Book On Creative Real Estate* will show you how! You will learn suggestions for finding the right properties, buying them quickly, and profiting ever quicker.

How To Pick Up Foreclosures
By Wade B. Cook

Do you want to become an expert moneymaker in real estate? This book will show you how to buy real estate at 60¢ on the dollar or less. You'll learn to find the house before the auction and purchase it with no bank financing-the easy way to millions in real estate. The market for foreclosures is a tremendous place to learn and prosper. *How To Pick Up Foreclosures* takes Wade's methods from *Real Estate Money Machine* and super charges them by applying the fantastic principles to already-discounted properties.

Owner Financing
By Wade B. Cook

This is a short but invaluable booklet you can give to sellers who hesitate to sell you their property using the owner financing method. Let this pamphlet convince both you and them. The special report, "Why Sellers Should Take Monthly Payments," is included for free!

Real Estate For Real People
By Wade B. Cook

A priceless, comprehensive overview of real estate investing, this book teaches you how to buy the right property for the right price, at the right time. Wade Cook explains all of the strategies you'll need, and gives you 20 reasons why you should start investing in real estate today. Learn how to retire rich with real estate, and have fun doing it.

REAL ESTATE MONEY MACHINE
BY WADE B. COOK

Wade's first best-selling book reveals the secrets of Wade Cook's own system–the system he earned his first million from. This book teaches you how to make money regardless of the state of the economy. Wade's innovative concepts for investing in real estate not only avoids high interest rates, but avoids banks altogether.

BLUEPRINTS FOR SUCCESS, VOLUME 1
CONTRIBUTORS: WADE COOK, DEBBIE LOSSE, JOEL BLACK, DAN WAGNER, TIM SEMINGSON, RICH SIMMONS, GREG WITT, JJ CHILDERS, KEVEN HART, DAVE WAGNER AND STEVE WIRRICK

Blueprints For Success, Volume 1 is a compilation of chapters on building your wealth through your business and making your business function successfully. The chapters cover: education and information gathering, choosing the best business for you from all the different types of business, and a variety of other skills necessary for becoming successful. Your business can't afford to miss out on these powerful insights!

BRILLIANT DEDUCTIONS
BY WADE B. COOK

Do you want to make the most of the money you earn? Do you want to have solid tax havens and ways to reduce the taxes you pay? This book is for you! Learn how to get rich in spite of the updated tax laws. See new tax credits, year-end maneuvers, and methods for transferring and controlling your entities. Learn to structure yourself and your family for tax savings and liability protection.

MILLION HEIRS
BY JOHN V. CHILDERS, JR.

In his reader-friendly style, attorney John V. Childers, Jr. explains how you can prepare your loved ones for when you pass away. He explains many details you need to take care of right away, before a death occurs, as well as strategies for your heirs to utilize. Don't leave your loved ones unprepared–get *Millions Heirs.*

The Secret Millionaire Guide To Nevada Corporations
By John V. Childers, Jr.

What does it mean to be a secret millionaire? In *The Secret Millionaire Guide To Nevada Corporations*, attorney John V. Childers, Jr. outlines exactly how you can use some of the secret, extraordinary business tactics used by many of today's super-weathly to protect your assets from the ravages of lawsuits and other destroyers using Nevada Corporations. You'll understand why the state of Nevada has become the preferred jurisdiction for those desiring to establish corporations and how to utilize Nevada Corporations for your financial benefit.

Wealth 101
By Wade B. Cook

This incredible book brings you 101 strategies for wealth creation and protection that you can't afford to miss. Front to back, it is packed full of tips and tricks to supercharge your financial health. If you need to generate more cash flow, this book shows you how through several various avenues. If you are already wealthy, this is the book that will show you strategy upon strategy for decreasing your tax liability and increasing your peace of mind through liability protection.

A+
By Wade B. Cook

A+ is a collection of wisdom, thoughts, and principles of success, which can help you, make millions, even billions of dollars and live an A+ life. As you will see, Wade Cook consistently tries to live his life "in the second mile," to do more than asked, to be above normal.

If you want to live a successful life, you need great role models to follow. For years, Wade Cook's life has been a quest to find successful characteristics of his role models and implement them in his own life. In *A+*, Wade will encourage you to find and incorporate the most successful principles and characteristics of success in your life, too. Don't spend another day living less than an A+ life!

BUSINESS BUY THE BIBLE
BY WADE B. COOK

Inspired by the Creator, the Bible truly is the authority for running the business of life. Throughout *Business Buy The Bible*, you are provided with practical advice that helps you apply God's word to your life. You'll learn how you can apply God's word to your life. You'll learn how you can apply God's words to saving, spending and investing, and how you can control debt instead of being controlled by it. You'll also learn how to use God's principles in your daily business activities and prosper.

DON'T SET GOALS (THE OLD WAY)
BY WADE B. COOK

Don't Set Goals (The Old Way) will teach you to be a goal-getter, not just a goal-setter. You'll learn that achieving goals is the result of prioritizing and acting. *Don't Set Goals (The Old Way)* shows you how taking action and "paying the price" is more important than simply making the decision to do something. Don't just set goals. Go out and get your goals, go where you want to go!

WADE COOK'S POWER QUOTES, VOLUME 1
BY WADE B. COOK

Wade Cook's Power Quotes, Volume 1 is chock full of exciting quotes that have motivated and inspired Mr. Cook. Wade Cook continually asks his students, "To whom are you listening?" He knows that if you get your advice and inspiration from successful people, you'll become successful yourself. He compiled *Wade Cook's Power Quotes, Volume 1* to provide you with a millionaire-on-call when you need advice.

LIVING IN COLOR
BY RENAE KNAPP

Renae Knapp is the leading authority on the Blue Base/Yellow Base Color System and is recognized worldwide for her research and contribution to the study of color. Industries, universities, and men and women around the globe use Renae's tried and true-scientifically proven-system to achieve measurable results.

In *Living In Color*, Renae Knapp teaches you easy to understand methods, which empower you to get more from your life by harnessing the power of color. In an engaging, straightforward way, Renae Knapp teaches the scientific Blue Base/Yellow Base Color System and how to achieve harmony and peace using color. You will develop a mastery of color harmony and an awareness of the amazing role color plays in every area of your life.

Y2K GOLD RUSH
BY WADE B. COOK

As we approach the end of the millennium, newspapers and television newscasters drone on about Y2K. Computers will read the year 2000 as 1900! The issue is a definite problem, but in *Y2K Gold Rush*, Wade Cook discounts the need for this hysteria. First, businesses and individuals alike have been preparing for this problem. Secondly, and more importantly, people are now buying gold to protect themselves against all types of potential problems.

This book is about how to invest in gold. By reading *Y2K Gold Rush*, you will understand the historical importance of gold. You will learn about the ownership of gold coins and gold stocks, and the benefits of both. You will see that adding gold to your investment portfolio will diversify your assets, safeguard you and your family against catastrophe, and add excitement and profits.

VIDEOS

DYNAMIC DOLLARS VIDEO
BY WADE B. COOK

Wade Cook's 90-minute introduction to the basics of his Wall Street formulas and strategies. In this presentation designed especially for video, Wade explains the meter drop philosophy, rolling stocks, basics of proxy investing, and writing covered calls. Perfect for anyone looking for a little basic information.

THE WALL STREET WORKSHOP™ VIDEO SERIES
BY WADE B. COOK

If you can't make it to the Wall Street Workshop™ soon, get a head start with these videos. Ten albums containing 11 hours of intense instruction on rolling stocks, options on stock split companies, writing covered calls, and eight other tested and proven strategies designed to help you increase the value of your investments. By learning, reviewing, and implementing the strategies taught here, you will gain the knowledge and the confidence to take control of your investments, and get your money to work hard for you.

THE NEXT STEP VIDEO SERIES
BY TEAM WALL STREET

The advanced version of the Wall Street Workshop™. Full of power-packed strategies from Wade Cook, this is not a duplicate of the Wall Street Workshop™, but a very important partner. The methods taught in this seminar will supercharge the strategies taught in the Wall Street Workshop™ and teach you even more ways to make more money!

In The Next Step, you'll learn how to find the stocks to fit the formulas through technical analysis, fundamentals, home trading tools, and more.

BUILD PERPETUAL INCOME (BPI)-A VIDEOCASSETTE

Wade Cook Seminars, Inc. is proud to present Build Perpetual Income, the latest in our ever-expanding series of seminar home study courses. In this video, you will learn powerful real estate cash-flow generating techniques, such as: power negotiating strategies, buying and selling mortgages, writing contracts, finding and buying discount properties, and avoiding debt.

CLASSES OFFERED

COOK UNIVERSITY

People enroll in Cook University for a variety of reasons. Usually they are a little discontented with where they are-their job is not working, their business is not producing the kind of income they want, or they definitely see that they need more income to prepare for a better retirement. That's where Cook University comes in. As you try to live the American Dream, in the life-style you want, we stand by ready to assist you make the dream your reality.

The backbone of the one-year program is the Money Machine concept-as applied to your business, to stock investments, or to real estate. Although there are many, many other forms of investing in real estate, there are really only three that work: the Money Machine method, buying second mortgages, and lease options. Of these three, the Money Machine stands head and shoulders above the rest.

It is difficult to explain Cook University in only a few words. It is so unique, innovative and creative that it literally stands alone. But then, what would you expect from Wade Cook? Something common and ordinary? Never! Wade and his staff always go out of their way to provide you with useful, tried-and-true strategies that create real wealth.

We are embarking on an unprecedented voyage and want you to come along. If you choose to make this important decision in your life, you could also be invited to share your successes in a series of books called *Blueprints For Success, Volume 1* (more volumes to come). Yes, it takes commitment. Yes, it takes drive. Add to this the help you'll receive by our hand-trained experts and you will enhance your asset base and increase your bottom line.

We want to encourage a lot of people to get in the program right away. You could save thousands of dollars, if you don't delay. Call right away! Class sizes are limited so each student gets personal attention.

Perpetual monthly income is waiting. We'll teach you how to achieve it. We'll show you how to make it. We'll watch over you while you're making it happen. Thank you for your consideration. We hope to see you in the program right away.

Cook University is designed to be an integral part of your educational life. We encourage you to call and find out more about this life-changing program. The number is 1-800-872-7411. Ask for an enrollment director and begin your millionaire-training today!

If you want to be wealthy, this is the place to be.

THE WALL STREET WORKSHOP™
PRESENTED BY WADE B. COOK AND TEAM WALL STREET

The Wall Street Workshop™ teaches you how to make incredible money in all markets. It teaches you the tried-and-true strategies that have made hundreds of people wealthy.

THE NEXT STEP WORKSHOP
PRESENTED BY WADE B. COOK AND TEAM WALL STREET

An advanced Wall Street Workshop designed to help those ready to take their trading to the next level and treat it as a business. This seminar is open only to graduates of the Wall Street Workshop™.

YOUTH WALL STREET WORKSHOP
PRESENTED BY TEAM WALL STREET

Wade Cook has made a personal commitment to empower the youth of today with desire and knowledge to be self-sufficient. Now you, too, can make a personal commitment to your youth by sending them to the Youth Wall Street Workshop and start your own family dynasty in the process!

Our Youth Wall Street Workshop teaches the power and money making potential of the stock market strategies of the Wall Street Workshop™. The pace is geared to the students, with more time devoted to vocabulary, principles and concepts that may be new to them.

Your children and grandchildren can learn these easy to understand strategies and get that "head start" in life!

If you're considering the Wall Street Workshop™ for the first time, take advantage of our free Youth Wall Street Workshop promotion and bring a son, daughter, or grandchild with you (ages 13 to 18, student, living at home).

Help make your children financially secure in the future by giving them the helping hand in life we all wish we had received.

FINANCIAL CLINIC
PRESENTED BY WADE COOK AND TEAM WALL STREET

People from all over are making money, lots of money, in the stock market using the proven bread and butter strategies taught by Wade Cook. Is trading in the stock market for you?

Please accept our invitation to come hear for yourself about the amazing money-making strategies we teach. Our Financial Clinic is designed to help you understand how you can learn these proven stock market strategies. In three short hours you will be introduced to some of the 11 proven strategies we teach at the Wall Street Workshop™. Discover for yourself how they work and how you can use them in your life to get the things you want for you and your family. Come to this introductory event and see what we have to offer. Then make the decision yourself!

THE NEXT STEP WORKSHOP
PRESENTED BY WADE B. COOK AND TEAM WALL STREET

An advanced Wall Street Workshop™ designed to help those ready to take their trading to the next level and treat it as a business. This seminar is open only to graduates of the Wall Street Workshop™.

THE ONE-MINUTE COMMUTE (TRADING AT HOME)
PRESENTED BY KEVEN HART

This one-day clinic will take you from being a semi-active investor to trading on a daily basis, giving you the freedom to dictate your own schedule and move forward on your own predetermined timeline. Trade from home and stay close to your family. This condensed training will get you where you want to go by helping you practice trading as a business, showing you which resources produce wealth through crucial and timely information, selecting appropriate strategies, qualifying your trades and helping you time both entries and exits.

EXECUTIVE RETREAT
PRESENTED BY WADE B. COOK AND TEAM WALL STREET

Created especially for the individuals already owning or planning to establish Nevada Corporations, the Executive Retreat is a unique opportunity for corporate executives to participate in workshops geared toward streamlining operations and maximizing efficiency and impact.

WEALTH INSTITUTE
PRESENTED BY WADE B. COOK AND TEAM WALL STREET

This three-day workshop defines the art of asset protection and entity planning. During these three days we will discuss, in depth and detail, the six domestic entities which will protect you from lawsuits, taxes, or other financial losses, and help you retire rich.

REAL ESTATE WORKSHOP
PRESENTED BY WADE B. COOK AND TEAM MAIN STREET

The Real Estate Workshop teaches you how to build perpetual income for life, without going to work. Some of the topics include buying and selling paper, finding discounted properties, generating long-term monthly cash flow, and controlling properties without owning them.

REAL ESTATE BOOTCAMP
PRESENTED BY WADE B. COOK AND TEAM MAIN STREET

This three to four day bootcamp is truly a roll-up-your-sleeves-and-do-the-deals event. You will be learning how to locate the bargains, negotiate strategies, and find wholesale properties (pre-foreclosures). You will also visit a title company, look at properties and learn some new and fun selling strategies.

BUSINESS ENTITY SKILLS TRAINING (BEST)
PRESENTED BY WADE B. COOK AND TEAM WALL STREET

Learn about the six powerful entities you can use to protect your wealth and your family. Learn the secrets of asset protection, eliminate your fear of litigation, and minimize your taxes.

ASSORTED RESOURCES

WEALTH INFORMATION NETWORK™ (W.I.N.™)

This subscription Internet service provides you with the latest financial formulas and updated entity structuring strategies. New, timely information is entered Monday through Friday, sometimes four or five times a day. Wade Cook and his Team Wall Street staff write for W.I.N.™, giving you updates on their own current stock plays, companies who announced earnings, companies who announced stock splits, and the latest trends in the market.

W.I.N.™ is also divided into categories according to specific strategies and contains archives of all our trades so you can view our history. If you are just getting started in the stock market, this is a great way to follow people who are doubling their money every $2\frac{1}{2}$ to 4 months. If you are experienced already, it's the way to confirm your feelings and research with others who are generating wealth through the stock market.

IQ PAGER™

This is a system which beeps you as events and announcements are made on Wall Street. With IQ Pager™, you'll receive information about events like major stock split announcements, earnings surprises, important mergers and acquisitions, judgements or court decisions involving big companies, important bankruptcy announcements, big winners and losers, and disasters. If you're getting your financial information from the evening news, you're getting it too late. The key to the stock market is timing. Especially when you're trading in options, you need up-to-the-minute (or second) information. You cannot afford to sit at a computer all day looking for news or wait for your broker to call. IQ Pager™ is the ideal partner to the Wealth Information Network™ (W.I.N.™).

THE INCORPORATION HANDBOOK
BY WADE B. COOK

Incorporation made easy! This handbook tells you who, why, and, most importantly, how to incorporate. Included are samples of the forms you will use when you incorporate, as well as a step-by-step guide from the experts.

Legal Forms
By Wade B. Cook

This collection of pertinent forms contains numerous legal forms used in real estate transactions. These forms were selected by experienced investors, but are not intended to replace the advice of an attorney. However, they will provide essential forms for you to follow in your personal investing.

Record Keeping System
By Wade B. Cook

A complete record keeping system for organizing all of the information on each of your properties. This system keeps track of everything from insurance policies to equity growth. You will know at a glance exactly where you stand with your investment properties and you will sleep better at night.

Travel Agent Information
By John Childers and Wade Cook

The only sensible solution for the frequent traveler. This kit includes all of the information and training you need to be an outside travel agent for a stable company. There are no hassles, no requirements, no forms or restrictions, just all the benefits of traveling for substantially less every time.

Explanations Newsletter

In the wild and crazy stock market game, *Explanations* newsletter will keep you on your toes! Every month you'll receive coaching, instruction and encouragement with engaging articles designed to bring your trading skills to a higher level. Learn new twists on Wade's 11 basic strategies, find out about beneficial research tools, read reviews on the latest investment products and services, and get detailed answers to your trading questions. With *Explanations,* you'll learn to be your own best asset in the stock market game and stay on track to a rapidly growing portfolio! Continue your education as an investor and subscribe today!

6

LATE BREAKING NEWS

Editor's note: A section similar to this was included in the original Wall Street Money Machine. *We thought this information in this section was important enough to include it again in the new edition.*

I'M CURRENTLY in my living room relaxing after a day at the lake. The book is complete and ready to go to press. A few days ago I was to go into the studio and do a taping for a new cassette tape entitled "Get Rich Steady"–a seminar on stock splits and options. I have done more extensive seminars on this topic in Zero to Zillions–a set of home study courses and The Wall Street Workshop™ Video; plus my instructors and I do several plays during the live Wall Street Workshops. That is why I'm awake right now. My body is tired but my mind is on fire.

You see, we just had an awesome two-day Wall Street Workshop™–doing practice trades, making money. Most people in the class were very enthused because they saw the amazing profit potential available in the stock market. That's why I can't sleep. It is a thrill to see people making so much money.

SAMPLE OF TRADES
APRIL 30, 1999

TICKER	COMPANY	REASON	BUY DATE	QTY	POSITION	PRICE	TOTAL	SELL DATE	PRICE	TOTAL IN	GAIN/LOSS	%	DAYS
C	CITIGROUP	CHART	19-Apr-99	10	MAY 65 C	10 1/4	$10,250.00	29-Apr-99	12	$ 12,000.00	$ 1,750.00	17%	10
CNXT	CONEXANT SYSTEMS	CHART	14-Apr-99	20	JULY 25 C	8 1/8	$16,250.00	28-Apr-99	17 5/8	$ 35,250.00	$ 19,000.00	41%	14
CIEN	CIENA CORPORATION	NEWS	14-Apr-99	10	JULY 15 C	7	$7,000.00	28-Apr-99	8	$ 8,000.00	$ 1,000.00	14%	104
WMT	WAL-MART	SPLIT	9-Apr-99	40	JUNE 52.50 C	3 1/8	$12,500.00	28-Apr-99	3	$ 12,000.00	$ (500.00)	-4%	17
QCOM	QUALCOMM INC	NEWS	13-Apr-99	10	MAY 165 C	16 3/8	$16,375.00	23-Apr-99	33	$ 33,000.00	$ 16,625.00	101%	10
CBS	CBS CORP	NEWS	8-Apr-99	20	JAN'00 35 C	6	$12,000.00	22-Apr-99	12 1/8	$ 24,250.00	$ 12,250.00	102%	104
CBS	CBS CORP	NEWS	8-Jan-99	20	JAN'01 40 C	6 1/2	$13,000.00	22-Apr-99	12 1/8	$ 24,250.00	$ 11,250.00	87%	104
DELL	DELL COMPUTER	CHART	20-Apr-99	20	MAY 35 C	3 7/8	$7,750.00	22-Apr-99	7 1/8	$ 14,250.00	$ 6,500.00	84%	3
F	FORD MOTOR CO	NEWS	4-Mar-99	10	SEPT 60 C	5 1/2	$5,500.00	22-Apr-99	7 1/2	$ 7,500.00	$ 2,000.00	36%	49
F	FORD MOTOR CO	NEWS	4-Mar-99	10	JUNE 55 C	6 1/4	$6,250.00	22-Apr-99	9 1/8	$ 9,125.00	$ 2,875.00	46%	49
IBM	IBM CORPORATION	CHART	30-Nov-98	10	JAN'00 190 C	15 1/4	$15,250.00	22-Apr-99	26 1/8	$ 26,125.00	$ 10,875.00	71%	144
BA	BOEING	CHART	1-Mar-99	30	JAN'01 50 C	4 1/8	$12,375.00	21-Apr-99	5 1/8	$ 15,375.00	$ 3,000.00	24%	51
BA	BOEING	CHART	1-Mar-99	10	JAN'01 30 C	11 3/8	$11,375.00	21-Apr-99	14	$ 14,000.00	$ 2,625.00	23%	51
BA	BOEING	CHART	1-Mar-99	10	JAN'01 40 C	6 3/4	$6,750.00	21-Apr-99	8 3/4	$ 8,750.00	$ 2,000.00	30%	51
QCOM	QUALCOMM INC	NEWS	13-Apr-99	10	MAY 160 C	19	$19,000.00	21-Apr-99	29 1/4	$ 29,250.00	$ 10,250.00	54%	8

These are some of our most recent trades showing a variety of the strategies used. They are for illustrative purposes only and should not be construed as a statistical sample of the corporate brokerage accounts of Wade Cook Seminars. Obviously, your returns may be different. Trades listed here are no guarantee of future success. We listed the actual date and purchase price so you could verify the trades. You should check with your professional regarding the risks and rewards in your personal account. Wade Cook Seminars and the instructors make no recommendations and give no advice. We teach correct methods and strategies and let people govern their own trades—and keep their own profits!

SAMPLE OF TRADES
MAY 14, 1999

TICKER	COMPANY	REASON	BUY DATE	QTY	POSITION	PRICE	TOTAL	SELL DATE	PRICE	TOTAL IN	GAIN/LOSS	%	DAYS
SCH	CHARLES SCHWAB	SPLIT	6-Apr-99	10	MAY 105 C	10 7/8	$10,875.00	13-May-99	14 1/4	$ 14,250.00	$ 3,375.00	31%	37
C	CITIGROUP	NEWS	16-Mar-99	10	JUNE 60C	8 1/2	$8,500.00	13-May-99	15 1/4	$ 15,250.00	$ 6,750.00	79%	58
BGEN	BIOGEN	SPLIT	16-Apr-99	20	MAY 105 C	7 7/8	$15,750.00	13-May-99	5 5/8	$ 11,250.00	$ (4,500.00)	-28%	27
QCOM	QUALCOMM INC	SPLIT	22-Apr-99	10	JULY 100 C	13 1/4	$13,250.00	12-May-99	22	$ 22,000.00	$ 8,750.00	66%	20
CSCO	CISCO SYSTEMS	CHART	30-Apr-99	10	JUNE 105 C	12	$12,000.00	12-May-99	14 5/8	$ 14,625.00	$ 2,625.00	22%	13
TLAB	TELLABS INC	SPLIT	20-Apr-99	10	MAY 95 C	9 7/8	$9,875.00	11-May-99	18 3/4	$ 18,750.00	$ 8,875.00	90%	21
VSTR	VOICESTREAM WIRELESS	NEWS	4-May-99	1000	STOCK	25 1/16	$25,062.50	7-May-99	29 1/16	$ 29,062.50	$ 4,000.00	16%	2
SCH	SEARS	NEWS	29-Dec-98	10	JULY 40 C	5 7/8	$5,875.00	6-May-99	9 3/8	$ 9,375.00	$ 3,500.00	60%	102
SCH	SEARS	LEAP	29-Dec-98	10	JAN'00 50 C	4 5/8	$4,625.00	6-May-99	5 1/8	$ 5,125.00	$ 500.00	11%	102
FDX	FDX CORP	NEWS	19-Apr-99	10	JULY 100 C	14 5/8	$14,625.00	6-May-99	16 3/8	$ 16,375.00	$ 1,750.00	12%	17
MSFT	MICROSOFT CORP	CHART	20-Apr-99	20	JULY 85 C	6	$12,000.00	4-May-99	4 1/8	$ 8,250.00	$ (3,750.00)	-31%	14
CAL	CONTENENTAL AIRLINES	NEWS	15-May-99	5	JUNE 35 C	9 1/2	$4,750.00	4-May-99	11 1/2	$ 5,750.00	$ 1,000.00	21%	19

These are some of our most recent trades showing a variety of the strategies used. They are for illustrative purposes only and should not be construed as a statistical sample of the corporate brokerage accounts of Wade Cook Seminars. Obviously, your returns may be different. Trades listed here are no guarantee of future success. We listed the actual date and purchase price so you could verify the trades. You should check with your professional regarding the risks and rewards in your personal account. Wade Cook Seminars and the instructors make no recommendations and give no advice. We teach correct methods and strategies and let people govern their own trades–and keep their own profits!

SAMPLE OF TRADES
MAY 21, 1999

TICKER	COMPANY	REASON	BUY DATE	QTY	POSITION	PRICE	TOTAL	SELL DATE	PRICE	TOTAL IN	GAIN/LOSS	%	DAYS
CMGI	CMGI INC	CHART	10-Mar-99	2	JUNE 200 C	50	$10,000.00	20-May-99	54 3/4	$ 10,950.00	$ 950.00	10%	71
APCC	AMERICAN POWER CONVERSION	CHART	9-Apr-99	20	JUNE 30 C	4 5/8	$9,250.00	20-May-99	5 1/4	$ 10,500.00	$ 1,250.00	14%	41
CPQ	COMPAQ COMPUTER	CHART	12-Apr-99	1000	STOCK	24	$24,000.00	20-May-99	25 9/16	$ 25,562.50	$ 1,562.50	7%	38
DJX	DOW JONES IND AVG INDEX	CHART	17-May-99	10	MAY 106 C	2 11/16	$2,687.50	20-May-99	3 1/4	$ 3,250.00	$ 562.50	21%	33
BRCM	BROADCOM CORP	CHART	6-May-99	10	JUNE 80 C	10	$10,000.00	18-May-99	21 3/8	$ 21,375.00	$ 11,375.00	114%	12
WOWS	WOWSTORES.COM	NEWS	6-May-99	100	STOCK	7 9/16	$756.25	18-May-99	10 1/2	$ 1,050.00	$ 293.75	39%	18
OEX	S & P 100 INDEX	CHART	17-May-99	10	MAY 665 C	11 1/4	$11,250.00	17-May-99	14 1/4	$ 14,250.00	$ 3,000.00	27%	1
OEX	S & P 100 INDEX	CHART	17-May-99	10	MAY 670 P	9 1/2	$9,500.00	17-May-99	10 1/2	$ 10,500.00	$ 1,000.00	11%	1
DELL	DELL COMPUTER	CHART	20-Aug-99	1600	STOCK	16	$25,600.00	14-May-99	41 5/8	$ 66,600.00	$ 41,000.00	160%	9 MONTHS
DELL	DELL COMPUTER	CHART	20-Apr-99	200	STOCK	37 1/2	$7,500.00	14-May-99	41 5/8	$ 8,325.00	$ 825.00	11%	25
QCOM	QUALCOMM INC	NEWS	21-Apr-99	500	STOCK	91 3/4	$45,875.00	14-May-99	110 15/16	$ 55,468.75	$ 9,593.75	21%	24
OEX	S & P 100 INDEX	CHART	14-May-99	10	MAY 675 P	8 3/4	$8,750.00	14-May-99	9 3/4	$ 9,750.00	$ 1,000.00	11%	1

These are some of our most recent trades showing a variety of the strategies used. They are for illustrative purposes only and should not be construed as a statistical sample of the corporate brokerage accounts of Wade Cook Seminars. Obviously, your returns may be different. Trades listed here are no guarantee of future success. We listed the actual date and purchase price so you could verify the trades. You should check with your professional regarding the risks and rewards in your personal account. Wade Cook Seminars and the instructors make no recommendations and give no advice. We teach correct methods and strategies and let people govern their own trades--and keep their own profits!

Sample of Trades
June 7, 1999

TICKER	COMPANY	REASON	BUY DATE	QTY	POSITION	PRICE	TOTAL	SELL DATE	PRICE	TOTAL IN	GAIN/LOSS	%	DAYS
C	CITIGROUP	SPLIT	26-May	20	JUNE 40 C	3 13/16	$ 7,625.00	1-Jun	4 5/8	$ 9,250.00	$ 1,625.00	21%	6
OEX	S&P 100 INDEX	NEWS	2-Jun	10	JUNE 650 C	15 1/8	$ 15,125.00	2-Jun	16	$ 16,000.00	$ 875.00	6%	1
AOL	AMERICA ONLINE	NEWS	2-Jun	10	JULY 110 P	12 3/4	$ 12,750.00	2-Jun	14	$ 14,000.00	$ 1,250.00	10%	1
UNH	UNITEDHEALTHCARE	CHART	3-Jun	200	STOCK	63 11/16	$ 12,737.00	4-Jun	65 1/8	$ 13,025.00	$ 288.00	2%	1
LXK	LEXMARK INT'L GROUP	SPLIT	3-Jun	10	JULY 125 C	14 1/4	$ 14,250.00	7-Jun	25	$ 25,000.00	$ 10,750.00	75%	4
IBM	INT'L BUSINESS MACHINES	SPLIT	25-May	10	JUNE 220 C	13 1/2	$ 13,500.00	26-May	20	$ 20,000.00	$ 6,500.00	48%	1
LXK	LEXMARK INT'L GROUP	SPLIT	12-May	10	JUNE 120 C	13 1/4	$ 13,250.00	26-May	20 3/4	$ 20,750.00	$ 7,500.00	57%	14
IBM	INT'L BUSINESS MACHINES	SPLIT	25-May	10	JUNE 230 C	7 7/8	$ 7,875.00	26-May	13 1/8	$ 13,125.00	$ 5,250.00	67%	1
C	CITIGROUP	SPLIT	26-May	20	JUNE 43 3/8C	1 7/8	$ 3,750.00	1-Jun	1 3/16	$ 2,375.00	$ (1,375.00)	-37%	6
LXK	LEXMARK INT'L GROUP	CHART	18-May	10	JUNE 125 C	12 1/2	$ 12,500.00	27-May	16 7/8	$ 16,875.00	$ 4,375.00	35%	9
COX	COX COMMUNICATIONS	CHART	20-May	20	JUNE 40 C	4 3/8	$ 8,750.00	25-May	2 9/16	$ 5,125.00	$ (3,625.00)	-41%	5
IBM	INT'L BUSINESS MACHINES	SPLIT	25-May	10	JULY 230 C	6 1/16	$ 6,062.50	27-May	7 3/4	$ 7,750.00	$ 1,687.50	28%	2
OEX	S&P 100 INDEX	NEWS	27-May	10	JUNE 650 C	17 1/2	$ 17,500.00	28-May	18 1/4	$ 18,250.00	$ 750.00	4%	1

These are some of our most recent trades showing a variety of the strategies used. They are for illustrative purposes only and should not be construed as a statistical sample of the corporate brokerage accounts of Wade Cook Seminars. Obviously, your returns may be different. Trades listed here are no guarantee of future success. We listed the actual date and purchase price so you could verify the trades. You should check with your professional regarding the risks and rewards in your personal account. Wade Cook Seminars and the instructors make no recommendations and give no advice. We teach correct methods and strategies and let people govern their own trades–and keep their own profits!

SAMPLE OF TRADES
JULY 12, 1999

TICKER	COMPANY	REASON	BUY DATE	QTY	POSITION	PRICE	TOTAL	SELL DATE	PRICE	TOTAL IN	GAIN/LOSS	%	DAYS
KO	COCA-COLA	CHART	1-Jul	10	AUG 70 P	6 1/8	$ 6,125.00	8-Jul	7 1/4	$ 7,250.00	$ 1,125.00	18%	7
LU	LUCENT TECHNOLOGIES	CHART	21-Jun	10	AUG 60 C	8	$ 8,000.00	9-Jul	12 3/8	$ 12,375.00	$ 4,375.00	55%	18
OEX	S&P 100 INDEX	CHART	6-Jul	10	JULY 715 C	13 1/4	$ 13,250.00	7-Jul	10 3/4	$ 10,750.00	$ (2,500.00)	-19%	1
BRCM	BROADCOM	CHART	22-Jun	10	AUG 110 C	18 3/4	$ 18,750.00	2-Jul	27 3/4	$ 27,750.00	$ 9,000.00	48%	10
QCOM	QUALCOMM	CHART	11-Jun	20	JULY 120 C	6 3/4	$ 13,500.00	1-Jul	24 1/2	$ 49,000.00	$ 35,500.00	263%	20
BRCM	BROADCOM	CHART	3-May	5	AUG 90 C	11 3/8	$ 5,687.50	1-Jul	49 1/2	$ 24,750.00	$ 19,062.50	335%	59
MSFT	MICROSOFT CORP	CHART	11-Jun	20	JULY 85 C	3 1/4	$ 6,500.00	1-Jul	5 5/8	$ 11,250.00	$ 4,750.00	73%	21
MSFT	MICROSOFT CORP	CHART	24-Jun	10	JULY 80 C	5 1/2	$ 5,500.00	1-Jul	10 1/4	$ 10,250.00	$ 4,750.00	86%	7
PFE	PFIZER	CHART	17-Jun	10	JULY 95 C	8 1/4	$ 8,250.00	29-Jun	9 7/8	$ 9,875.00	$ 1,625.00	20%	12
SCH	CHARLES SCHWAB	CHART	23-Jun	10	JULY 90 C	9 3/8	$ 9,375.00	1-Jul	14 5/8	$ 14,625.00	$ 5,250.00	56%	9
SCH	CHARLES SCHWAB	SPLIT	23-Jun	10	JULY 95 C	6 3/4	$ 6,750.00	1-Jul	10 7/8	$ 10,875.00	$ 4,125.00	61%	8
QCOM	QUALCOMM	CHART	24-Jun	5	JULY 120 C	14 3/4	$ 7,375.00	1-Jul	24 5/8	$ 12,312.50	$ 4,937.50	67%	7
CL	COLGATE PALMOLIVE	SPLIT	23-Jun	80	JULY 47.5 C	3 1/4	$ 26,000.00	1-Jul	1 9/16	$ 12,500.00	$ (13,500.00)	-52%	8
MSPG	MINDSPRING	CHART	22-Jun	10	JULY 70 C	10 1/4	$ 10,250.00	24-Jun	15 7/8	$ 15,875.00	$ 5,625.00	55%	2
OEX	S&P 100 INDEX	CHART	24-Jun	10	JULY 675 C	12 1/4	$ 12,250.00	25-Jul	13	$ 13,000.00	$ 750.00	6%	1

These are some of our most recent trades showing a variety of the strategies used. They are for illustrative purposes only and should not be construed as a statistical sample of the corporate brokerage accounts of Wade Cook Seminars. Obviously, your returns may be different. Trades listed here are no guarantee of future success. We listed the actual date and purchase price so you could verify the trades. You should check with your professional regarding the risks and rewards in your personal account. Wade Cook Seminars and the instructors make no recommendations and give no advice. We teach correct methods and strategies and let people govern their own trades–and keep their own profits!

SAMPLE OF TRADES
AUGUST 9, 1999

TICKER	COMPANY	REASON	BUY DATE	QTY	POSITION	PRICE	TOTAL	SELL DATE	PRICE	TOTAL IN	GAIN/LOSS	%	DAYS
BAMM	Books-A-Million	CHART	12-Jul	5	Aug 12.50 C	3/16	$ 93.75	2-Aug	1 3/4	$ 875.00	$ 781.25	833%	21
JWN	Nordstrom	CHART	26-Jul	10	Aug 35 P	3 5/8	$ 3,625.00	4-Aug	4 5/8	$ 4,625.00	$ 1,000.00	28%	9
YHOO	Yahoo!	CHART	26-Jul	5	Sep 140 P	14 1/8	$ 7,062.50	5-Aug	20 1/4	$ 10,125.00	$ 3,062.50	43%	10
OEX	S&P 100 INDEX	CHART	4-Aug	10	Aug 675 C	13 1/4	$ 13,250.00	5-Aug	16 1/2	$ 16,500.00	$ 3,250.00	25%	1
OEX	S&P 100 INDEX	CHART	22-Jul	10	Aug 675 P	10	$ 10,000.00	5-Aug	15 1/4	$ 15,250.00	$ 5,250.00	53%	3
OEX	S&P 100 INDEX	CHART	22-Jul	10	Jul 705 P	24 1/2	$ 24,500.00	5-Aug	41	$ 41,000.00	$ 16,500.00	67%	14
CREE	CREE RESEARCH	CHART	27-Jul	20	Aug 32.50 C	4 1/2	$ 9,000.00	2-Aug	13/16	$ 1,625.00	$ (7,375.00)	-82%	6
NXLK	NEXTLINK COMMUNS.	CHART	12-Jul	10	Aug 90 C	12 1/2	$ 12,500.00	29-Jul	16 3/4	$ 16,750.00	$ 4,250.00	34%	17
LU	LUCENT TECH.	CHART	21-Jun	10	Oct 65 C	7 5/8	$ 7,625.00	20-Jul	9 1/2	$ 9,500.00	$ 1,875.00	25%	29
QCOM	QUALCOMM	CHART	12-Jul	10	Aug 140 C	19 3/8	$ 19,375.00	20-Jul	28	$ 28,000.00	$ 8,625.00	45%	8
OEX	S&P 100 INDEX	CHART	22-Jul	10	Aug 700 P	15 1/8	$ 15,125.00	23-Jul	14	$ 14,000.00	$ (1,125.00)	-7%	1
QCOM	QUALCOMM	CHART	3-Jun	10	July 100 C	14	$ 14,000.00	16-Jul	52 1/2	$ 52,500.00	$ 38,500.00	275%	43
QCOM	QUALCOMM	CHART	3-Jun	10	July 120 C	6 3/4	$ 6,750.00	16-Jul	35	$ 35,000.00	$ 28,250.00	419%	43
MSFT	MICROSOFT	CHART	7-Jun	10	July 90 C	1 3/8	$ 1,375.00	16-Jul	4 7/8	$ 4,875.00	$ 3,500.00	254%	39
MSPG	MINDSPRING	CHART	26-May	20	July 35 C	6 1/8	$ 12,250.00	16-Jul	13 1/4	$ 26,500.00	$ 14,250.00	116%	46

These are some of our most recent trades showing a variety of the strategies used. They are for illustrative purposes only and should not be construed as a statistical sample of the corporate brokerage accounts of Wade Cook Seminars. Obviously, your returns may be different. Trades listed here are no guarantee of future success. We listed the actual date and purchase price so you could verify the trades. You should check with your professional regarding the risks and rewards in your personal account. Wade Cook Seminars and the instructors make no recommendations and give no advice. We teach correct methods and strategies and let people govern their own trades—and keep their own profits!

I asked our Team Wall Street in our W.I.N.™ (Research) department to take several of our last trades and calculate the rate of return. This time I wanted an annualized calculation. Yes, we were in and out in a matter of days; and we have done many more trades than what you see listed and we didn't put in some of the best ones. On the tape I mentioned a few potential losers. We have a few from time to time, but the two options which are down right now still have about two months to recover. Maybe I won't lose on them after all. But the story behind the dozens and dozens of winners shouts out to be told.

Here's what we did to calculate the returns. If we purchased an option for $3 (10 contracts would be $3,000) and sold them seven days later for $5 ($5,000) we'd have a profit of $2,000. Then we divide the profit by the investment and get a rate of return. In this example it would be $2,000 ÷ $3,000 = 66%. Then we divide seven days into 365 and multiply that number (52) by the percent return (66%) to get the annualized return (3,432%).

These are exciting. Look at the diagram on the preceding page. It lists the news, the buy date, strike price and option price, then the sale date and sale price, the rate of returns for how many days, and then the annualized returns. *Pretty awesome, isn't it?*

I surely don't want you to take this lightly, so I'm going to put the annualized rates of return on the next page–*really big*–so you'll catch the magnitude of this formula. And let me put in a plug, once again, for the Wall Street Workshop™. You simply can't afford to miss this remarkable workshop. After today, and as I think back on all the classes, I'm convinced the tuition is the value of the century. Yes, it's expensive, but I'll never promise that which I can't deliver and I'll always deliver more than I promise. I just wish you could hear the comments of the attendees, tears in their eyes, squeezing my hand so hard I thought they'd crush it, thanking me for the information, the practice deals done in class, and finally the knowledge which lets them substantially improve where they are. They didn't come for a motivational seminar. They came to make money, and make money they did. Options and optimism have the same root word.

Again, here are the returns.

QUALCOMM	*1,205%*
TELLTABS	*1,530%*
BROADCOM CORP.	*3,420%*
US ROBOTICS	*6,604%*

If this doesn't get you excited, check to see if you have a pulse!